Remapping Bolivia

School for Advanced Research
Global Indigenous Politics Series

James F. Brooks
General Editor

Remapping Bolivia

Resources, Territory, and Indigeneity in a Plurinational State

Edited by Nicole Fabricant
and Bret Gustafson

SAR
PRESS

School for Advanced Research Press
Santa Fe

School for Advanced Research Press
Post Office Box 2188
Santa Fe, New Mexico 87504-2188
www.sarpress.sarweb.org

Managing Editor: Lisa Pacheco
Editorial Assistant: Ellen Goldberg
Designer and Production Manager: Cynthia Dyer
Copy Editor: Cecile Kaufman
Proofreader: Kate Whelan
Indexer: Margaret Moore Booker
Printer: Cushing Malloy, Inc.

Library of Congress Cataloging-in-Publication Data

Remapping Bolivia : resources, territory, and indigeneity in a plurinational state / edited by Nicole
Fabricant and Bret Gustafson.
     p. cm. — (Global indigenous politics series)
  Includes bibliographical references and index.
  ISBN 978-1-934691-51-9 (alk. paper)
 1. Indians of South America—Bolivia—Politics and government. 2. Indians of South America—
Bolivia—Government relations. 3. Indians of South America—Bolivia—Ethnic identity. 4. Indigenous
peoples—Bolivia—Politics and government. 5. Morales Ayma, Evo, 1959- 6. Bolivia. Asamblea
Constituyente (2006-) 7. Bolivia—Politics and government—2006- 8. Bolivia—Race relations.
I. Fabricant, Nicole. II. Gustafson, Bret Darin, 1968-
  F3320.1.P56R45 2011
  984—dc22
                                    2010053948

 This book was printed on 10% PCR paper with soy-based inks.

Cover illustration: Chile Pepper Production, Movimiento Sin Tierra, Gran Chaco. Photo by Kara
Panowitz, August 2007.

Contents

Photo Essay: Envisioning Bolivia

(Photos follow page 67.)

Acknowledgments

The initial impulse for this volume came out of the conference "Decolonizing the Nation, (Re)Imagining the City: Indigenous Peoples Mapping a New Terrain" organized by Nicole Fabricant and held at Northwestern University in 2008. We thank Northwestern University's Roberta Buffet Center for International and Comparative Studies, Weinberg College of Arts and Sciences, and the Department of Latin American and Caribbean Studies and Department of Spanish and Portuguese. For guidance at various stages of the conference and volume, we appreciate the support of Josef Barton, Micaela di Leonardo, Brodwyn Fischer, and Mary Weismantel. Thanks also to participants whose contributions impacted this work, including Robert Albro, Waskar Ari, Douglas Hertzler, Juan Arbona, Julieta Paredes, Kathryn Hicks, Daniel Goldstein, Stephen Scott, Andrew Orta, Elizabeth Monasterios, Tara Daly, Raquel Alfaro, Estelle Tarica, and Jorge Coronado. We also thank Charles Hale for agreeing to offer reflections on Bolivia in the context of wider Latin American transformations. *Remapping Bolivia* owes its publication at SAR Press to the support of Catherine Cocks (former executive editor) and to Lisa Pacheco (managing editor) and Lynn Baca (director), who guided it to completion. We are grateful for their enthusiasm and professionalism. Translations were done by Carlos Freytes and Bret Gustafson (Chapter 2); Bret Gustafson and Nicole Solawetz (Chapter 3); Eugenia Mitchelstein and Nicole Fabricant (Chapter 4); and Salvador Vásquez de Mercado and Nicole Fabricant (Chapter 6). We thank Patty Heyda for her work on the figures and maps and Nicole Solawetz for transcriptions. Finally, we admire and appreciate the Bolivian scholars, activists, and organizers who contributed to this volume directly and indirectly. We are inspired by your daily labor to transform Bolivia, and we look forward to future collaborations.

Introduction
New Cartographies of
Knowledge and Struggle

Bret Gustafson and Nicole Fabricant

The election of Evo Morales to the presidency of Bolivia in 2005 was a critical and historic moment of political and cultural transformation in the country. At the head of a party called the Movement to Socialism (Movimiento al Socialismo, MAS), Morales, coca farmer, peasant union leader, and Aymara Bolivian, became the first indigenous president of the country.[1] By sociohistorical (rather than biological) criteria, he is the first indigenous president in the history of the Americas. But Morales did not emerge from an "ethnic" movement. Backed by lower- and middle-class leftist, nationalist, indigenous, and labor organizations, Morales led a broad-based democratic challenge to a political system long dominated by entrenched elite parties. His election brought to an end two decades of free-market or "neoliberal" economic policies that had privatized state industries, deregulated production, increased labor flexibility, and encouraged foreign investment in natural resource extraction and exportation. After neoliberalism, the indigenous- and social movement–led rise of Morales is yielding a deep rethinking and remapping of Bolivia into what is being called a "plurinational" state.

These emerging changes create new expectations for Bolivian social movements and new analytical challenges for researchers. The free-market era had seen an official turn toward interculturalism as a strategy for "including" the country's long subordinated indigenous majority. As many analysts noted, interculturalism across the Americas was a social movement demand that was instrumental in making claims for human, cultural, and indigenous rights (Gustafson 2002; Postero 2006; Rappaport 2005; Sieder 2002; Warren 1998; Warren and Jackson 2002). Yet, as state policy, neoliberal interculturalism as a managed form of "inclusion" did not radically deepen democracy or decolonize state forms. Furthermore, free-market policies exacerbated poverty and deepened inequalities. The array of social movements supporting Evo Morales and his political party thus represented an alternative set of visions that have now taken the fore. These include a nationalist turn toward state sovereignty and natural resource control aimed at state-led wealth redistribution and industrialization policies. A new constitution approved in 2009 moves beyond interculturalism to the idea of plurinationalism, with explicit support for robust indigenous rights and forms of indigenous self-determination or "autonomy." Beyond interculturalism, the constitution and government now back the idea of "decolonization"—of education, the economy, law, the state, and society—promising to dismantle centuries of racialized and racist cultural, legal, and political-economic state form and practice. It is unclear whether Morales and the Movement to Socialism (MAS) party can meet the rising expectations generated by this ambitious "democratic cultural and political revolution" that is euphemistically called the "process of change" (*proceso de cambio*) in the country. Still, Bolivia has embarked upon a series of momentous transformations that call for new forms of political and intellectual activism and practice.

This volume, *Remapping Bolivia: Resources, Territory, and Indigeneity in a Plurinational State*, examines this rapidly changing historical moment by focusing on the emerging cultural politics of territoriality and indigeneity in relation to state change and globalized struggles over Bolivia's natural resources. We do not pretend to offer prescriptive policy suggestions, nor simplistic evaluations of Bolivia's current moment. Rather, the chapters that follow seek to capture emerging trajectories of change tied to two broad shifts in the country: one, the turn toward a state-led economic model based on aggressive natural resource extraction and, two, the shift toward a pluralist vision of decolonization and plurinational governance that radically alters the official and unofficial grammars of race, rights, identity, and territory in the country. For indigenous and nonindigenous Bolivians alike, the cultural and political upheaval has certainly unsettled existing symbolic orders and opened the hope for new possibilities of material change. There also emerges a new, complex, and often conflictive geopolitics of space that involves remappings of territorial orders across multiple scales, from the microspaces of daily life in the homes, markets, and streets of the cities to macroregional struggles over jurisdiction, resource control, and sovereignty. These are struggles tied to material concerns entangled with competing cultural and epistemic models for reshaping political, social, and economic orders. If territorial orders during the neoliberal era were reshaped to facilitate trade liberalization and market-oriented accumulation (with labor flexibility and rural dispossession), the reconstitution of a sovereign developmentalist state and the recognition of the country's indigenous majority have fueled a new array of remappings emerging both from official policy and from social movement struggle. In this volume, we explore these remappings, which are changing both the shape of cultural politics and the direction of research agendas for the country.

Through case studies of emerging territorial and cultural-political dynamics around the country, our purpose is to analyze, critique, and establish points of intellectual and political solidarity with the wider process of change underway in the country. There is clearly a sense in our collective work that after more than three decades of free-market neoliberal reformism, the "process of change" offers much promise and hope. Yet, this does not suggest a naïve embrace of the MAS regime, nor of "Evo," as he is affectionately known in Bolivia. The politics of change are not as simple as being "for" or "against" indigenous rights, nor even for or against "neoliberal" or "state-centric" development models on the global capitalist stage. The MAS regime faces intense opposition from right-wing business elites, especially those tied to agribusiness in and around the city of Santa Cruz (and their backers in the US foreign policy circles). It also faces criticism from left-wing sectors dissatisfied with the pace of change. Although the nationalist turn to recover state control of natural resource wealth was widely popular—and the flood of new rents to the state treasury circulates to assuage opposition from all sides—the turn to indigenous rights has been widely questioned, even by inner circles of the MAS regime. As observers also point out in Ecuador and Peru, Bolivia's efforts to re-capitalize the country through natural resource extraction have generated tensions with indigenous movements and local community organizers, potentially creating new ecological and social violences that replicate the rapaciousness of the neoliberal turn (Bebbington 2009; Farthing 2009). At the outset, then, we take a position of critical solidarity, avoiding the reductionist readings of Bolivia as simply populist, ethnicist, or resource nationalist. We seek to capture the fluidity and complexity of these changes. At the same time, we support the deeper projects of transformation that go beyond Evo Morales and the temporal conjuncture of MAS party rule.

Globally, Bolivia has garnered much deserved attention as an icon of social movement and popular resistance and of indigenous struggle. Yet, although unique, Bolivia also reflects a conflict between a global onslaught on natural resources by wealthier countries—including Europe and the United States but also new powers such as India, China, Russia, and Brazil—and efforts by national movements to reconstitute sovereignty as something more than an instrument of extraction in the wake of the destructive impacts of neoliberalism. If, from within Bolivia, there is a great reservoir of visions about progressive transformation for the future, from without, the country is often represented merely as one of many troubled, poverty-stricken regions marked by "underdevelopment" (and, paradoxically, lots of resources). Such countries are framed in the wealthy imaginary as targets—with their internal histories and movements as "obstacles"—for access to resources. Long-time Bolivianists and Bolivians now see the country thrust into the media imaginary of the wealthy North as a site of "lithium" dreams or as merely another peripheral country treated as a place needing "help" to "manage" its national and natural resources (that is, open access to them from the North).[2]

What is at stake in Bolivia? Beyond lithium that has excited Japan and France, iron ore in the country's east is disputed by China, Venezuela, and India. Minerals in the high Andes are targeted by France, Japan, Canada, Australia, and the United States. Land in the east is already under significant control—via soy marketing and export—by Monsanto, ADM, and South American soy capital. With high global prices of crude oil and excessive use of fossil fuels, soy and sugar lands in Bolivia are now imagined globally as a new opportunity for biodiesel production. Water resources in the Amazon basin of the east (in stark contrast to the crisis of water scarcity in the Andean west) are slated to be dammed and turbined for electricity production for Brazilian energy consumption. Conversely, water scarcity has yielded the threat of "market-based" solutions that attract foreign capital eager to profit from human need—and against human right. And, central at the moment, the immense natural gas reserves along the Andean foothills are coveted by Brazil and Argentina, with Russian, British, American, and Spanish capital, with their own dreams of gas liquefaction and export to Europe or the United States. The global onslaught has not been slowed by nationalization, as detractors have shrilly argued. What is more significant is whether and how these resources might contribute to more equitable development patterns and democratizing processes without yielding new socioenvironmental crises or new authoritarian or militarist regimes. It is in this wider context that we take a critical stance of solidarity with the process of change in Bolivia, arguing that Bolivia's struggle to sustain its own forms of democratic governance against global and national legacies of coloniality may offer lessons in a world marked by intensifying lines of racialized and gendered class inequality, the effects of market-led exclusionary growth patterns, and the social and ecological effects of environmental degradation. Our purpose is thus to explore the promise and contradictions of a wide array of social movement efforts to *vivir bien* (live well) with sovereignty and self-determination.

Indigeneity—its contested meanings, its divergent expressions, and its implications in relation to the reordering of citizenship, territory, and state form—is at the heart of this text. Indigeneity not only represents the presence of "ethnic" politics but also offers a cultural and knowledge-centered challenge to conventional Western paradigms through which state transformations are debated. Old debates pitting the state against the market as key development actors are now confronted by a third field of epistemic, territorial, and ideological challenges to development and the state itself. With rethinkings and remappings shaped by indigenous philosophical tenets, cultural ideas, and social models of territorialized governance, the question becomes not merely whether indigenous rights might be recognized, but how the turn toward a more robust recognition of indigeneity might yield creative national transformations in law, economics, and social relations. Again, this is not to suggest an acritical embrace of all things "indigenous"—since indigeneity bears its own risks of fundamentalism, commodification, or simply, as with neoliberal interculturalism, masking stasis with the rhetoric of change. Rather, this is to suggest that the cultural and epistemological reservoir of difference in Bolivia—now exercised as a decolonizing thrust—might yield ideas about pluralist democracy in a world hungry for scarce natural resources. Our "remapping" of Bolivia is not, then, a colonialist effort to prescribe change, nor a romantic embrace of indigenous utopia, but an attempt to engage in dialogue about possibilities in a complex scenario of political and social transformation ridden with tensions and frictions.

The history of this collection has some bearing on its form and content. *Remapping Bolivia* originated at a conference organized by Fabricant at Northwestern University in 2008. The conference, "Decolonizing the Nation, (Re) Imagining the City: Indigenous Peoples Mapping a New Terrain," brought together US and Bolivian scholars and indigenous intellectuals to cross the North–South divide (between Bolivian and predominantly North American researchers) and disciplinary boundaries (between anthropologists and their colleagues in geography, urban planning, literature, and political science). This volume builds on the conference to explore interdisciplinary research trajectories articulated with political processes in Bolivia. Working largely through ground-level, ethnographically situated viewpoints, this book embraces engaged, collaborative, and activist research. We thus acknowledge and activate the links between academic and grassroots modes of knowledge production and cultural-political transformation (Hale 2006b; Rappaport 2005, 2008). This volume includes work rooted in the ethnographic traditions of anthropology (Fabricant's chapter 7, Gustafson's chapter 8) in dialogue with urban planning (Kirshner's chapter 5; Revilla's chapter 6), literature, history, and postcolonial studies (Garcés's chapter 3, Soruco Sologuren's chapter 4), and sociology (Mamani Ramirez's chapter 2). We have also included interludes—called "Visions from the Ground"—to destabilize the often monologic form of research dissemination. These segments capture indigenous and other Bolivian voices speaking of their ongoing struggles for and against change in the country.

This dialogic and reciprocal style of engagement between knowledge and political work also characterizes movement and intellectual practice in Bolivia, a phenomenon we seek to emulate here. The sometimes rowdy embrace of polyvocality is a direct challenge to the depoliticizing turn of the neoliberal paradigm, as well as the reductionist embrace of formulaic models, methods, and theories that has taken over much academic labor, missing, in the process, the chance for deeper and transformative understandings of cultural politics. Here we eschew an attempt to reduce Bolivia to a singular narrative, while critically embracing a range of epistemic, discursive, and historical reserves that characterize Bolivian modes of reimagining and debating change. This dialogic, if often conflictive, embrace of epistemic creativity—much like the Andean ritual of the *tinku*[3]—may, as many of our contributors highlight, represent one of the country's most significant resources as it moves toward the future.

In more conventional academic terms, the volume is situated within the anthropology of the state, social movements, and globalization that focuses on the cultural politics of territory and nature as contested spaces constituted through struggle. This shift moves to reground social and cultural analyses spatially and materially in an era in which resources and territoriality are returning (or at least reappearing in our research) to occupy a center point in the study of power and meaning. This is not a claim to novelty, but rather a suggestion that questions of identity, subjectivity, and the body—and assumptions about neoliberal globalization's erasure of categories such as state, nation, class, and place—have dominated the study of power in recent years. Yet, in this era of widening inequalities and intensified resource struggles, we must move to reconnect these questions in a more explicit way without returning to crude materialist or rationalist models or their inverse, a culturalist or ethnicist myopia, to understand what is going on in places like Bolivia. By the same token, the wider Andeanist frame for producing knowledge about Bolivia is clearly no longer sufficient for speaking of the cultural politics of indigeneity or of Bolivia itself. Several of the chapters here explore the changing positionality of indigeneity in Bolivia and the shifting meanings of Andeanness within the country.

Given the new role of the state in economic production and redistribution, this focus on territoriality and indigeneity is situated within consideration of what might be tentatively called a post-neoliberal era. As a descriptor of free-market policies, techniques, and processes that have entrenched themselves deeply in people's lives and in state and economic forms, "neoliberal" has taken prominence in academic and political discourse. We realize that merely labeling Bolivia "post-neoliberal" is at best hopeful, because neoliberal practices coexist with nationalist extractivism and state-led developmentalism elsewhere. However, scholars working in places such as Venezuela, Ecuador, and Bolivia have recently defined a post-neoliberal order as "a hybrid state formation that has mounted certain challenges to the neoliberal paradigm but which remains subject to the internal and external constraints of global capitalism" (S. Fernandes 2010:23). In Bolivia, this is marked by social movement efforts to reground sovereignty, refound the state, and remap Bolivia, as well as by our own attempts to trace and understand these processes. Together, these chapters suggest new directions for anthropologists of Bolivia and beyond as neoliberalism gives way to new modes of social struggle, redistributive and egalitarian utopias, reactionary violence, and emergent models of pluralist statecraft.

The sections that follow introduce the concerns of this volume across three conceptual fields: the remaking of Andeanism as a marker of scholarship, polity, and indigeneity in Bolivia; the articulation of resources, territorialities, and movements involved in the remaking of the state; and the rethinking of knowledge production as collective and collaborative engagement.

Remapping Andeanism: Between Indigeneity, Mestizaje, and Race

The contested meanings of the Andes and the Andean—*lo andino*—deeply inflect the academic imaginary and the public politics of mobilization in Bolivia. In academia, Bolivia has long been positioned in an Andean slot, such that those who work and study there are assumed to be Andeanists and, as far as politics and indigenous issues go, most research has concentrated on the Andean Quechua and Aymara peoples. This reflects the demographic centrality of the Quechua and Aymara, who together number more than four million, as well as their political and historic centrality in indigenous and popular movement struggles and Bolivian nation-making. Yet, Andeanism also reflects a longer tradition of ethnological area studies that have sought to understand peoples in relation to ecologies, often in deterministic ways, and have deemphasized dynamics of wider political-economic change. Though much of Bolivia is, in fact, Amazonia—and a good part is in the Chaco—this culturalist Andeanization of Bolivia has left a lasting imprint on internal cultural politics and academic paradigms and continues to influence area-centric models of policy making and analysis.[3]

In anthropology, the rethinking of Andeanism began with Orin Starn's (1992) essay, which argued that theoretical concerns with cultural phenomena such as dual organization, the *ayllu* (community), ritual, and the supposed durability of timeless cosmological and social orders had generated a kind of anthropological blindness to broader political-economic processes, exchanges, and relationships.[4] What has since resulted, in some ways, is a retreat from Andeanism and locality and movement toward the study of transnationalisms and politics of various sorts. To highlight but a few, these studies include accounts of transnationalized Andean communities (Bigenho 2002; Colloredo-Mansfeld 1999; Orta 2004); rural–urban and transnational migration (Goldstein 2004; Pribilsky 2007); and of late, the rise of Andean movements engaged with transnational development and state reform (among others, Becker 2008; Colloredo-Mansfeld 2009; García 2005; Goodale 2008; Lazar 2008; Lucero 2008). This burgeoning work transcends a traditional focus on community life and has opened a vibrant, interdisciplinary space bridging anthropological concerns with cultural politics and wider debates on citizenship, pluralist democracy, inequality, and the state. As a precursor to this volume, this remaking of lo andino has added complexity to our understandings of indigeneity in Bolivia and beyond. Even so, as we explore here, uniquely Andean symbols, epistemologies, and social forms are still central, perhaps more than ever, to the remapping of Bolivian political spaces and imaginaries.

Yet, there are two dimensions of the rethinking of lo andino that have yet to be explored. The first entails articulating lo andino analytically with the "other" parts of Andean countries like Bolivia. The Amazonian and Chaco lowlands are now, especially in light of the rush on resources such as oil and gas, taking a central role in the political and cultural dynamics of Andean-centered Bolivian (and Peruvian and Ecuadoran) statecraft. We highlight articulations across these spaces—national, regional, ethnolinguistic, and social—acknowledging a wider history of (pluri)national state formation that has long bridged arbitrary geographic divides. A second and closely related issue involves examining the reaction to lo andino within Bolivia, a phenomenon quite distinct from the comfortably distanced squabbles of academics. In both cases, there emerge articulations of conflict and engagement that involve rethinking and remapping lo andino in relation to a wider panoply of places, peoples, and politics in Bolivia.

This latter point was most abruptly brought to international attention by an unlikely agent: Miss Bolivia 2004, Gabriela Oviedo, a celebrated daughter of the city of Santa Cruz. During that year's Miss Universe pageant in Quito, Ecuador, the otherwise elegant beauty queen resignified the Andean character of her country for the world by answering journalists' queries in this way:

> Unfortunately, people who don't know Bolivia very much think that we are all just Indians from the west side of the country, that is, La Paz …poor people and very short people and Indian people. I'm from the other side of the country, the east side, and it's not cold, it's very hot, and we are tall and we are white people and we know English, so all that misconception that Bolivia is only an Andean country, it's wrong. [Wall 2004]

Dressed in an outfit with indigenous (non-Andean) Guaraní motifs during the national costume portion of the pageant, Oviedo, perhaps unwittingly, embodied a phenomenon that we explore here: the racialized rejection of a certain kind of indigeneity—that of the Andean Aymara and Quechua—by the eastern regionalist opposition to the MAS; and the appropriation and subalternization of another kind of local indigeneity, that of the Guaraní, Chiquitano, and other native peoples of eastern Bolivia. This claim for a local kind of *mestizaje* with "our" Indians but not "those" Andean ones (and its attendant racism) unsettles simplistic readings of indigeneity and race (Lowrey 2006). For the right-wing elite of the east, the rejection of all things Andean helps fuel the reaction against the MAS, seen as neither Bolivian nor national, but as Andean, or *Colla* (or *Kolla*, referring to people of Andean origin; see figure 7, in the section "Envisioning Bolivia"). This reaction against lo andino and the appropriation of local indigeneity serves the interest of regional business elites and their ultimately anti-indigenous political projects in eastern Bolivia. Illustrative of this stance, whereas indigenous intellectuals speak of decolonizing the country by dismantling racialized inequality, reactionary intellectuals of the east speak of decolonization as a need to "de-Andeanize" eastern Bolivia. What is clear is that contested meanings of indigeneity—as both a positive and negative referent—take center stage in attempts to contest and change the exercise of state sovereignty, nation, and state.

Much of this new politics is interpreted as a conflict between the central government in La Paz and the agro-industrial city of Santa Cruz in the eastern lowlands. With the post–World War II economic boom in eastern

Bolivia, Santa Cruz took on increased importance. Today, much like conservative Texans, fueled by oil profits and an exaggerated sense of their individualist origins and nation-like particularity, Santa Cruz's civic elites—with the backing of middle and lower classes sparked by fears of insecurity—are at the forefront of the challenge against the nationalist-indigenous turn. As scholars of Bolivia who did not work in the Andes have observed, people of eastern Bolivia have long been unsettled by Andean migrations from the highlands to the lowlands (Fifer 1970; Gill 1987; Heath, Erasmus, and Buechler 1969; Henkel 1982; Stearman 1985). Yet, only now, with the election of an indigenous president hailing from the Andes, the long simmering regionalist sentiment in Santa Cruz has revived past dreams of separatism that not only reject *andinocentrismo* but also question the foundations of the Bolivian state itself.

In this context, the figure of the colla (Andean) invader is represented by some in the east as an *avasallador* (subjugator, invader, dispossessor). The once quietly cursed is now publicly denigrated (see figure 8). This reaction to the Andean is, at its crudest, an expression of racialized fear about public space and jobs that often manifests itself through violence. Yet, this anti-Andean reaction also has an intellectual expression. Editorialists and writers opposed to the MAS project are analyzing Andean heritage—and its contemporary bearers, the Aymara and Quechua—as subjects and spaces culturally rooted in authoritarian, bureaucratic, and antidemocratic matrices bequeathed by the Incan and Spanish empires and a hostile natural environment (see, for example, Mansilla 2004). This reading recovers outdated culturalist and ecological (and racialist) idioms of traditional ethnology. Against the "low-oxygen" Andes, deemed detrimental to cognitive development, such works describe the places and peoples of the east, especially Santa Cruz, in part because of its tropical clime, as centers of liberal, entrepreneurial, pioneer-like citizens, the vanguard of Bolivian modernity and democracy. This erudite discourse—ostensibly liberal yet ultimately racist—revives a longer Bolivian intellectual tradition that denigrated Andean indigeneity and racial mixing (Arguedas 1982[1910]). The reaction to lo andino is now politically productive as a reaction against redistributive nationalism and popular democracy and the rise of alternative models of indigenous territoriality. Anti-Andean racism lends support to the idea of sub-state models of *regional* governance, a neo-neoliberal strategy for localizing and maintaining market-oriented resource extraction in articulation with transnational capital (Escobar 2008; Gustafson 2006).

Although the MAS is not an ethnic party and Evo Morales is more versed in labor union struggle than the language of indigenous revindication, the MAS project is deeply imprinted by Andeanist scholarship and discourse.

This support for Andean philosophy, knowledge, and languages is denigrated by critics as a facile *pachamamismo* for its embrace of the *Pachamama*, or Mother Earth. But it is here that the decolonization of public reason and the official embrace of lo andino energize and transform philosophical debates about law, rights, and polity. The Pachamama is now part of the new constitution, and Andean idioms of reciprocity, exchange, solidarity, and complementarity are making their way into a multitude of official texts and discourses. We engage this bifurcation created by both positive and negative reifications of lo andino and seek to transcend it here by highlighting articulations rather than fixating on putative cultural and geographic dichotomies.

The contest over lo andino and the conflict between tropical east and Andean west are thus more complex than an overt rejection of indigeneity, evidenced in the beauty queen's stylized Guaraní dress and renewed talk about mestizaje as an alternative to the indigenous turn. As in Guatemala, indigenous resurgence is confronted by the intensification of discourses about mestizaje, a supposed process of racial and cultural mixing that has yielded neither Indians nor Whites but *mestizos* as the model of the national citizen. Mestizaje discourses emerge from both the left and the right in Bolivia today. The idea of mestizaje ostensibly embraces indigeneity and critiques Euro-Bolivian privilege. However, the notion of mixing ultimately reaffirms the primacy and superiority of European and "Western" things and ideas in governance, mobilizes an implicitly racist biological model of race, and denies particularity of *rights or difference to those Bolivians long subjugated as indios* (del Valle Escalante 2009). One banner hung by the women's civic chamber in Santa Cruz for the city's two-hundredth anniversary read in late 2010, "We are a mestizo race, without lament or rancor." Yet, this seemingly inclusive call to mestizaje marks a refusal to recognize entrenched privileges long constructed in opposition to the category of indigeneity and indicates a refusal to recognize indigenous peoples—as peoples—themselves.

At the national level, mestizaje is also being revived by conservative intellectuals as a means of undermining the epistemological stance of indigeneity and the decolonizing turn. For instance, conservatives have used census and polling strategies and data to argue that Bolivia is a majority mestizo country (Toranzo 2008). The 1992 census, based on languages spoken, yielded a count of around 60 percent of the country speaking an indigenous language, hence the oft heard assertion (with which we agree) that indigenous peoples are a majority in the country (Albó 2008). How-ever, a 1996 poll by the United Nations Development Program (UNDP), similar to a later study headed by a Vanderbilt University team, allowed people to refer to themselves as "mestizo" or "white." This poll generated results suggesting that Bolivia was 16 percent indigenous, 67 percent mestizo, and 17 percent white (Toranzo 2008:37). In 2001, the census allowed people to self-identify with a particular ethnolinguistic group (Quechua, Guaraní, Aymara, or other), again generating a response of roughly 62 percent indigenous. Though linguistic origins and self-ascription tend to affirm the predominance of indigeneity as a marker of identity, it is not our purpose to enter this debate over the fixing of categories (for a rebuttal, see Albó 2008; Mamani Ramirez, chapter 2, this volume). This would mean engaging the spurious assertion that if indigenous peoples are minorities, then their claims to rights should somehow have less importance. What is illuminating is how racial anxieties are translated into new battles over public categories. The renewed embrace of mestizaje and now frequent assertions that Bolivia suffers from "reverse racism" (indigenous peoples against nonindigenous) suggests what Hale (2006a) refers to as a "preemptive strike" against indigenous claims and the antiracist decolonizing agenda. These seething debates highlight disputes within and against the MAS project about whether and how Bolivian "indigeneity" offers a platform for remaking the Bolivian state, a question we explore herein.

Amid these debates, most indigenous movements generally argue that it is the state, not indigenous peoples, that must change and adapt to reality. Indigenous movements from across the country are already reshaping the state in articulation with new and emergent expressions of indigenous and popular (class-based) movements of peoples displaced and dispossessed in rural and urban peripheries and city centers. These movements are at times rooted in conventionally understood indigenous territorialities marked by sociocultural and linguistic particularity (especially in the lowlands) and at times based in a more diffuse claim to indigeneity tied to a sense of popular subaltern belonging. Along with a long-standing presence of indigenous Bolivians in cities large and small, this complicates conventional readings of indigeneity as fixed in specific, usually "rural" territorialities (and cultures or cosmologies). It calls for creative thinking about how legal frameworks of indigenous rights designed for minorities might work in a country in which those with reasonable claims to be indigenous are in the majority. There are also alliances and tensions between Andean and lowland indigenous organizations, migrant settlers, and farmers' unions that complicate any facile reading of an indigenous agenda. Though key alliances led to the new land reform, there is now a split between small farmer settlers who seek individual landholdings and lowland indigenous peoples demanding collective territorialities—often in the same regions.[5] The political and intellectual work behind the rise of MAS has involved, in large part, the strategic articulation of these diverse indigenous expressions with popular movements and a nationalist and redistributive agenda. This process relies on decolonizing notions of identity—from races to peoples—while maintaining a national frame of a sovereign national *pueblo* (people) that highlights the language of class struggle. This decolonizing view of indigeneity (see Garcés, chapter 3, this volume) stands in stark contrast to the efforts of the conservative intelligentsia, who resuscitate colonial idioms of race, Andean primitiveness, and mestizaje to selectively contain or reject "their" and "other" kinds of Indians in defense of existing orders of status, inequality, and territory.

Without reviving the culturalist models of the past, there is thus a case to be made that "Andean" cultural traditions and idioms continue to shape rural and urban life and public politics across Bolivia, with lo andino mobilized in positive and negative terms as part of the changing public sphere of politics, law, and culture. What are the implications of this discussion for representing and contextualizing Bolivia and its multiple forms of indigeneity and other emergent political identities? One response, attempting to redirect the Starn critique, has been to suggest a return to the role of cultural symbolism in the shaping of a deterritorialized, neo-indigenous cosmopolitanism (Goodale 2009). This envisions indigeneity as no longer rooted in territorial fixity (or even non-Western alterity) but as expressed in a hybrid "cosmopolitan" liberalism that transcends both the class-based utopias of the past and the decolonizing epistemological utopias of the present. Yet, this liberal reframing fails to capture the intensely grounded ways that collective indigenous and popular agendas are not merely problems of individual freedom and identity, but of unfinished historical and epistemological struggles that entail territorial reconfigurations, radical structural and symbolic changes, and the literal and figurative "remapping" of the state.

On the other hand, some academic approaches to cultural and political change in Bolivia have embraced a newly politicized stance linked to the "decolonial" option. This idea—evidenced in some of the chapters in this volume—argues that rethinking the state entails transcending not only neoliberal modernization of the right but also the Westernizing and homogenizing mindset of a traditional statist left (see Arnold and Yapita 2006; Gustafson 2009a; Mignolo 2005). Yet, this decolonial option also brings risks of a new kind of essentializing that reduces indigenous complexities to certain epistemic tenets—ontological predation, communitarian reciprocity, non-Western cosmologies, and so forth. This reflects the discourse of some sectors of the state and indigenous movements—as with the romanticizing of pachamamismo—as a kind of catch-all solution to the ecological and social challenges of capitalism. Although decolonizing Western categories is crucial, essentialism of indigenous knowledge is not a useful way of engaging the complexities of Bolivian indigenous subjectivities and politics.[6] We embrace the creative potentiality of indigenous epistemologies, but we are critically wary of attempts to transform indigenous cultural alterity into instrumental ideological doctrine. To do so is to risk contributing to new forms of reductionism that echo—in the name of critique—the grammars of colonial and patriarchal violence and exclusion itself.

Against attempting to redefine the Indian—whether as the hybrid cosmopolitan, the revolutionary militant, or the telluric native—what we seek is a vocabulary in which culturally and politically significant practices marked by a claim to "indigeneity" become imbricated in socially, politically, and economically salient struggles. This approach does not seek to reinscribe a timelessness to cultural forms or to define the indigenous, Andean or otherwise, but to trace recontextualizations and deployments in distinct political moments. We also seek to understand the ways in which these real and imagined cultural forms and practices inform material issues linked to resource redistribution. This includes questions such as the centrality of the ayllu and its reimagining in highland and now lowland settings in the context of land reform (see Albro 2005; Fabricant, chapter 7, this volume); the redeployment of cultural models of reciprocity and complementarity in the new constitution and in notions of indigenous autonomy (Garcés, chapter 3, Fabricant, chapter 7, Gustafson, chapter 8, this volume); the rethinking of models of economy, exchange, and nationalist resource control that shape the work of Bolivian and indigenous intellectuals (Gustafson, chapter 8, this volume); the rethinking of practices of citizenship and democracy in relation to hybrid cultural models (Lazar 2008; Revilla, chapter 6, this volume) and the prospects and risks involved in proposing a path to decolonization that highlights (or absolutely denies) the "indigenization" of the country (Mamani Ramirez, chapter 2, Soruco Sologuren, chapter 4, this volume). It is more productive to view Andean and other indigenous cultural matrices not as restrictive or deterministic frames but as knowledge networks that are immersed in movement, repositioning, and rearticulation with a range of reterritorializing projects and other knowledge forms.

This moves our discussion toward a more grounded yet translocally networked, rather than localist, understanding of cultural production as political practice, which allows us to focus on intersections between cultural production, territorializing processes, and multiscalar political-economic transformations and articulations (Escobar 2008; Tsing 2004). This also entails rethinking context, to delink geography and culture from their connectedness in racialist, evolutionary, and essentialist forms, while leaving room for the emergence of territorially specific, collective political projects, indigenous and otherwise. These projects produce authenticity and legitimacy, not by virtue of replication of the past but through processes of political articulation, negotiation, and exchange in the present.

Remapping Resource Politics: Between Dispossession and the New Extractivism

Political geographers have suggested that recent resource conflicts are the result of long histories of uneven geographic development. These can be interpreted as the product of a differentiated diffusion process from the center that leaves behind residuals from preceding eras. Harvey, in *The New Imperialism* (2003), reworks Marx's fundamental construct of "primitive accumulation," the process of forced dispossession and transformation of modes of production, as in the British enclosure movement or the European conquest of Latin America, which enabled early capitalist growth. He describes this process as longer-term accumulation by dispossession endemic to all capitalist expansion. This encapsulates the contemporary moment of the triumph of exchange over use value, or in other words, the commodification and privatization of land and forceful expulsion of peasant populations. Such accumulation-by-dispossession cycles have specific effects in shifting national and global spatialities (di Leonardo 2008; N. Smith 1990).

In the case of Bolivia, contemporary scholars have used this framing to understand the emergence of movements against dispossession to reclaim control over natural resources such as water and gas from transnational corporations (Spronk and Webber 2007). A wealth of popular and academic scholarship emerged after the "Water War" of 2000, exploring how and why the privatization of water sparked new forms of politics across identitarian, class, and regional distinctions.[7] What emerged were understandings of distinctive strategies of movement building that differed from a previous generation of organizing and academic thinking concerned with privileging class or ethnic identity. As Albro (2005) and Olivera and Lewis (2004) have noted, the Water Wars effectively mobilized a discourse centering on the defense of the "traditional use and distribution of water" as a collective cultural right based on *usos y costumbres* (uses and customs). In this case, Andean cultural identities, in a complex and networked way, became a critical frame of reference for reclaiming water as part of a wider trans-Andean commons. Similarly, what might be called the "coca" wars, waged against the US-backed plans to eradicate coca in the 1990s—which effectively threatened to dispossess peoples already dispossessed from their prior labor as miners—had mobilized the symbolism of a "millenarian leaf" against imperialism, conflicts that ultimately propelled Evo Morales to the status of national hero and, later, president.

Three and a half years after the Water Wars, when former president Gonzalo Sánchez de Lozada proposed to export Bolivia's gas in a pipeline through Chile, distinct groups, this time centered in the largely Aymara city of El Alto, came together to resist dispossession and the alienation of resources in the "Gas War" of 2003. Analyses of the Gas War highlighted the ways that local movements articulated around a national frame to recover control over a resource that was seen as the country's national patrimony (Arbona 2006; Kohl and Farthing 2006). Demands for the nationalization of gas were discursively bundled with other demands, indigenous and otherwise, including calls for the refounding of the country, greater democratization based on new forms of social organization, greater indigenous representation, and the rewriting of the constitution. Importantly, these demands came from the Aymara and Quechua organizations, as well as from urban labor and popular unions, middle classes, and lowland indigenous peoples (Perrault 2006). The nationalization of gas, though questioned by left and right for different reasons and generative of new lines of struggle, appears to be consolidated. But the unfinished debate over the rewriting of the constitution and its implementation in relation to indigenous and other autonomy agendas will be conflictive and complex. It is this unfinished remapping, the jostling between nationalist and indigenous projects against conservative reaction, as well as the ongoing struggle to meet basic daily needs faced by a majority of the country's population, that will shape the next decades in Bolivia.

Land and gas represent two examples of the friction between an extractive and transnational model of economic development, state-based redistributive agendas, and territorially situated indigenous projects.[8] In a recent essay, Linda Farthing (2009) astutely highlights the essence of this dilemma: on one side of the continuum lies the social and economic pressure to satisfy the country's immediate needs through extractive industries, and on the other, the environmental and social demands of indigenous movements, NGOs, and certain intellectuals. One environmental organizer describes it thus:

> Just look at the National Development Plan, and even the new constitution passed at the beginning of the year. In some parts of both, a "strong development at whatever cost" orientation predominates, and in others there is more emphasis on protecting resources. [Farthing 2009:29]

Defending nature—and finding space for robust indigenous projects of self-determination—in a wider battle against a voracious and destructive capitalism has been central to the public discourse of MAS and of Evo Morales (see the interview in the "Visions from the Ground" following this chapter). Yet, with Bolivia positioning itself as a global center for energy and other resources—water, lithium, gas, steel, and soy—wider forces may destabilize the attempt to consolidate an alternative political project already confronted by local and transnational opposition and internal divisions between productivist nationalism and indigenous decolonization. This volume explores transformations underway as struggles against dispossession arise, articulate, and enter into tension with the new national model of state-led natural resource extraction and growth.

Remapping and Reterritorializing Identity: Between Locality and Articulation

Work on social movements in the 1990s and 2000s focused primarily on identity. We follow its evolution into the analysis of governmentality, the state, and citizenship by relinking culturally mediated movement agendas with political-economic and reterritorializing processes (see Escobar 2001; Escobar and Alvarez 1992; Lucero 2008; Offen 2003, Postero 2007; Yashar 2005). Several chapters in this volume speak directly to emergent identities that surfaced as a result of the deterritorialization and reterritorialization of rural, mining, and indigenous communities in the wake of neoliberal structural adjustment. The economic restructuring of the 1980s led to the relocation of ex-miners from highland communities and small-scale subsistence farmers from the lowlands to urban peripheral spaces. Migrants found jobs in the expanding informal economy as domestic servants and street vendors and frequently moved in search of employment. The social and economic fragmentation and intensified poverty produced by the reterritorialization of miners and peasants created a difficult environment for union-based organizing. As with the expressions of the Water and Gas Wars, neither the Marxian frames of the once powerful miners' unions nor the varied indigenous positionings of many farming communities proved effective for confronting broader national processes of urban spoilage and marginality, underemployment, and landlessness that affected Bolivians across multiple lines of identity.

On the other hand, the neoliberal disruption and its attendant reforms —most crucially, municipal decentralization, or "Popular Participation" (1994)—led to the emergence of new types of groups that mobilized around territory and space. These territorially based yet not "traditionally" rural or indigenous organizations, such as the Federation of Neighborhood Councils (FEJUVE) in El Alto, the coca-growers' movement (cocaleros) in Cochabamba, and the Landless Movement (MST) of the peasants in Santa Cruz, all multiplied—somewhat paradoxically—in the context of neoliberal municipal decentralization. In contexts like Chapare, pan-municipal alliances around the MAS party as an "instrument" created a platform for propelling Evo Morales to the presidency. In the Andes, municipal politics yielded new indigenous organizations such as CONAMAQ while position-ing older ones in new posts of control over public goods. In the lowlands, the effects were uneven for indigenous peoples, who were often minorities in municipal jurisdictions, though they appropriated in distinct ways the "communal lands of origin" (TCOs) offered by the neoliberal state. Reformers' intentions during the neoliberal era were to channel demands to the local level in order to reduce pressure on the central government and break up union organizations and frames of contestation that had coordi-nated past challenges to the state. As Arbona (2008) and Yashar (2005) note, however, the decentralization process had unintended consequences: it created relatively autonomous governance spaces that facilitated the for-mation of organizational structures focused on territorializing rights—specifically, access to basic services, the right to farm coca, and land as a space for small-scale production.

Thus, a renewed embrace of popular power (from below) merged with ongoing demands for the redistribution of property and rights (from the state, above), prominently including land and the surplus of national resources such as gas. From these new clusters of movement articulation, a wider politics of rearticulating and refounding the state unfolded from the ground up. This entailed a simultaneous embrace of the "local," in which claims to rights took on an intensely territorial sense, and a tactical and multiscalar pursuit of "articulation," in which a shared recognition of the role of the state—albeit from multiple loci of enunciation—yielded a com-mitment to processes such as the constitutional assembly and the national-ization of gas. All of the chapters are positioned between these movement processes of localizing territoriality and trans-scalar articulations with and via the state.

Distinct from the struggles of some indigenous movements to defend and recover their traditional or ancestral territorial spaces, entities such as FEJUVE in El Alto, the *gremios* (merchant trade unions) in Santa Cruz, the coca-growers' movement, and MST become hybrid spaces of displaced and dispossessed peoples, collective organizations through which differently positioned experiences forge new political identities yet do so around terri-torializing logics and agendas. Urban satellite cities like El Alto now house informal workers, ex-miners, mestizos, and indigenous Aymara. This is not, as the liberal theorists of mestizaje argue, representative of some moderniz-ing rupture with some generic indigeneity rooted in the past or in rural areas. Lazar (2008) describes how women still own land in the countryside and, more often than men, return to help with agricultural duties such as sowing potatoes and quinoa. In effect, they rely on rural strategies of sur-vival, combining urban informal labor and rural subsistence work. These women have built a multivocalic political identity that borrows from rural Aymara farming communities and Andean social organization and kin-based structures, but their political agenda is very much centered on their everyday struggles in urban, impoverished El Alto. These processes push analysts and activists to further decolonize stubborn dichotomies of rural and urban, individual and collective, or proletarian and peasant, which obstruct more creative political thinking about indigeneity, as well as emergent and alternative models of polity and economy.

Arturo Escobar (2008) has foregrounded such networks of territorialized and territorializing projects as central sites where the rethinking of the epistemological bases of production, sociality, and life are unfolding and which are critical to shaping ecologically and socially revindicatory struggles of the twenty-first century. Community-based studies of these diversely territorialized movements—some operating from "traditional" areas of occupation, as with much of lowland Bolivia, others mobilizing from marginal spaces that are the product of displacement and dispossession or migration—have rightly highlighted the importance of materiality and territoriality, in both political and analytical terms. Yet, there are also risks in the localization of politics—or the romanticization of locality—which can lead to what Michael Watts (2004), in the distinct case of Nigerian oil politics, refers to as the breakdown of wider secular nation-building frames. The risk is present in Bolivia, where territorializing projects are targeted for appropriation and containment by defenders of the status quo, especially within the framework of regionalism. Localist projects also raise the possibility of the mobilization of new languages of racialized exclusion, the purification of place-specific rights to belonging, and forms of ethnic or social cleansing. On the one hand, some indigenous visions in the Andes speak of displacing the "mestizo" (see Mamani Ramirez, chapter 2, this volume), whereas, more frequently, nonindigenous provincial and regional elites stake their claims to power on birthrights that delimit citizenship rights and seek to contain and exclude that deemed an indigenous, primitivist threat (as discussed by Soruco Sologuren, chapter 4, this volume). We must analytically distinguish, therefore, models of localist politics that maintain an openness to articulation in tandem with alternative models of production, exchange, and distribution that contest the logics of extraction and accumulation, from models of equally localizing politics that retrench systems of extraction, exploitation, and accumulation. The distinction is crucial when speaking of relations between place, territory, and movement agendas and between these and the possibility of rethinking the wider (pluri)nation-state itself.

The territorializing and rearticulation of movements, old and new, can thus be seen as a wider set of counter movements (Polanyi 1944) that must be read across scales and forms of articulation as much as through local frames. These counter movements consist of a range of ideologies, from social justice frameworks and an environmentalism of the poor (Bebbington 2009) to movements concerned with increased state access to and control over natural resources (see Escobar 2008; Peluso and Watts 2001; Watts and Peet 1996). Among others, geographers have highlighted the creative work of these movements, which do not simply occupy space as territorial conquest or seek to capture stable institutions of power but which mobilize within and through territorializing projects to transform society by reimagining links to territory. As Raul Zibechi describes it, these movements are in large part the product of the "social earthquake" generated by neoliberalism, the processes of deterritorialization that unsettled forms of "production, reproduction and territorial and symbolic orders," followed by attempts to reconfigure, reconquer, and recover space. They represent an "active resituation of popular sectors, frequently located in the margins of cities and in rural zones of intensive production" (Zibechi 2003:185–186). This rebuilding of power from below, yielding networks of clusters and nodes that are undermining traditional power relations, is ripe for engagement with a wider MAS strategy to "articulate pluralities" (Prada 2007), even though they are not ideologically or organically united in party form.

We maintain here, then, a focus on these dislocations and reterritorializations among a variety of popular movements, as well as attention to how issues of territory, identity, and resources are brought into focus in relation to the particularities of more conventional approaches to indigenous rights. Bolivia, indeed, was the first country to adopt the United Nations Declaration on the Rights of Indigenous Peoples into national law. As has been much celebrated, Evo Morales's indigenous identity has generated its own "social earthquake" in Bolivia, creating, as Mamani Ramirez highlights in chapter 2, an irreversible turn toward the reconfiguration of Bolivian society and public life. A number of other recent volumes have examined at length the issue of indigenous rights in Latin America, in Bolivia and beyond (Dean and Levi 2003; Postero 2006; Rappaport 2005; Sieder 2002; Urban and Sherzer 1991; Varese 1996; Warren 1998; Warren and Jackson 2002). We do not pretend to replay here the debates over the legal definitions of indigeneity on the global stage, nor conceptualize our work as an evaluation of policies to judge whether these debates' objectives have been achieved.[9] Such an effort would be premature, in any case. We do, however, seek to open space for a rethinking of some of these central and contested categories—indigeneity, territoriality, resources, and autonomy—and highlight emerging trajectories and risks as Bolivians mobilize on new terrains of struggle.

Remapping Engaged Research: Between Detachment and Engaged Struggle

Anthropology has undergone self-examination and remapping in recent decades derived from its historical complicities with colonialist forms of knowledge production and its own decolonizing thrust. But it is still the case that institutional forms of academic knowledge production and circulation tend to replicate hierarchies of place, power, and voice. By the same token, transformative processes underway in Bolivia are pushing to decolonize knowledge production and relations of inequality by remapping territorial orders and redistributing rights to speak, know, and live well. We acknowledge the significance of these decolonizing moves by highlighting alignments (and distances) between the ethnographic venture and the processes on the ground. Just as grassroots organizers seek to remap the nation-state and disrupt hierarchies produced by extractive economies, we hope to remap knowledge production to disrupt traditional forms of research and open up spaces for new kinds of collaborations across the North–South divide.

In the case of this volume, such a remapping effort entailed a critical dialogue between US-based and Bolivian authors, movement theorists, and indigenous organizers. Many of these conversations and critiques are reflected herein—including our own eagerness to emphasize that we do not, by any means, propose a prescriptive remapping of Bolivia as a neo-imperial venture. More importantly, many of the volume contributors have collaborated with movements through on-the-ground relations of ethnographic knowledge production, exchange, and practice, which has influenced the ways in which they think about and reflect upon the changes occurring in Bolivia. After Dwight Conquergood, we seek to do the intellectual and political labor of finding out what it means to be "radically engaged and committed, body-to-body, in the field and in the academy…a politics of the body deeply in action with Others" (Madison 2007:827). The research and writing thus reflects how the remapping struggles on the ground intersect with local and nonlocal processes of knowledge production. This entails highlighting how academic knowledge filters into local fields of struggle at the same time that indigenous and grassroots concepts, epistemes, and visions nurture and transform academic practice, as seen in the space opened here for genres, languages, and registers of knowledge production that readers will easily recognize as distinct. Bolivia provides a distinctive opportunity for this approach because of the intensely reflective way in which activists and intellectuals, many of whom now occupy positions of state or movement power, fuse social analysis with cultural-political practice. This is a legacy of

Bolivia's history of combative intellectualism in opposition to technocratic neoliberalism, as well as the influence of indigenous-led critical and decolonizing thought. The Bolivian experience can potentially serve as inspiration for similar discussions across universities and fields of movement practice elsewhere in the world. Because we are moving toward an era of scarce resources and environmental degradation, our intellectual work must move beyond the academy and across our traditional disciplinary bounds. In these new times, the blind faith in techno-science and rationalist positivism as the hope for humanity must be challenged by a pluralist orientation to knowledge production and distinct visions of ecological and social challenges, within the academy and between the academy and its others. As indicated above, this knowledge dialogue is pursued here through an experimental component, the inclusion of textual and visual material in dialogue with the chapters. Drawn from indigenous and other voices of Bolivian society, these include multilingual excerpts from editorials, manifestos, testimonials, communiqués, and legal documents that serve, in a minimally mediated way, as expressions of knowledge at work. Such creative and performative "stuff" of culture and politics does not always fit into academic analyses or do so in ways that impoverish their performative power. We hope that the multiple voices and conversations in the volume reflect and inspire the opening up of new spaces for rethinking the future directions of the country.

The Structure of the Book

The first three chapters shed light on wider frames of state and regional re-mappings of indigeneity and (de)coloniality. Pablo Mamani Ramirez (chapter 2) outlines this territorializing shift as an Aymara sociologist and intellectual, a view in which indigenous peoples—and a more diffuse expression of indigeneity—establish themselves within the state and through the multiple interstices and fractures of power in spectacular and quotidian ways, remaking the very fabric of Bolivian society. Mamani Ramirez's chapter, as much manifesto as analysis, may strike some readers as intensely charged. Yet, echoing del Valle Escalante (2009), who argues that Western intellectuals have long been licensed to speak in racialist and exclusionary terms about the indio, with their biases enshrouded in the language of science, Mamani Ramirez offers a distinct perspective on the present moment, one in which a kind of assertive indigenous reconquest of space is underway, a process that is, inescapably, deeply charged. Chapter 3 (Fernando Garcés) delves into some of the hopes and limits of this indigenous reconquest in the legal and constitutional arena of state–indigenous relations. One of the most significant dilemmas of the indigenous movement is its long struggle to inscribe robust self-determination rights in the constitution. Garcés examines this effort and its dilutions, which were produced out of the negotiation between the MAS government and the right-wing opposition. In addition to offering an insider's account of an unprecedented historical process of alliance building between peasant and indigenous organizations, Garcés details how indigenous positions were transformed and translated—or excluded—from the country's new constitution approved in January 2009. Ximena Soruco Sologuren (chapter 4) examines the tragic massacre of eleven peasant and indigenous activists in Pando in September 2008. Soruco explores the event by juxtaposing the effects of dismantling traditional forms of power and subjectivity with a critique of the emergent language of individualist autonomy, which seeks to establish new forms of violent exclusion and negation of the Other. Each of these three chapters, in a distinct voice and register, is written from deep within Bolivian histories and struggles, evoking the intensely charged positionalities through which broader processes remapping the country are experienced, analyzed, and interpreted.

Following a photo essay including maps and images that illustrate the chapters and offer their own forms of "Envisioning Bolivia," chapters 5 (Joshua Kirshner) and 6 (Carlos Revilla) take us into two very different urban spaces: Santa Cruz in the lowland east and El Alto in the Andean west. Here, territorializing projects and dilemmas of urban growth and inequality are tied to planners and politicians' attempts to contain Andean migrant subjects deemed dirty and threatening in Santa Cruz and to reclamations of rights by the marginalized communities of El Alto. As we look through the lens of markets in Santa Cruz and neighborhood movements in El Alto, we gain a better understanding of the complexities of indigeneity as it relates to transformations of daily life and public political relationships in two contrasting urban spheres. Whereas Santa Cruz elites seek to project an image of modernity and civilization through municipal campaigns aimed at controlling (largely Andean) migrants, El Alto organizers embrace the "dirtiness" or "disorder" of their city by focusing on structural and environmental inequalities as reasons to mobilize—dynamics that, in both cases, are marked by and generate new kinds of political tensions and conflicts over territorialities, writ large and small.

Chapter 7 (Nicole Fabricant) and chapter 8 (Bret Gustafson) similarly juxtapose two expressions of mobilization on the peripheries of the lowland east—one of the MST Landless Movement, the other of the Guaraní. Fabricant focuses on how the expansion of soy as creative destruction (the loss of jobs, destruction of natural and built environments, and ecological degradation) leads to a new politics of seizing and occupying latifundio land in the Oriente and emergent attempts to create small-scale farming cooperatives or agro-ecological communities. Gustafson considers the Guaraní movement to reconstitute its nation and claim its own forms of indigenous "autonomy," juxtaposing these efforts against those of its detractors on the regional stage. The chapter considers the prospects and limits offered within the new constitution's dual approach to redistribution and recognition in the model of a productivist developmentalist state.

Chapter 9 (Charles Hale) discusses the volume and the debates it raises—political, analytical, and theoretical—surrounding the legacies of neoliberal multiculturalism, the intensification of racialized polarization, and the contradictions of the current political moment. Hale focuses on the racialization of contemporary struggles over resources, territory, and indigeneity while drawing attention to the risks of banal (multi)culturalism or a naïve embrace of "Indianism." This call for thinking more deeply about race and the risks of culturalist projects—as well as confronting the racist reaction of right—converges with our own concern with the ecological and socioeconomic challenges posed by the paradox of abundant resources and increasingly fragile human livelihoods and natural landscapes. Rather than position this volume as the expression of a singular response to this challenge, we hope that the chapters and the multiple voices provoke critical reflections on the current complexities of Bolivian resource politics and point to future possibilities. We also hope that by mapping out models of engaged research, we can (in a very modest way) contribute to new forms of solidarity and research that confront the tensions and risks posed by the present moment. In a small way, following Hale, after Martin Luther King, this may help push the bending arc of the moral universe toward justice.

Notes

1. The MAS was founded in 1998 as a heterogeneous alliance of social movements, left-leaning and nationalist intellectuals, and indigenous theorists and leaders. Here and throughout this text, we do not capitalize *indigenous*. It is sometimes common in English-language writing, especially when used as a legal category, to capitalize *indigenous*. We recognize the political significance of such usages as a reference to a shared historical experience of coloniality. However, in contrast to *Native American* or *American Indian*, *indigenous* is also a descriptive label that refers to a range of colonial histories and political relationships. We have chosen not to capitalize it to avoid imputing a generic racial, ethnic, or cultural essentialism and obscuring the particularities of distinct native peoples (Aymara, Quechua, Guaraní, and others). This also avoids obscuring the distinct usages of the term in Bolivia, as discussed below.

2. Among others, see Wright 2010 for "lithium dreams"; N. Klein 2010 on Bolivia's environmentalist challenge; and *The New Yorker's* racialist darkening of Evo (alongside Mahmoud Ahmadinejad and Hugo Chávez) in the issue of December 7, 2009. Against both sovereignty and indigeneity, Collier (2010), speaking in the name of a wealthy "we," offers economistic prescriptions to "manage nature for global prosperity."

3. Ritual combat in which exchange, not defeat is the goal; also, an amorous encounter.

4. The Andes, in US-based national security policy, continues to be viewed as a problematic region, with implicit assumptions about the political threat of Andean peoples, by virtue of their (non-Western) ethnicities. This frame for production of "intelligence" about the Andes—which seems to view all change as inherently threatening—tends to fuse indigenous movements and the MAS regime with a panoply of other "risks." Here, Andeanism is defined by "physical insecurity," "risks" to democracy, "violent conflict," and "porous borders that enable the easy movement of drugs, arms, and conflict." Bolivia, in particular, is seen through this lens as a country "where almost everything is going wrong" (Council on Foreign Relations 2004:1–9, 10; see also Gamarra 2007).

5. Starn (1999:19–22) later qualified his critique as somewhat exaggerated in its portrayal of the contributions of an earlier generation of Andeanist anthropology.

6. This ongoing conflict led to the recent ouster of a much respected Vice Minister of Lands, Alejandro Almaráz. Almaráz, who supported collective territorial rights, was replaced by a proponent of individual titling, and tensions now exist between sectors of highland Andean organizations and the lowland CIDOB, accused of demanding "too much land for too few people." Paradoxically, this parcelization push from some sectors of the MAS (which contradicts Evo's own statements, as in the interview following this chapter) echoes emerging neoliberal discourse on the "liberation" of indigenous peoples through individualized private property. As with the US Allotment Act in 1887, Bolivia's own Ley de Desvinculación, 1874, and the 1952 Reform, the dogmatic embrace of private ownership led to *de jure* and *de facto* dispossession. For the neoliberal view in Peru, see De Soto 2010; on complexities articulating individual and communal holdings, Hvalkof 2008; on Bolivia, Almaráz 2010.

7. By *pachamamismo* we refer to a stereotyped set of (generally Andean Aymara) discourses defending the power of Mother Earth, the harmonious social order of indigenous societies, and protesting the sins of Western capitalism, modernity, and development. The reactionary right attacks pachamamismo as primitivist romanticism invented by Euro-American anthropologists. Although Bolivia's new left is taking a decolonial and ecological turn, some left-leaning theorists also attack pachamamismo as an ethnicist or culturalist, if not reactionary, response to the challenges of capitalism (Stefanoni 2010). In contrast, for a classic if sometimes forgotten articulation of the Pachamama and militant politics, see Nash 1979.

8. The Water Wars unfolded in Cochabamba in 2000 as public resistance to a government attempt to privatize water delivery (Albro 2005; Assies 2003; Dangl 2007; Farthing and Kohl 2001; Finnegan 2002; Perrault 2006; Spronk 2007).

9. The land wars in the eastern region have been a backdrop to battles over water and gas (see Mendoza et al. 2003; Orduña 2001; Tamburini and Betancur 2001).

10. Two other recent collections include Grindle and Domingo's *Proclaiming Revolution* (2003), which contains (mostly sympathetic) evaluations of the reformist policies initiated by the MNR during the 1990s. Crabtree and Whitehead's *Unresolved Tensions* (2008) offers insightful macrolevel framings of current debates over the MAS project through a juxtaposition of polarized viewpoints. Save exceptions, in both collections the scholars are also politically "engaged," albeit mostly from positions of power, distinct from the grassroots-level positionings we explore here.

Visions from the Ground
A Conversation with Evo Morales

¡Viva La Revolución Agraria!

In June of 2006, at a large gathering in the city of Santa Cruz, Evo Morales declared that he would modify the 1996 National Agrarian Reform Law, or Ley INRA, implemented by the right-leaning government of Gonzalo Sánchez de Lozada. Evo's government named the new proposal the "Law for the Communitarian Redirection of Agrarian Reform." The phrase *communitarian redirection* symbolized a shift from reform that prioritized the creation of a free market in land, toward reform that included redistributive concerns aimed at meeting social and community needs. The new law included four pillars distinct from its predecessor. One, social and economic function: all land that does not fulfill a social and economic function—that is, serving only as a speculative or unproductive large-scale holding—is subject to expropriation by the state and redistribution to peasants. Two, mechanization: tractors and other equipment will be provided to small-scale farmers. Three, credit: an Agricultural and Rural Development Bank will lower interest rates for small scale producers from 20 percent to 6 percent. Four, eco-markets: the state will support development of foreign markets for ecological products (organics) and develop options for long-term sustainability. At the event and in the presence of approximately one hundred thousand supporters, Morales also presented official land titles representing more than 7.5 million hectares to sixty small-scale farming communities. Morales said that he hoped to distribute an additional 20 million hectares of land to the nation's mostly poor peasant and indigenous communities over the next five years.

However, by October 2006, the draft of the New Agrarian Reform Law was stalled on the Senate floor. The members of the right-wing PODEMOS (Poder Democrático y Social, or Social and Democratic Power) party—which still held a controlling vote in the Senate—refused to support the new legislation. The opposition had also organized spectacular performances of resistance to the law—deemed communistic—in the cities of Santa Cruz and Tarija. In response, landless peasants and lowland indigenous communities came together from around the country to launch the fifth Annual March for Land and Dignity. (The first had been in 1991 with the others in intervening years, though this was the first in support of, rather than in resistance to, government proposals). They walked for twenty-eight days from Santa Cruz to La Paz to pressure senators to pass the law. On November 29, 2006, with La Paz's Plaza Murillo crammed with people, the Bolivian Senate approved it. The interview that follows took place in the Presidential Palace nine months later, as right-wing resistance to land redistribution continued.[1]

"I Am Evo Morales Ayma, for the Moment, President of the Republic"

NICOLE FABRICANT: Well, we could start with your name, Mr. President, and maybe go from there to the issue of the landless movement?

EVO MORALES: Sure, thank you very much. Well, I am Evo Morales Ayma, [*he smiles and pauses*] for the moment, President of the Republic. We are here, as always, struggling, in search of justice. In the past as a leader and now as president, in search of equality, in search of justice. If we speak about the theme of land and the landless movement, these are unfolding through an agrarian revolution, to guarantee the total elimination of the unproductive latifundio (large underproductive landholdings) in our country. Why an agrarian revolution? Because we differentiate it from the so-called agrarian reforms of '52, of '53.[2] In those times, our grandfathers, our ancestors rose up, rifle at the shoulder, to recover the lands held by the *patrones* (landlords). And the MNR [Movimiento Nacionalista Revolucion-ario]? The only thing they did was to try to legalize an armed uprising with the distribution of land. One of the errors of the reform was the individual parcelization, the lack of respect for the communitarian lands of origin. Another error was the creation, in the altiplano and the valleys, of the *minifundio*, or the *surcofundio* as some of our brothers say,[3] and in the east, *latifundio*, where by the end there was no agrarian reform at all. To differentiate ourselves, we speak of agrarian revolution…[which] aims to provide land to those people without lands or with insufficient lands, through state assistance…

The resistance [to this agrarian revolution] attempts to divide peasant movements or to create parallel organizations and movements. There are never lacking among our brothers, whether indigenous, campesinos [peasants], colonists, those who become involved in these [divisive] strategies. And I am sorry to say—since you are from the United States—well, no matter, that the United States also manages a lot of money and uses it to divide organizations. It is impressive. They manage around $100 million used to divide the labor organizations, and if some of our brothers enter into that game, they do it for money. It [money] is the best instrument. But for the majority [of the people], there is a great consciousness and dignity, so as not to fall into that trap.

Second, the media are against the agrarian revolution. The media, by and large, are owned by the landowners or by the opposition. Here in Bolivia, it turns out that media programming is paid for by private interests—the landlords, capitalists, corrupt politicians. And, unfortunately, the United States also pays ex-ministers, Goni [Gonzalo Sánchez de Lozada], ex-cabinet ministers, who now work as commentators, analysts, and economic analysts in the media. They are all paid by the United States Embassy. That is another way they defend themselves and stand against [the agrarian revolution].[4]

Another is the fact that some Bolivians, for money, and some NGOs, some, not all, to be clear, have other development objectives with their programs. I saw this personally in the so-called alternative development programs [in the Chapare].[5] A program has 70 percent or 80 percent for overhead, expenses for their employees. For travel costs, per diems, salaries. And 20 percent or 30 percent? Not even for investment, but for workshops, training, seminars. That is how the money of the United States is spent, the so-called cooperation of USAID. And the problem is that there is no control. These are all the best instruments of defense of the oligarchic sector, the landlords, against the agrarian revolution.

What is my vision for this country? To, little by little, reduce the asymmetries—from family to family, from department to department, from municipality to municipality, and why not, from continent to continent…. What are we talking about? Equality. Justice. Complementarity. I am talking, in other words, about a socialism [un socialismo]. I continue to be convinced that capitalism is the worst enemy of humanity. Why do I say that to you? I, for example, if I want to concentrate capital in my power or in my family—or if I, as president, want my country to be capitalist…I have to invent wars, invade, exploit, humiliate, and turn people into slaves. The life of others is of no interest to me, as long as I have money.

If we begin with basic things, equality, justice, eliminating individualism, greed, sectarianism, regionalism, eliminating that way of thinking just about ourselves and not about everyone—we will have to change all that. That is why I say to my ministers, if we want to change Bolivia, we have to change ourselves. If we do not change and we continue being egotistical, individualistic, *ambiciosos*,[6] we'll never change anything. So we start changing ourselves, we change our region, our nation, and why not say it, we change humanity and we change the thinking of everyone.

Notes

1. Interview by Nicole Fabricant, La Paz, August 17, 2007.

2. The reference is to the Revolution of 1952, after which the Nationalist Revolutionary Movement (MNR)—under pressure from peasant unions—carried out a sweeping land reform in the Andean western part of the country, but with little effect in the east (see Grindle and Domingo 2003; Malloy 1970).

3. Minifundios are properties of 1 or 2 hectares, insufficient for subsistence, as contrasted with latifundio, large-scale holdings of the wealthy that were maintained in the Oriente (eastern Bolivia). Surcofundios, from the word *surco*, for "row," is a colloquialism that refers to the fragmentation of land through inheritance, leading to properties of only one or two hand-hoed rows.

4. He refers here to long-standing accusations—many substantiated—that programs like USAID, the National Endowment for Democracy, and the International Republican Institute contribute money to support antigovernment movements and leaders.

5. In the Chapare, where Morales lived and emerged as a political leader of the coca growers' movement, USAID's heavily funded alternative development programs ostensibly sought to incentivize crops other than the coca leaf.

6. *Ambicioso* (ambitious) in the Bolivian sense means avaricious, self-serving, and greedy.

2 Cartographies of Indigenous Power

Identity and Territoriality in Bolivia

Pablo Mamani Ramirez

In this chapter, I argue that a profound territorial and social transformation is underway in Bolivia, one that unfolds largely in spatial and geopolitical terms and manifests itself in ethnocultural, racial, and class conflict surrounding the reterritorializing tactics of indigeneity and indigenous peoples across the country.[1] Some of these shifts occur at the level of everyday life, in relation to mundane conflicts, for instance, the diffusion of Andean cultural practices in eastern Bolivia. Others are large-scale, momentous clashes—such as the 2003 Gas War and the 2008 clashes over autonomy in the east—which are dramatically reordering power relations in the country. Whereas critics assert that indigenous peoples' visions and demands for recognition as *peoples* are essentialist, implying that we ignore internal complexities and relations of class hierarchy within indigenous populations, I argue here that a broader pattern of ethnoracial domination and inequality between indigenous peoples and the criollo-mestizo elites is most significant for understanding Bolivia today. I also argue that this history and relationship of inequality and domination is being questioned and dismantled. The indigenous resurgence is thus simultaneously transforming state and territory, yielding new cartographies of indigenous power, a distinct remapping of Bolivia—while also dismantling a longer historical relationship based on white-mestizo dominance. Ideally, we are in transition to a more robust expression of what we might call an ethnic democracy, though this is a conflictive process marked by painful legacies of colonial racism and exclusion, as well as future uncertainties.

A New Historical Moment

Bolivia, or Qullasuyu to indigenous campesinos, is at the center of a profound historical event. Like a volcano—or several of them—the country is erupting and fully active, transforming the depths of ethnic domination and exploitation suffered by the majority of the population, the indigenous peoples, a majority that until five years ago was treated as a simple political minority. Historically, indigenous peoples were made invisible—treated as peoples without history, without memories of struggle, without territories, without leadership. Now, the political domination and ethnicized economic exploitation of indigenous peoples have become irreversibly tangible, visible, and real before the eyes of indigenous and nonindigenous Bolivians alike.

Until recently, even Indians themselves saw their exploitation as a "natural" fact, sanctioned by God, from the day of their birth to the day of their death. It was as if indigeneity was a kind of divine punishment that one should be born and live in the lowest levels of society. This was understood to be part of natural reality, never seen as a condition created by men and women. Indigeneity was synonymous with inhuman, uncivilized, savage, irrational, idolatrous, brutal, incompetent, retrograde, and antimodern.[2] In contrast, in Bolivia today the Indians (indios) or indigenous peoples (*pueblos indígenas*) have become geopolitically strategic actors, even extending across Latin America. This is due, in part, to their great capacity for collective mobilization, a power and practice enhanced by complex systems of discursive strategies and tactics of collective action. This national and transnational significance is further mediated—as I discuss below—by their territorial positioning in distinct regions of state territory, their demographic dynamics, and the strategies of episodic regional and local uprisings. Most recently, the indigenous resurgence has unfolded through electoral results. This phenomenon is confirmed by the colossal triumph of Evo Morales in Bolivia's presidential election on December 25, 2005, which he won with 54 percent of the general vote, and his reelection in 2008, in which he garnered more than 60 percent of the popular vote. The triumph of Evo Morales has definitively contributed to the national reterritorialization of a longer historical state–indigenous conflict in Bolivia (*Ayra* 2006). That is to say, the entirety of Bolivian state territory and modes of territorial occupation, governance, and organization are now being fundamentally questioned from the position of alternative indigenous rationalities and ways of thinking.

These aim to reconstitute, from various positions, new territorialities and territorial orders as spaces of contestation and reappropriation.

This is an unfolding process in tactical terms and a strategic fact from a political perspective. In a sense, there is an ongoing reoccupation of the great indigenous territory that the white-mestizo state (*estado blanco-mestizo*) had disarticulated through state formation during its 180 years as a republic. In some ways, state legitimacy has collapsed; in others, it is being reconstituted by both new and re-emergent movements. This process is reconfiguring the concept of the state in relation to territory. What were once historically understood as the centralization of power and the abusive use of "legitimate" physical violence, we now see as the production of a new concept of the state as a space for the decentralized institutionalization of territorial and political power(s), with the possibility of sharing power among distinct regions and specific localities.

In my previous work (P. Mamani 2004, 2005), I argued that Bolivia is undergoing a profound process of territorial resignification and demographic re-occupation of state territory by multiple social movements. Among these movements, I argue, the indigenous-originary-peasant world (*mundo indígena campesina originaria*) predominates. This also implies that we are witnessing a sort of "revolution of the body." An indio, the bearer of an Indian body and originary discourse, had never been elected as president in the 180 years of the Republic. Never before had an indigenous person without a college education become the president of the Republic. To have been born in the ayllus, or in indigenous cities has always been a factor of racial segregation. To wear hand-knit sweaters and the jackets or overcoats popular among indigenous people was considered a sign of degradation, especially in the spaces of public power. Dark skin has always been a limiting factor and a source of economic and social discrimination and exploitation in Bolivia. Speaking Spanish without the "proper" articulation in fluid and "correct" form has also been a central factor of Latin American apartheid, a form of society and government in which the indigenous people were included so as to be discriminated against. But now these signs on certain bodies have been converted into positive signs marking triumph and success. They are increasingly signs of social acceptance and recognition. This fundamental and positive valuation of the indigenous social world is wholly new in Bolivia. If, in the past, deep walls had gone up between indios and non-indios, now many people want to be indios, or at least dress like them or live as one with them without being indigenous. Of course, none of this was a gift given by the dominant groups. It was a painful, bold, and astute re-conquest carried out by these once reviled bodies.

There are many who do not wish to recognize this fact, and the new sociopolitical dynamic is not entirely embraced or understood. For instance, many members of Evo Morales's political circle are white and mestizo, or as the Aymara call them, *q'ara*. His is not, then, an indigenous cadre. This suggests that there is still a gap between the new sociopolitical dynamic and the leadership groups of the Movement to Socialism party (Movimiento al Socialismo, MAS). This reproduces a sort of "internal colonialism" within Morales's government. Yet, in spite of this, we are witnessing a historical moment that will have a significant geopolitical impact on the different states and peoples of so-called Latin America. Indigeneity (including those of African descent) has become the reference point for a new articulation of alternative projects, feelings, orientations, and diffuse actions that, little by little, have been building and claiming political spaces in this part of the world. What is happening today in Bolivia is of great importance, and its effects will be felt in some form in other latitudes as well.

Legacies of Ethnoracial Inequality and the Invisible Indio

Indigeneity (*lo indígena*) or Indianness (*lo indio*) has become a center point of social conflict in that it is central to social and power relations. Although critics of the indigenous resurgence often accuse indigenous peoples of essentializing their identity, this is an accusation that usually comes from those who essentialize themselves. That is to say, we often hear essentialist claims about core meanings and values of the "West" and "Western knowledge" and "modernity" from those who consider themselves to be the so-called members of "Western" society. Yet, despite attempts to deny the fact that there is an indigenous majority of Bolivia and attempts to revive arguments about the inevitable mixing (mestizaje) of the country (for example, Toranzo Roca 2008), there is an undeniable historical reality: the Aymara and Quechua are peoples that belong to an Andean civilization of great historical depth, peoples that now live in both the cities and the rural areas. Although there are many poor Bolivians who are not indigenous and, for a long time, indigenous rural peoples referred to themselves (and were referred to) as peasants (campesinos), there is no way to deny either the existence of indigeneity or its salience in relations of power. In Bolivia and in all colonized countries, including ongoing modern forms of colonization, there are three clear lines of domination: that of ethnicity or race, that of class, and that of gender. In Bolivia, the privileging of the classist vision—or the category of class—has always been used to obscure the ongoing, and always painful, ethnic and national domination of the indigenous peoples.

This fact cuts through multiple facets of Bolivian life and life elsewhere in the world, shaping historical process through a conflictive dialectic between the scales of extraordinary events and those microevents of every-day social life. The extraordinary events are those important moments, such as indigenous mobilizations or uprisings, that are charged with profound political and historical meaning. The everyday events are those changing relations that unfold and are embedded in the microevents of daily life. Social conflict takes place in both spheres, separately and together, and in both cases, I argue that these are largely characterized by their ethnic conditions, combined with important degrees of class conflict, events large and small that are now emerging with force in various centers of power. Two primary elements, cultural and economic, thus organize the complexities of social conflict. This is a multifaceted social reality because the borders between culture and economy are often undifferentiated and blurred, such that, for instance, class domination is naturalized as a relationship between unequal ethnocultural groups. In the past, these conflicts were always thought of as the expression of class struggles. Today, however, the ethnic and racial characteristics of these conflicts have become increasingly visible as well.

Arguably, relations of power and force between the indigenous-popular and white-mestizo worlds (particularly of the white-mestizo elites) are charged with different historical and social rationalities. Indigenous peoples organize their time and space cyclically and in terms of communitarian, as well as individual, actions (Hylton and Thomson 2007; Lazar 2008). The white-mestizo world, especially its upper class, is defined by the individualistic, linear, and instrumental rationality that is part of a positivist, liberal philosophy. The conflict is ethnicized or racialized because dominant groups define themselves in terms of a dominant common sense based on defining the color of their skin as "white" (even when it is not really so), whereas the indios or indigenous people define these relations in terms of their own common sense, based on the color of "dark" (morena) skin. This reading may make some uncomfortable, but it is a quotidian reality that skin color is perceived as an objective indicator of profound ethnic and social differentiation. Power relations are thus expressed in what we define as a pyramid of ethnic and racial domination.

Sociologically speaking, this pyramid graphically expresses different hierarchical levels on which state and society are organized, with three major structures or spaces, each one with its own internal complexities. The first element is the structural base of the pyramid. The indigenous people are situated at the base of the pyramid, with a population (6,371,230 inhabitants) close to 77 percent of the total national population of 8,274,325 (Bello and Rancel 2000; INE 2002a, 2002b, 2003).[3] There are, of course, exploitative relationships among the indigenous people within this population. The next element is the intermediate space. The middle class, which constitutes between 17 percent and 20 percent of the population, occupies the intermediate position. This intermediate space has its own complexities as well because there are ethnic and economic differences within it. A considerable part of this middle class acts as the "moral cushion" (*colchón moral*) of ethnic domination. That is to say, the middle class has historically been the main intellectual defender of the dominant social order, contributing to the domination of the groups in power. The final element is the space at the top of the pyramid, constituted by the white-mestizo elites and the oligarchy, with some traits of a bourgeoisie,[4] and defined around several subgroups. Its population represents approximately 8 to 10 percent of the national population (661,946 inhabitants). This is the organizing nucleus of social hierarchies and relations.

Out of this pyramidal structure and through these spaces, ethnic domination is generated and legitimized. These are also the loci where the organization of social life is pursued through the means of different technologies of power—what Foucault (2000) calls the government of populations (classificatory systems, juridical bodies, and exclusionary practices) and biopolitics (control of the birthrate, the census, and the discourse of hygiene). These strategies for the organization of power produce and reproduce ethnic boundaries, such that the society has been historically separated conceptually and institutionally between a massive indigenous population and a minority population descended from European colonizers. One ongoing illustration of the production of these boundaries is the biological reproduction of the oligarchy, which is predicated on the logic of endogamy. The oligarchs of La Paz, for instance, do not marry with the *qamiri* (moneyed Aymara) of the neighborhoods of the Garita de Lima or Buenos Aires Avenue or the Uyustus in La Paz.[5] The same goes for the nonindigenous elites of the wealthy neighborhoods of Equipetrol in Santa Cruz or Calacala in Cochabamba. They marry among themselves. They would rather marry an Italian or North American, but never an indio. And the indigenous people do the same. Cultural mestizaje can be observed, but—at least among these social strata—not biological mestizaje.[6]

In the political field, these social relations manifest themselves even more crudely. The original indigenous demographic majority has been reduced to a political minority by means of the civilizing discourse of modern citizenship. The indigenous majority was made to be invisible in the public space, in spite of being the true moral and economic foundation of the white state. By this I mean that indigenous peoples—despite their public invisibilization by the mestizo-white majority—have historically expressed the needs of the entirety of society through collective mobilization, such as the Gas War of 2003 (or their massive participation in the

Chaco War in the 1930s).[7] The Gas War, for instance, was a national project led by the people of El Alto. In economic terms, the indigenous have also always been the support of the state through the provision of cheap manual labor and natural resources from within their territories. This historical invisibilization—in contrast to the reality of indigenous peoples providing the moral and economic foundation of the country—was something like a mental state or imaginary of the elite, because in objective social relations and in the history of the Republic, indigenous people have always been at the center of quotidian and extraordinary moments, whether in political revolutions or in daily life, whether in the cultural or economic realms.

Despite these empirical and historical realities, the public intellectual field is another space through which images of the defeat of indigenous peoples—part of the strategy of invisibilization—have always been produced. One example of this in the intellectual arena is the cartography and historiography of domination—the ways that indigenous history has been (re)mapped and (re)written from the locus of domination. This has yielded what we refer to as a trans-writing (*transescritura*) of indigenous history, the writing of indigenous history as a secondary or distorted version of history, one with little historical value. In this sense, many historians, sociologists, literati, poets, and anthropologists have become ventriloquists (Guerrero 2000). They speak, write, and perform in the name of indigenous people without being indigenous themselves, and they do so from the space and institutions of ethnic domination. This fact has prevented indigenous people from writing and speaking about themselves. The ventriloquists have appropriated the dominated bodies to infuse them with a dominant republican discourse.

New Cartographies of Indigenous Power

What is remarkable today is that this pyramid of ethnic domination—and this colonial legacy of invisibilization and political minoritization—is being profoundly challenged. From dominated positions, that is, from the bottom of the pyramid, or from the interstices of these spaces, indigenous peoples are assuming a leading role, becoming social and political actors of transcendent historical importance. They have reasserted their status as the country's moral foundation. As a demographic majority, indigenous peoples are now becoming a political majority, although one as yet institutionalized at the level of the state. As Bengoa (2000) describes it, this is part of a wider (re)emergence of indigeneity in Latin America. From invisibility, indigenous people have made themselves visible before the world, the state (and its functionaries), and the dominant groups.

Accompanying this process—and against the historical weight of the inequalities described above—indigenous people have developed their own strategies of counter-power. Although there are certainly degrees of cooptation and party-based clientelism, at the same time there are instances of collective self-assertion as an alterity within the spaces of the dominant power. In these relationships, indigenous people are not passive actors, but rather profoundly active ones, because from and through the interstices of ethnic domination they are reaffirmed as indigenous peoples and reconstruct their power, establishing what we might call new "cartographies of indigenous power." The creation of counter-power strategies is a territorialized and territorializing fact that becomes inscribed in the geographical and social spaces of the indigenous world, part of the wider reterritorializing phenomenon to which I refer above.

One of these spaces is the school. The state has tried to impose by way of the school the values of Western civilization. Indigenous people have replied with their own rationalities by appropriating others' values according to their own cultural technologies, their own languages, knowledges, and histories (Gustafson 2009a). Another key dimension of this revolt of meanings is the remaking of the cities as indigenous cities. Here—in Otavalo in Ecuador or El Alto in Bolivia—indigenous people, in spite of the discourse of the Western modernity that presumed that indigeneity would disappear with urbanization, now construct their own urban or inter-neighborhood social relations within big cities. In these cases, urban social relations and organizing patterns are being remade by indigenous peoples who are bearers of distinct values and social relations.[8]

Social and personal identity can also be seen as subjected to a new remapping, a new cartography of the body. Compared with the immediate past, it is evident today that many people define their social relations based on their indigenous social identity instead of the historically dominant notion of white-mestizo citizenship. Because of this, many Bolivians are now defining themselves as derivations of the indigenous, understood as a sector of society, distinct from others, that is a significant component of the whole. Hurtado's (1986) forecast, that in the future many people would feel proud of being the descendants of native women, has been fulfilled. Today, thousands feel proud of being Aymaras, Qhiswas, Urus, Chipayas, Guaraníes, Lecos, Mojeños, Chiquitanos, and so forth. As these identity claims express themselves in the assertion of distinct forms of social organization or knowledge production, they undermine processes such as the state's expansion in recent years through the tactic of "popular participation"[9] and other mechanisms of government. This also yields new territorializations of identity based on the making visible of a demographic majority and on the reinterpretation of the historical meanings of the indigenous world. There are, of course, elements of cultural ethnogenesis in this process, not merely a "return" to tradition. It is a reterritorializing process that unfolds in both open and concealed forms as an indigenous counter-power develops from within the very centers of cultural and economic domination.

In this vision, indigenous people are constructing power from within the spaces of dominant power and as a substantial element of these relations. This construction of counter-power has, then, two conditions: (a) it occurs from the interstices of ethnic domination, and (b) it happens through social and geographic separation, from an ethnic frontier.

This is an exercise of power to overturn ethnic domination. One of the main loci of this strategy is the co-production of identity and territoriality. How is indigenous identity made territorial? The answer can be found in a geopolitics of the indigenous populations, a strategy to occupy diverse social and territorial spaces. For instance, starting around fifty years ago, the *qulla* (Andean, also spelled *Colla*, herein, or *kolla*) population, composed mainly of Aymara and Quechua, by its own means and through state policies of colonization, has been extending its presence in the territories and towns of Amazonia and Chaco (P. Mamani 2005; see also Gill 1987; Stearman 1985). Today in these regions, these populations have become protagonists of mobilizations and confrontations with local power groups, the landlords. This is, for example, the case of the events of May 2005 in Yuquises, north of Santa Cruz, led by the Landless Movement (Movimiento Sin Tierra, MST; see Fabricant, chapter 7, this volume). In this instance, land was occupied using quasi-military strategies in tandem with claims made through legal channels. In this way, indigenous populations appropriate organizational and territorial resources that are key to their cultural, biological, and economic reproduction.

This reappropriation takes place with more force within the Andean regions themselves, although it is concentrated in large and medium-size cities. To objectively capture this phenomenon, it would be interesting to do a visual and mental exercise of an imaginary low-level flight over the territory of the country. It would be easy to see, in this way, that there are indigenous peoples of the Andes, Amazon, and Chaco in El Alto, La Paz, Potosí, Oruro, Cochabamba, Alto Beni, Chapare, San Julián, Santa Cruz, Plan Tres Mil of Santa Cruz, the rural provinces of Santa Cruz, and even the first peripheral ring of Santa Cruz.[10] It is clearly evident that there is a massive indigenous presence across the territory of the state, a presence that is a direct expression of a new social reality.[11] Thus "discovered" and now more visible than ever, these populations have become social and political actors engaged in productions of indigenous territoriality—expressed in these places through commercial, sport, and festival events, obviously with local economic and regional variations. There are thus, in these places, major cultural and political disputes between these populations and the local white-mestizo dominant groups, especially in the Amazonia and Chaco regions (Kirshner, chapter 5, this volume). In the Andean altiplano and the valleys of the Andes, this indigenous territorialization is more intense because there are now few mestizo-white landowners' descendants in these places. The landlords abandoned the indigenous communities or ayllus when faced with emergent indigenous power and the force of identity, making room for the emergence of politicized communities. Although some still call themselves peasants (campesinos), there is in these regions a clear positioning of the indigenous as the structuring element of the local social reality.

This new cartography of indigenous power unfolds in ritual public cultural forms as well. One can observe how indigenous people, in particular the Aymaras and the Quechua, reproduce their own festivities in the places they inhabit. This can be seen—again, in our flyover of the country, in both historically indigenous city-regions and in new settlement areas, as well as in cities that long represented themselves as "white" (such as Tarija and Santa Cruz). A variety of folkloric festivities, the *morenada*, *tarqueada*, and *moseñada*, among others, are now organized in these places. This leads to the infiltration of originary indigeneity at various levels of social relations, with increasing influence and power, even when it does so without conscious intention or political motivation. These ritual practices—often unfolding today as expressions of urban belonging in the culture of the public streets—emerge out of the dynamics of the populations themselves and the practice of making space a place through which identity is defined and where the reorganization of the structures of social organization, as well as the rituals of the earth and the re-identification of *wak'as* (sacred places or objects) as an expression of collective belonging to those territories, takes place.

This echoes the ongoing reality that territory maintains its centrality as a cultural and strategic factor because it contains the language of indigenous memory, of indigenous agricultural and medicinal technologies, and of indigenous cosmology. In several places, one can observe that the names of the hills and mountains have a deeper significance, such as *awicha* (older grandmother), *achachila* (older grandfather) (both major figures of indigenous memory and ritual), and those of minor divinities, all of which are central to the biological and cultural reproduction of peoples and indigenous populations. This is part of the representation of Pachamama (Mother Earth), *uywiris* (creators of life), and *jiliris* (older brothers and sisters). In each one of these places, collective memory and indigenous knowledge and practical wisdom are inscribed. These include economic, political, cultural, and social expertise and technologies. In sum, territory is the space defined by the indigenous world's multiversal knowledge. Its geography is inhabited not only by human populations but also by the gods. Territory, then, is a part of life—human and nonhuman—and of the active social life of the Andean and Amazonian worlds. In this way, territory is not only a space for the exploitation of natural resources but also the space for the reproduction of social and religious life. Clear examples of this are innumerable. For instance, the sites of Qalachaka and Pachjiri in the province of Omasuyus are spaces of Aymara religiosity where commemorations to past and present political struggles are carried out through ritual, such as those on August 1 and April 9, the latter in memory of those killed in the Aymara uprising of 2000 (Mamani Ramirez n.d.). In Kurahuara de Karangas, the hills of Monterani and Thikhapani (Man and Woman) represent the force of the ayllus. The people engage the high mountains in dialogue between the ayllus, spirits, and their authorities before going out to road blockades or before inaugurating new political authorities. In other cases, these sites are like markers of a life plan, places to which people go to ask for health, well-being, money, love, or other desires. In the tropical regions of Yungas, around Carañavi, the colony-communities have hills that refer to Pächata—a sacred and respectable place. In the Chapare, the mountains and woods are places in which the Andean and Amazonian gods are present. In El Alto, Waraq Achachila and La Ceja are references to this meshing of religious, social, and territorial meanings.

The same happens with the indigenous people of the Amazonia and Chaco. In these regions, the Guaraní or Chiquitano dispute systems of representation and historical projects with the white elites of European origin. These struggles produce new scenarios of discourse and strategies of counter-power whose political dimension is characterized by the public symbolic performance of identity. For instance, the indigenous people of the Andes and Amazonia represent their identity by means of the *wiphala* (multi-colored flag of Andean indigenous movements) and other symbols. The "others" who defend the privileges of the mestizo-white elite, such as the so-called Camba Nation (Nación Camba), define themselves through regional symbols such as the green and white flag of Santa Cruz. Thus, each of them, considered in the past as indios, now disputes cultural tastes with the dominant groups. If, in the past, owning a new car or an SUV was the privilege of the white-mestizo, now the moneyed indigenous people can also treat themselves with the same vehicles as part of their economic and symbolic capital. Some descendants of the landowners, who still live in these places, in particular in the valleys, feel a certain uneasiness when observing how the Indians are no longer so Indian, how the Indians are even better off than they are, now that Indians have economic and cultural power. This does not mean that in these social spaces economic exploitation is no longer present. Rather, the indigenous people are no longer crying over themselves (*llorosos*), as in the past, but present themselves as proud, entrepreneurial (*emprendedor*), and defiant. Such pride is disconcerting to the groups once in power, to the so-called "decent" people (*gente decente*),[12] because they find that Indians are no longer the same as Indians fifty years ago, but are now entrepreneurial and savvy.

Symbolic performances as occupations of public space and natural territory and the acquisition of new economic positions are accompanied by another mode of remapping cartographies of power, that of remaking spaces of governance. Indigenous peoples have expanded their capacity for leadership in private and public organizations, in particular in the administration of local public policies at the municipal level. Fifty years ago, it was unthinkable that an indigenous person could be a municipal authority. Today, even if these positions are still defined within the logic of the state, indigenous peoples control municipal councils in much of the country (Albó 2002). This involves the capacity to define and manage state territory as a strategic exercise in order to build identity and power from that position. It is part of building an indigenous universe or multiverse based upon local and regional worlds. Even if certain municipal administrations have been criticized because of poor performance, which is part of the learning process, it is also well known that in several places the good indigenous administration of public affairs has gained prestige. This is the case, for example, in the municipality of Kurahuara de Karangas. It reminds us that indigenous people construct their alterity both within and outside relations of domination. For some, this process of municipalization is seen as a factor legitimizing ethnic domination, which may be true. But it is also evident that this is an example of indigenous counter-power as part of the struggle against ethnic domination. It is a space that, in spite of all its problems, might be the leading example of possible indigenous states, which could be the result of a sort of indigenous assault on town administrations and territories. Although local, this indigenous power has the capacity to rebuild new places and then rebuild the geographic fabric of indigeneity. Because these are specific places of indigenous territoriality, the possession of them generates feelings of collective and individual belonging, of becoming, as Yampara (2001) points out, *uraqpacha* (a whole) of men and women, everything that surrounds and belongs to the soil and everything that belongs to and surrounds the space.

In this way, territory becomes a direct expression of the world and of power. If, following de Certeau (2002), a strategy consists of defining a place in order to act from there to deploy or counter tactics and techniques of power, then these acts of defining one or several places—of remapping or reterritorializing—are a mode of political struggle. In this case, geography is being transformed into a reference of identity as part of the memories and cartographies of indigenous power. A strategy for building counter-powers from different geographical places is an effective way of fighting ethnic domination. These struggles take different forms and meanings. Sometimes they occur by means of violence, other times by way of negotiation, and still other times indigenous people continue to bow their heads to negotiate their survival. From this place of occupied geography, indigenous people, once vilified, rebuild an alternative and litigant body (*un cuerpo alterno y litigante*).

It should be understood, then, that the geopolitics of indigenous populations is a field of counter-power and identity and cultural struggles, all of which are part of a construction of indigenous hegemony and an effect of the exercise of power through reterritorializing techniques. Not only must "geopolitics" be understood as a kind of strategic planning from the center of the state or governmental power, but also the state must acknowledge that the population has the capacity to produce its own geopolitics from its own cultural matrices—in this case, out of indigeneity. Therefore, identity and culture are not only produced by the capitalist system, as Patzi (2004) argues—or through the tactics of governmentality described by Foucault (2000)—but also emerge through individual, collective, and material subjectivities, manifesting themselves as a concrete materiality via the social action that is part of the system of power, along with the economic factor. This echoes Foucault's notion of a microphysics of power—invisible, interwoven threads that have, among their practical effects, that of indigenous counter-power—albeit in forms distinct from that of the state. This kind of geopolitics has two sets of conditioning factors: one, that it is part of a process of cultural and territorial reappropriation, and the other, that it is a part of an ongoing negotiation with the dominant power. The cause of this remapping of indigenous power is the valorization of indigenous identity as a result of indigenous struggle.

Indigenous Identities, Ethnic Democracies

For these reasons, the white-mestizo identity (as a sign of prestige and social recognition) appears now as a universal referent with very little social foundation (but see Toranzo Roca 2008). In contrast, indigeneity, or lo indígena, has become a positive collective marker, despite the historical discrimination associated with the word *indígena*, or worse yet, the word *indio*. The indigenous particular is becoming a universal, one that according to our understanding, would be part of the multiversal, a referent of multiversity, that is, an approach to understanding the world from different points of view (Mamani, Quisbert, and Callizaya n.d.). This acknowledges and makes visible a richer and more complex reality of indigeneity, but one with a specific trunk or core founded in indigenous common sense. In this sense, we do not understand the word *indígena* as it is usually understood, that is, as a social being ostracized in the distant rural mountains (as was understood by white-mestizo *indigenism*). Rather, the indígena is that being who proudly takes a walk through the physical spaces of domination, such as the Plaza Murillo, the seat of government in La Paz. The concrete manifestation of this is that indigenous people now tacitly occupy, with their bodies and the signs of their bodies, the physical spaces of dominant power.

Against accusations that we are essentialists, we therefore do not understand identity as a static or immobile essence. It may be true that a kind of strategic essentialism—claims to absolute alterity, authenticity, or purity—is often a mode of political and cultural negotiation. However, and even though indigeneity has a substantial core—a particularity and a specificity rooted in history and place—identity emerges as the product of relations of force between the indigenous-originary world and the white-mestizo world, as well as the overlaps within and between them. I say worlds because each space has its own rationalities, identities, and economic and political relations. Identities in plural are the products of these power relations.

In sum, the originary indigenous populations in Bolivia have become strategic populations because they occupy immense territories and social spaces where indigenous identities and territorialities are under reconstruction. These spaces are at stake in power struggles. If the ongoing process of constitutional transformation does not recognize this dynamic, it may easily reach its own limits and be succeeded by a process of unforeseen political violence, creating conditions for the amplified reproduction of ethnic conflict expressed in different spaces of society and its territory.

This brings us again to our starting point: the driving force of this process is the populations' increasing identification with references to the *popular* and to indigeneity (*lo indígena* and *lo popular*). An Aymara, Evo Morales, is now the direct representation of this. The conditions for the production of an indigenous self-government on a national scale have spread across the whole space of the territory of the state, in spite of the fact that those in positions of leadership have yet to make sense of these emergent territorial articulations. There is a feeling of owning those territories, and in those spaces, the privileges once held by the white-mestizo are now questioned, especially those gained by the exploitation of indigenous labor and natural resources in those territories. This critique, questioning, or delegitimation of privilege also refers to the dismantling of the white-mestizo logic of relations that operates through a logic of alienation (*enajenación*) of resources without sharing with the rest of society, or, in economic terms, through those who refuse to redistribute the economic surplus (*excedente económico*). As the indigenous person and indigeneity have become the structuring elements in the new social and political reality in Bolivia, it is not surprising that we have an Aymara or indigenous president in Bolivia, breaking the logic of white-mestizo presidents that had long been the norm in the history of the Republic.

As some argue, we are establishing an ethnic democracy to break with the white-mestizo ethnic dictatorship. This may, in time, lead to the constitution or the reconstitution of a grand indigenous state with its own specificities, such as territorial confederations. Such an indigenous state might be organized according to the logic of indigenous counter-power—building on the model of the ayllus—with a rotating government, with turns of sharing authority, with obligatory service, and with the representation and participation of diverse parts and regions. Against those who critique and dismiss the possibility of indigenous reterritorializations or a remapping of indigenous cartographies of power, it is necessary to highlight these dynamics emerging from indigenous geopolitical productions rather than merely reproduce the middle-class entelechies that currently dominate debates on the future of the Bolivian state and society.

Notes

1. This is a translated and revised version of a manuscript originally titled *Cartografías del poder indígena*.

2. The notion that indigeneity was linked to a repulsive, inferior body derives, in part, from the ongoing legacy of intellectuals such as Alcides Arguedas, who, in works such as *Pueblo enfermo* (1982[1910]), imagined that the social, political, and economic ills of a "sick" society derived from indigeneity. —Eds.

3. This calculation reflects the 1992 census, which, by virtue of languages spoken, calculated that approximately 60 percent of Bolivia's population was indigenous. This excluded children under fifteen, suggesting a higher total, as indicated here. The 2001 census asked people which ethnic group they belonged to; 31 percent identified as Quechua, 25 percent as Aymara, and 6 percent as various lowland indigenous, yielding approximately 62 percent of the total population (Albó 2008; INE 2002a, 2002b; see Gustafson and Fabricant, chapter 1, this volume).

4. I say "some traits" of a bourgeoisie because they are not completely bourgeoisie in the sense of being industrious and modern, because they maintain neocolonial logics in their social and economic life.

5. These refer to predominantly Aymara middle-class commercial neighborhoods in La Paz.

6. Felix Patzi, personal communication, 2005. For a comparative parallel on elite reproduction, racism, and endogamy from Guatemala, see Casaus Arzú 1992.

7. For the background to the Gas War of 2003—including a series of mobilizations that were not tied to indigenous populations or claims—see Dangl 2007; Garcés, chapter 3, this volume; Kohl and Farthing 2006.—Eds.

8. For views of El Alto and Santa Cruz as more hybrid expressions of both indigenous and nonindigenous modes of social organization, see Kirshner, chapter 5, and Revilla, chapter 6, this volume, and Lazar 2008. —Eds.

9. Popular participation refers to the 1994 Law of Decentralization, which devolved certain administrative powers to the municipal level, encouraging some new expressions of democratic practice but also imposing a standardizing template of governance. —Eds.

10. See figure 3, a map of Santa Cruz. The first ring (*primer anillo*) of Santa Cruz refers to the concentric rings of avenues that encircle the city center. The first or inner ring is deemed the most urban—and thus the least indigenous—by city dwellers. —Eds.

11. This process of indigenous-popular reappropriation does not occur in some social spaces inhabited by the more elite strata of the white-mestizo populations, such as the residential zones of La Paz—Calacoto, San Miguel, Obrajes, Equipetrol in Santa Cruz, and the "distinguished" (*distinguidos*) neighborhoods of Sucre or Cochabamba.

12. The phrase "decent people" (gente decente) is used by nonindigenous and indigenous alike to refer to the moneyed classes, implicitly white or mestizo.—Eds.

3 The Domestication of Indigenous Autonomies in Bolivia

From the Pact of Unity to the New Constitution

Fernando Garcés

> It is one thing when [people] themselves break the feudal yoke through their
> own collective impulse and quite another when they are let go through a verti-
> cal act, that is to say, by something that does not come from themselves.
> Exogenetic freedom produces only formal freedom.
>
> —*René Zavaleta*, The State in Latin America.

The ongoing debate over the reterritorialization of Bolivia revolves, in large
part, around the political status of indigenous territories (as a demarcated
geophysical region) and territorialities (as a more networked sense of spatialized indigenous practices of daily social and economic life, political participation, and self-determination that may extend beyond particular
geophysical regions). While much has been made of the turn in support of
indigenous rights—a position voiced most prominently by Evo Morales—
the political situation on the ground is infinitely more complex than this

rhetoric suggests. Doubtless, important gains have been made by indigenous peoples, central among these, the advances in the constitution put into place in 2008 after a long and conflictive process of national debate. A central category of this new constitution is "indigenous autonomy"—a legal possibility more than a concrete expression—which offers the possibility that indigenous peoples establish certain territorialized modes of governance that are distinct from the wider templates of department, provincial, and municipal administration.

However, as of this writing, no actual cases of indigenous autonomy have been mobilized into processes of implementation. And, as I argue in this chapter, analysis of the Constitutional Assembly process reveals a series of "domestications" of the idea and potential form and practice of indigenous autonomy—maneuvers by the government and the right-wing opposition to limit and restrict indigenous demands. For indigenous organizations, mobilized in a historic Unity Pact (Pacto de Unidad), the Constitutional Assembly was to be a foundational political moment, one that was truly *constitutional*, in which social movements, indigenous and others, rather than conventional political parties, would literally "refound" the state. This would make of the constitution an "originary" document, rather than one derivative of the existing system, and would open space for the remapping of state territoriality, including a robust approach to indigenous self-determination and autonomy. Nonetheless, as I explore here, various factors worked to moderate this pro–indigenous rights stance. This produced a constitution that was derivative of the current political order—that is, emerging from already constituted powers rather than those rising up through social mobilization. The process and the outcome illustrate the ways through which indigenous demands were negotiated—and sacrificed—to favor a more conservative defense of existing state forms.[1]

The Pursuit of Unity: Peasant, Indigenous, and Originary

The creation of the Constitutional Assembly in Bolivia in 2006 resulted from a long process of mobilizing distinct actors whose origins lie in a deep history of social memory and struggle, as well as more recent phenomena (Garcés 2008a). In recent history, for instance, the Water War in 2000 against privatization was followed by demands by the urban leaders of the movement for a Constitutional Assembly that would be a mechanism for the Bolivian people to claim decision-making power over their resources. The Indigenous People's March for Sovereignty, Territory, and Natural Resources in 2002 had three objectives: land for indigenous peoples (indígenas) and the peasantry (campesinos); respect for the territory of indigenous peoples;

and the installation of a Constitutional Assembly with the participation of originary (*originario*) indigenous peoples as indigenous peoples (rather than as represented by parties or labor unions). The Gas War in October of 2003 ultimately centered around hydrocarbon nationalization, an explicit and forceful demand that was followed by the call for a popular Constitutional Assembly and the expulsion of then president Gonzalo Sánchez de Lozada.[2] As I describe in this chapter, another historic process unfolded, the formation of an Indigenous, Originary, and Peasant Unity Pact (Pacto de Unidad Indígena, Originario y Campesino), beginning in September of 2004. This pact proposed as its central objective the call for a sovereign Constitutional Assembly that would be both "participatory" and "foundational." The creation of the pact was followed by massive collective mobilizations in May and June of 2005 demanding the immediate convocation of the Constitutional Assembly and the nationalization of hydrocarbons.

The Unity Pact articulated the demands of social organizations with various historical trajectories and revindicatory platforms including issues tied to indigenous movements, but also issues not specific to them. Though converging around recent events and representing an entirely new coalition, the Pact had its roots in movements of the 1990s. For example, even before the Water War, during which positions congealed around the rejection of the neoliberal water privatization legislation, there had been in 1998 a similar process of collective construction of a proposal for a social law on water. This effort included organizations such as the CSUTCB (Confederation of Peasant Workers of Bolivia), the FNMCB-BS ("Bartolina Sisa" National Federation of Women Peasant Workers of Bolivia), the CIDOB (Confederation of Indigenous Peoples of Bolivia), and the CSCB (Confederation of Unionized Colonists of Bolivia). Similarly, the same can be said about an articulation referred to as the Bloque Oriente (Eastern Block), an alliance of indigenous and peasant organizations on one side, with urban and rural organizations on the other, that emerged in the late 1990s to cross ethnic lines and address issues of popular concern in eastern Bolivia. The Bloque Oriente was the protagonist of the 2002 march. By the same token, national indigenous and popular movement organizations had organized, as of 2002, a National Communication Plan. The tenor of these alliances among organizations was to respect the autonomy of each while working together on common demands and proposals.

In September of 2004, in the city of Santa Cruz, a Pact of Programmatic Unity was created during another institutionalized moment of articulation, the National Encounter of Peasant, Indigenous, and Originary Organizations. At this meeting—preceding, it should be noted, the election of Evo Morales—the participants wrote out a draft proposal for a Ley de Convocatoria a la

Asamblea Constitutyente, a law that would call for the creation of a Constitutional Assembly. More than three hundred representatives of various movements were present at the event. These included the peasant and colonist settlers' unions (CSUTCB, CSCB, FNMCB-BS) and lowland indigenous organization (CIDOB) mentioned above, as well as regional indigenous and peasant organizations such as the Assembly of Guaraní People (APG), from the southeast; the Central of Ethnic Moxeño Peoples of Beni (CPEMB) and the Confederation of Ethnic Peoples of Santa Cruz (CPESC), from the eastern lowland departments; the National Confederation of Quechua and Aymara Ayllus (CONAMAQ), from the Andean altiplano; the Landless Movement (MST), from eastern Bolivia; the Block of Indigenous and Peasant Organizations of the Northern Amazon (BOCINAB), from the Pando region; and the Salaried Rural Workers' Union of Santa Cruz (CDTAC), which had organized laborers in agro-industry (see García Linera et al. 2004; Pacto de Unidad 2004, n.d.).

In initial phases, the other movements of salaried and landless workers were instrumental, but when the process of preparing a proposal for the Constitutional Assembly began in 2006, the channels of organizational representation were consolidated into umbrella organizations. Some organizations withdrew, leaving broadly three kinds of organizations. Although this categorization masks complexities of identity in practice, it is useful for considering how the legal category of autonomy would later arise in debate. First were those who emphasized their peasant (campesino) identity and thus the category of social class, the outgrowth of the process of peasantization that emerged from the revolution of 1952. These would include the CSUTCB, FNMCB-BS, CSCB, and MST. A second would be those who emphasized the idea of indigenous identity using the term *originaria*, a largely Andean usage that derived from the revision of the category of peasant and its ethnicization—or indigenization—during the process of territorial transformations that had been underway during the 1990s. This included CONAMAQ. Finally, there were indigenous organizations who had long mobilized around the category of *indígena*, primarily those of the eastern lowlands. These included the CIDOB, CPESC, CPEMB, and APG.

It is in this wider context that the formation of the Unity Pact has a unique and particular importance, because it made the indigenous, originary, and peasant movements one of the most important—and certainly the most representative—social actors behind the Constitutional Assembly. But three other points also bear mention. In the first place, the Pact was an articulation of organizations that, despite sharing many common interests and themes, did not have a tradition of common dialogue or of propositional construction of their ideas and demands. This strategy of articulation revealed both the possibilities and the limits of broad-based social movement alliances in the historical moment. Second, the Pact was a space that was constitutive of a new political subject expressed in the category—strange, for some—of "indigenous originary peasant" (*indígena originario campesino*), which presupposed a number of tensions that cannot easily be reduced to a simplified understanding of questions of indigenous rights, territorial and resource rights, or land reform, the most crucial issues for these organizations. Finally, the Pact constructed a proposal that came to be, after a year of debates and discussions, also full of tensions. It at times saw strong disagreements, as well as a congealing of core positions, around the core issues confronting the interests of the actors: autonomy, natural resources, political representation, and social control as the "fourth power" of the state (beyond the executive, legislative, and judicial).

In what follows, I explore these debates and tensions—both within the Unity Pact and against its positions. In the first section, I describe the proposal of this new political subject. Then, in broad strokes, I discuss how the theme of autonomies took shape in the constitutional text. I conclude with some critical observations about the transformation process of organizational proposals into what René Zavaleta (1989) would call "state matter" (*materia estatal*), or what I refer to as the domestication of indigenous rights and demands.[3]

Central Themes: Plurinationalism and Autonomy

Throughout the process through which the Unity Pact developed its constitutional proposal, between May of 2006 and May of 2007, the common articulatory theme of all the various groups was the position that Bolivia be referred to as a "plurinational" country. All the organizations brought this idea in their respective proposals, but none had as yet given the idea explicit meaning or form. Most sought to descriptively characterize the country as *plurinacional*—as compared to the way in which the neoliberal era had described the country as *pluricultural* in the 1994 constitution—but only the CSUTCB had proposed that the official name of the state itself include the descriptor *plurinational* (as, in effect, it does today). There was an intense labor of debate to this end, a process formalized in a text presented to the members of the Constitutional Assembly in August of 2006 titled, "What Do We Understand by Plurinational State?" (CSUTCB et al. 2006). In what follows, I examine the ideas that emerged from this labor of collective construction.

The text published by the CSUTCB begins by outlining the challenge of refounding the country through the participation of the indigenous peoples as *peoples* (pueblos), that is to say, as collective constructors of a plurinational state that transcends the model of the liberal and mono-cultural state founded on the individual citizen. This assertion relies on recognizing, and departing from, the critical supposition that, historically, the Bolivian state had constructed a liberal model that imposed Western culture (*cultura occidental*), which had weakened indigenous political and juridical systems. In its wake, a uniform juridical system was imposed, one through which the administration of justice favored the interests of the market and deprived the peoples of their means of subsistence. In addition, the political-administrative division of the country had fragmented the territorial unity of the peoples, breaking down autonomy and control over land and natural resources. Nonetheless, despite these impositions and mechanisms of domination, the indigenous peoples had resisted and had maintained their identities. For that reason, one can affirm that in Bolivia there are diverse nations, peoples, and cultures with the right to a peaceful and solitary coexistence, what we refer to as *convivencia*. The idea of the Unitary Plurinational State was proposed from this critical sense and historical positioning.

This foundational critique is interrelated with the establishment of the political identities being put forth within the framework of the Unity Pact. That is to say, given the historical configuration of the organizations that made up the Pact, one of the conflictive themes was the definition of the political subject. The intense debate that developed around this theme generated the somewhat unwieldy formulation of a legal category now inscribed in the constitution: Indigenous-Originary-Peasant Nations and Peoples (*naciones y pueblos indígena originario campesinos*, NPIOCs). This category has its origin in ongoing debates over the past decades that re-emerged in the internal discussions of the Unity Pact. Some indigenous peoples of the lowlands pointed out the difficulty of recognizing themselves as *nations* because they had, in many cases, small populations. On the other hand, the Quechua, Aymara, and Guaraní did recognize themselves as originary nations (*naciones originarias*). Hence, both *indigenous peoples* and *originary nations* referred to those who embraced indigeneity as a central category of self-identification. The organizations that refer to themselves as indigenous or originary have strongly criticized the category of the "peasant" (campesino). Yet, the "peasant" organizations—including the organizations that emerged out of settler populations and communities that had migrated from the Andes to the Chapare or to the east—argued that their communities maintained their originary cultural forms and territorial organizations despite being subjected (in terms of both land ownership and legal discourse) to a process of peasant-ization (*campesinización*) by the state in the wake of the revolution of 1952. As such, they maintained a claim to indigeneity despite their reterritorialization in new geohistorical spaces. Nonetheless, as I discuss further below, the category of class maintains centrality in discourse, in their lived experience as rural small-scale farmers, and in the wider structural position of their organizations. The term *peasant* (campesino) reflects a historical and ideological positioning, with implications for a wider articulation in practice and policy between decolonization and the struggle against inequality.

This pluralist formation of indigenous identity, which nonetheless congealed around a shared effort of political coalition, quite logically also demanded a pluralist model of autonomies. For this reason, the Unity Pact came to conceive of the plurinational state as a model of political organization that would have as its end the decolonization of the indigenous peoples and nations. The goal centered, in large part, on recovering, reaffirming, and strengthening territorial autonomy to "live well" (vivir bien) with a "vision of solidarity" (*visión solidaria*). This phrasing was crucial in balancing the idea of plurinationalism (and indigenous autonomies) with the sense of a unitary nation-state tied to living well and in solidarity with all Bolivian citizens and peoples. Thus, it was proposed that the indigenous peoples would be the drivers of unity and well-being of *all* Bolivians, guaranteeing the full exercise of *all* rights, rather than those particular to indigenous peoples. This pluralist model also relies on the idea of juridical pluralism, which is fun-damental as a guiding principle of the idea of the plurinational state. Indigenous, originary, and peasant juridical systems would coexist, within the plurinational state, alongside the Western juridical system. These are envisioned as existing (eventually) within a framework of equality, respect, and coordination. Judicial pluralism would parallel territorial and political pluralism, such that a plurinational state, based in indigenous, originary, and peasant autonomies, would be a pathway toward self-determination (*auto-determinación*) as nations and peoples who would be able to define their own juridical systems.

However, the idea of the plurinational state implies thinking about an asymmetric territorial organization. Some territorial entities would still be organized around the foundational base of a colonial and republican state (the departments, municipalities, and provinces). Other territorial entities would eventually be organized around the territories of the indigenous peoples, according to their ancestral or actual uses. The conflict between these asymmetries remains central to the ongoing battle over the remapping of the country. Additionally, as argued by the Unity Pact, the exercise of the right to land and natural resources in these territories was fundamental. It meant that the Pact envisioned the end of large-scale, speculative, and unproductive landholdings (latifundia), a reality, especially in the east, that had led to the concentration of land in few hands. The claim for resource control was also tied to envisioning the end of private monopoly control over resources used to benefit private interests.

Juridical and territorial pluralism would be paralleled by political pluralism. Within indigenous autonomous territories, indigenous structures of government and means of electing authorities would also be reaffirmed as part of the move toward self-determination. At the national level, the Pact proposed that the structure of the new state would include direct representation of the indigenous, originary, and peasant nations and peoples, as peoples, with representatives selected according to their own norms and modes of selection. In sum, the organizations of the Unity Pact proposed a state form in which political collectives—rather than individuals elected, for instance, by political parties—could express agreement and make decisions about the core issues of the state. These positions put into question the idea that the state has unique and absolute sovereignty over its territory and raised the possibility of creating plural forms of self-government (within indigenous peoples' territories) and co-government (between the indigenous peoples and the plurinational state) (Máiz 2008).

The proposals—as yet solidified in legislation or practice—revolved around central conceptual platforms that defended the idea of the plurinational state in the proposal of the Unity Pact. These included the following.

The exercise of the right to self-determination and the right to indigenous autonomies. The right to self-determination is the fundamental collective right that indigenous peoples demand, based on their existence as collective subjects that pre-exist the formation of modern states. It is the right from which all others derive, including the rights to territory and jurisdiction over economic, social, and political issues (López 2007).

Simultaneous inclusion and redistribution to abolish exclusion and inequality. The juxtaposition of political and economic claims to equality was tied to the attempt to resolve, and overcome, both classist and culturalist (ethnicist) reductionism by recovering the theory of the "two eyes" (Sanjinés 2004). The idea of seeing with two eyes dates to the rise of indigenous movements such as the Kataristas in the 1970s, who used the concept to refer to a temporal and political stance that merged issues of class inequality with ethnoracial exclusion. The act of seeing both issues simultaneously positioned movements as articulating both a subjectivity (who we are) and a historicity (from where we emerge and act). This also tied anticolonial struggle of a much earlier date to revolutionary nationalist struggle of more recent origins. In the context of the Unity Pact and the new constitution, seeing with two eyes implied, according to participants, learning to move within the semantic duality of the concept of the nation. One side maintained the vision of the "national-popular" idea of class struggle and national liberation that is part of the recent collective memory of the indigenous peoples and a large segment of the Bolivian society in general (Rivera 1993; Zavaleta 1986). The other defended the historical sense and long-term memory of indigenous communities who pre-existed the state and who emphasized difference and co-government in terms of sovereign control over territory.

Collective rights as having—at the least—equal hierarchy to individual rights. To achieve equal hierarchy in relation to the liberal political system that has deemed individual rights as the supreme value of humanity, the Pact demanded the exercise of collective primary rights of indigenous peoples (De Sousa Santos 2007)—including rights to exercise internal restrictions that may not be accepted by the liberal opening described by Kymlicka (1995). Here, as below, I refer to Kymlicka's (1995:8) argument that external protection of minorities' rights from injustices should not preclude the overarching liberal legal system from exercising "internal restrictions" on "minorities" to control putative infractions of individual rights within minority communities. This liberal opening to collective rights, in fact, maintains the hierarchy described here. The position invokes the historical memory of similar liberal efforts we might recall in this regard, such as the Law of Expropriation of 1874 (Ley de Exvinculación), which offered recognition of citizenship rights to indigenous peoples, but only as a means of dispossessing indigenous adults of communal lands (Regalsky 2003; Rivera 2004). As the position of the Pact implied, these individual rights—as expressed in the notion of a hierarchy between liberal and collective rights—have been the guarantors of private property as a means of plundering collective, public, and family property in indigenous and originary lands and territories.

Nonetheless, the exercise of primary rights of indigenous peoples—that which they exercise as peoples—does not imply negating the development of collective derived rights that may not be limited to indigenous peoples. That is to say, such collective derived rights of the rest of—or all of—the Bolivian population would be exercised as a collectivity that still moves within the frames of the nation-state. The Bolivian plurinational state should thus articulate both kinds of collective rights as a means of exercising a kind of plural sovereignty, a sovereignty of access to determined benefits of surplus capital and circulation in the country. This crucial point—like seeing with two eyes—breaks down the false dichotomy that sees collective rights as the terrain (only of) racialized and ethnicized peoples and sees liberal individual rights—associated with whiteness and the West—as somehow more modern, so "modern" subjects might not claim collective rights (to health, to water, to well-being) such as those tied to Bolivian nationhood.

Recognition of juridical pluralism. As discussed above, juridical pluralism would allow the exercise of juridical, epistemic, political, and economic normativity in equal hierarchies, again moving beyond the multiculturalist gaze that tolerated so-called "external protections" but not "internal restrictions" that indigenous peoples might exercise in their territories. This is the limit of liberal tolerance proposed by Kymlicka (1995). It is not possible, according to him, for there to be dissent against individual rights and a Western framework of "justice" within different forms of (indigenous) self-government. Yet, for the Pact—and precisely for this reason—juridical pluralism implied that the decisions of indigenous juridical systems would not be monitored by the legal norms of the central state.

Redistribution of ownership of land and territory. The Pact demanded redistribution of land and territory so that their use, control, and management—based on the practices of the indigenous peoples—could be solidified. This has been a central platform of the indigenous, originary, and peasant struggle in Bolivia in the past few decades. This is a fight for the recovery not only of ancestral indigenous territory but also of land, by way of land reform, understood as a mechanism for expropriating grand concentrations of land held by the landlords of the eastern lowlands. Again— marking the fusion of "indigenous" and "peasant" positions—this did not refer simply to the acquisition of individually held property, but also to the struggle for territory, as the mechanism for exercising the indigenous right to self-determination. Admittedly problematic—and still conflictive in practice—the demand for self-determination and autonomies was made not solely with the goal of recovering land and territory, but to create a framework, both conceptual and legal, to be able to make decisions about natural resources through a double perspective: both as a territorial right of indigenous peoples and as resources that belong to all Bolivians.

These conceptual orientations underpinned the overarching demand for indigenous autonomy, or, given the pluralist reality, autonomies of different sorts. Two paradigms shaped understandings. In one, autonomy exists as part of a decentralized system that proposes self-government of territorial entities within a liberal, monocultural, and Western civilizational paradigm. In another, autonomy is part of a process of territorial (re)distributions of power in a plural form (Paz 2008). *Plural* in this sense refers both to numerical status (more than one) and to a diversity of civilizational paradigms (of more than one kind). In the first case—autonomies of a singular form within a monocultural state—we are speaking of a mononational federal model. In the second, of autonomies linked to diverse peoples and nations, we are speaking of the construction of a plurinational state (Máiz

2008). The legislative and policy implications are clear. In the first case, one might argue simply for deepening mechanisms of decentralization. In the second, transformation would require strengthening forms of self-determination within the framework of a state that recognizes the forms of governed society of, by, and for the peoples and nation(s) that compose it (Paz 2008).

The proposal of the Unity Pact was clearly aimed at the second model. Autonomies were understood as a mechanism of and for the territorial reordering or remapping of the state to suture the wounds of colonialism and to recover the sovereignty of these self-named peoples and nations. The indigenous autonomies, therefore, were proposed as forms of government that opened spaces in—and ruptured existing forms of—the imaginary and practice of a nation-state in crisis. These were not simply accommodations to the liberal system that was ultimately founded in an approach to achieving "equilibrium" in state and political systems, as proposed by Kymlicka (1995) and Safran (2002).

It is probably useful here to clarify, given the frequent objections by some intellectuals (Bolivians and otherwise) to the multiculturalist character of indigenous autonomies proposed by the Unity Pact. Some liberal critics—and critics on the left—argue that plurinationalism would balkanize the country, fragmenting it into ungovernable entities while promoting ethnic conflict.[4] Yet, some who are also proponents of decolonization and supporters of indigenous peoples have argued that recognition of the indigenous territories would end up "minoritizing" indigenous peoples of Bolivia, when these are, in reality, majorities (Rivera 2008). Although the indigenous peoples in Bolivia make up 62 percent of the population (according to the 2001 Census), they are not a homogeneous unit. In the eastern lowlands, indigenous peoples constitute true minorities for whom self-government would be crucial to defend land and territory against agribusiness and cattlemen's power. In the Andean western part of the country, the possibility that the Bolivian state might abandon its historical colonial form and take on, somehow, an Andean political form would depend not only on the correlation of forces—that is, a conjuncture of conflict and power relations that is as yet present—but also on the hegemonic capacity that the proponents of indigenous government have to expand their administrative habitus, their distinct visions and practices of governance, into the state apparatus. Neither of these conditions as yet exists. For these reasons, defending the idea of indigenous territorial autonomies does *not* mean ignoring the risk that subaltern segments of society fragment and begin to function according to a logic of entrenched and territorialized self-defense rather than through wider coalitions of (national) solidarity.

From Concept to Proposal: The Unity Pact and Indigenous Autonomies

In August of 2006, the Unity Pact presented a proposal to the Constitutional Assembly gathered in Sucre, suggesting three types of autonomies: indigenous-originary-peasant autonomies; urban peasant autonomies; and regional autonomies. Later, after a year of work, the proposal was refined and a more complex design emerged, including indigenous originary territories; indigenous originary peasant municipalities; intercultural municipalities; indigenous originary peasant regions; intercultural regions; and departments. Note that, in both cases, what was being proposed was a system of autonomies *for the whole country*, distinct from the nonindigenous proposals for departmental autonomy, a vision of radical federalism supported by conservative business elites in the eastern city of Santa Cruz. This conservative vision of autonomy was unable to transcend a regionalist orientation that sought primarily to rearticulate (or remap) Bolivian territorial orders so that political power corresponded with existing departmental boundaries and their city-centric economic leadership articulated to global capital.[5] On the other hand, it is important to note that the Unity Pact also emphasized the significance of regional autonomies—with "region" being an intermediary category between (or crossing) jurisdictions of department and municipality. Regional autonomies, both indigenous and intercultural (ethnically mixed), were thought of as spaces for the articulation of wider solidarities and political alliances. Such regional autonomies could be formed out of combinations of lower-level indigenous or municipal autonomies and were envisioned as a means to impede the creation of autonomies of the "trenches"—that is, those closed off to others and thus closing off the "minorities." By the same token, the region became a spatial category that would enable a demand for reterritorialization proposed by indigenous and originary organizations, a demand that transcended the limitations of existing municipal jurisdictions.

As one might imagine, the debates within the Unity Pact were marked by tensions over points that highlighted myriad conflicting interests. For example, there was debate on whether the Unity Pact should include in its proposal the category of "departmental autonomy," because this had been appropriated by the powerful right-wing segments of the so-called "half-moon" (*media luna*), the group of four eastern departments (Pando, Beni, Santa Cruz, and Tarija) that spearheaded the radical federalist vision. Against the idea of departmental autonomy, some argued that the departmental spaces should be drastically transformed as part of a process of reterritorialization of the country guided by the criteria of recovering ancestral territories of indigenous peoples, rather than by the logic of existing jurisdictions. There was also a debate over whether the authorities of newly created indigenous autonomies would be the same as the authorities and leaders of existing socioterritorial organizations of the indigenous originary and peasant peoples and nations. Were these merged, some argued, there would be a risk of "statizing" the organizations. Some suggested that newly created autonomous authorities be elected according to particular norms and procedures distinct from the existing communitarian or organizational authorities, so as to avoid the risk of leaders becoming both judge and jury within the state structure. Finally, there was intense debate over the control and ownership of natural resources. This confronted difficult positions, in the sense that some argued that indigenous peoples should have total control (dominion, property, and benefits derived from exploitation) and others proposed rights of use and usufruct of renewable natural resources in indigenous territories with only a binding vote—the right to veto or say no—over the exploitation of nonrenewable natural resources in indigenous territories. This long process of collective construction led to further conflict and dialogue as the proposal of the Pact of Unity entered into the arena of wider national debate within the Constitutional Assembly.

Autonomies in the New Constitution

The proposal of the indigenous and peasant organizations confronted a range of other actors within the context of the Assembly. These included representatives from opposition conservative parties, representatives of the ruling MAS party, and advisors for various entities (Bolivian and European constitutional experts and NGOs). The Unity Pact proposal was virtually the only one that had a wide national, nonsectorial vision—despite its origins as an indigenous project—as compared with proposals tied to one or another interest such as agribusiness or labor. The document thus generated a broad space of discussion, yet one that greatly complicated what activists refer to as the spaces of *incidencia*, that is, the spaces within which one can defend or negotiate his or her position. In the end, the MAS—the dominant force in the Assembly—adopted the proposal of the Pact, and the assembly members of the MAS took it on as an important component for the development of what were called "majority opinions"—the positions on constitutional points held by the MAS, as opposed to the "minority opinions" put forth by various other political blocks. The original constitutional text approved in Oruro in December of 2007 reflected, in large part, the proposal of the Unity Pact. However, the later text, now called the "negotiated" text,[6] which emerged from high-level discussions between the MAS and the right-wing opposition in October of 2008, departed in major ways from the position of the Unity Pact, significantly domesticating the issue of autonomies.

The constitutional text finally approved by national referendum on the 25th of January of 2009 proposed a territorial organization based on departments, provinces, municipalities, and indigenous originary peasant territories (Art. 269.III).[7] With these four types of autonomy, the text specifies that each autonomous regime implies direct elections of authorities, the administration of economic resources, and the exercise of legislative, regulatory, fiscal, and executive powers (Art. 272). An important aspect of the constitution is the nonsubordination between distinct autonomies, which are all given equal hierarchy (Art. 276). This was a blow to the elite proposal for departmental autonomy, which sought to subordinate indigenous autonomies to departmental authority.

Of the four autonomous forms, the weakest, without doubt, is regional autonomy. The category of "region" was relegated to the then as yet approved passage of legislation that would put the process into implementation (the Ley Marco de Autonomías y Descentralización, passed in August 2010). Such regions would theoretically consist of various municipalities or provinces that have geographic contiguity and share culture, language, history, economy, and ecosystem but can surpass departmental limits. The region is conceived, fundamentally, as a space of planning and management (Art. 280.I), although it can become a regional autonomy (Art. 280.III). It is so weak that the constitution assigns it no attributes (Art. 301). As such, a category deemed crucial to articulating cross-ethnic alliances and reconstituting indigenous territorialities beyond existing jurisdictions was significantly restricted.

With respect to indigenous autonomy, this was defined as "consisting in self-government as the exercise of free determination of the indigenous originary peasant nations and peoples [NPIOC, or Naciones y Pueblos Indígenas Originarios y Campesinos], whose population shares territory, culture, history, languages, and their own economic, social, political, and juridical organizations and institutions" (Art. 289). The text also affirms that the formation of indigenous autonomies will be based on ancestral territories actually inhabited by the NPIOC and will be established according to the will of the people expressed through consultation (Art. 290.I). Self-government is to be exercised through their own norms, institutions, authorities, and procedures, but according to attributes and powers determined by the constitution and the law (Art. 290.II). In addition, the constitution makes explicit the procedures to follow in case indigenous autonomies affect district or municipal limits and in the case that various autonomous territories seek to become an autonomous region (Arts. 291–295).

This formulation of indigenous autonomies is part of a political agreement that was made in the national Congress—not within the deliberative space of the Constitutional Assembly—in October of 2008. There the Congress also agreed on the law that would call for a referendum on the constitution (and on the revocation of authorities), a law signed by President Evo Morales that same month. To achieve this political agreement, a commission of senators and deputies of the four most important political parties (MAS, PODEMOS, UN, and MNR)[8] modified the constitutional text approved by assembly delegates in Oruro, changing more than one hundred articles of the document created by the Constitutional Assembly. This— what we now call *metiendo mano*, or sticking their hands into a finished text—meant that the constitutive character of the entire constitutional process was erased. In other words, the constitutive power, of which Negri (1999) speaks, was disarticulated. They neutralized the potential of a process unleashed by the mobilizations that began in 2000, which had opened a range of political possibilities. In effect, the entire mobilizational process was taken over by the already constituted powers—the existing structure of political parties.

It must be said that important elements were maintained that allow advances in terms of the conquest of rights in a legal sense. If we follow the letter of the constitution, we see achievements in elements such as the recognition of the precolonial existence of the NPIOC (Art. 2), the opening to juridical pluralism (Art. 178), and the official re-designation of the state as "Plurinational" (Art. 1). All of these gestures will facilitate what de Sousa Santos (2007) refers to as the continued designing, thinking, and even experimenting with another state form. The issue, however, is not the letter of the law, but the seriousness of the fact that the process was derailed, or de-constituted. In what follows, I describe some of the more troubling changes that were introduced in the negotiated, now official, text.

For instance, though the principal of juridical pluralism was maintained, the possibility that indigenous jurisdictions not face review and control by ordinary jurisdictions was removed (Art. 192 of the original version). This impinges directly on the establishment of mechanisms of control in the exercise of direct democracy and indigenous originary representation as peoples and nations. That is to say, the exercise of direct democracy is diminished because it restores indirect government through the delegation of sovereignty to the state (Art. 7). By the same token, the exercise of direct democracy (by referendum, citizen initiative, revocatory referendums, assemblies, *cabildos* [town meetings], and prior consultations) is all derived —that is, assigned not to the peoples, but to the state—since it is to be regulated by law (Art. 11). As for the election, designation, or nomination of representatives of the indigenous originary peasant nations and peoples, it will be done through their own norms and procedures, but in conformity with the law (Art. 11) and under supervision of state electoral commissions (Arts. 26 and 211). The representation of indigenous peoples in the Plurinational Assembly is also restricted. Indigenous circumscriptions cannot cross departmental limits, and they are to be established only in the rural area and in departments where the indigenous peoples are a minority (Art. 146). This implies that some indigenous peoples will elect representatives through special electoral districts and others will compete within existing electoral districts.

The two most complicated areas are those of autonomies and territory. In the case of autonomies, the participation of indigenous peoples in departmental assemblies is assured when they are minorities in these departments (Art. 278). In the case of the regions, which could in theory have become spaces for translocal indigenous autonomy projects, they are, as described above, being constituted not as entities possessing their own political authority, but as spaces of planning and management. Although the "official" text opens the possibility that regions take on an autonomous status based on member municipalities (Art. 280.III), their functions and administrative attributions will be determined by a two-thirds vote in the Departmental Assembly (of the surrounding departmental jurisdiction). This is a virtual impossibility because departmental assemblies are unlikely to cede territory and authority to what would, in effect, be seceding portions of their own territory. As for indigenous autonomy, the "consolidation of ancestral territories" is eliminated, giving way only to the ancestral territories actually occupied by the NPIOC (Art. 290). The possibilities of reterritorialization are also limited; any claim for indigenous originary peasant autonomy that affects municipal boundaries must be subjected to approval by the (state-level) Plurinational Assembly (Art. 293). At base, indigenous originary peasant autonomy is being given the status of a municipality (Art. 303) and contained within the limits of existing TCOS (Tierras Comunales de Orígen, or communal lands of origin).

In relation to territory and land, the central issue was the weakening of mechanisms aimed at the redistribution of large concentrations of landholdings, the revolutionary attempt to dismantle the latifundias described above. In effect, the means for maintaining a highly unequal agrarian structure of land ownership were restored. In the area of land, the central state maintains the power over "general policies of lands and territory, and their titling" (Art. 298.I.17), and control of the "land regime" (Art 298.II.28) becomes one of the exclusive attributes of the central level of the state. (This was a power that departmental business elites sought for themselves with their own claims for "autonomy"). However, power over land regime issues can be transferred as regulatory and executive capacities to other levels of government (including the departments). The same can be said of forest policy (Art. 2989.II.7), of water resources (Art. 298.II.5), and others. This opens the possibility that future governments unsympathetic to indigenous and popular issues will rapidly revert to a federalist system that undermines indigenous and peasant advances. A related theme pertains to regulation of the environment. The "official" text removed the robust designation of crimes against the environment as imprescriptible (Art. 112 in the original text) and paved the way for the possibility of introducing transgenics into the country, albeit regulated by law (Art. 409).

The most serious issue of this shift in relation to land is that the limits placed on latifundia—individual holdings are now restricted to 5,000 hectares—are not retroactive (Art. 399). This means that existing landholdings larger than 5,000 hectares are not subject to expropriation and redistribution, unless they are deemed unproductive, counter to social benefits, or sites of slave-like or debt peonage labor relations. The ongoing cadastral processes involving the titling of large landholdings, as well as those latifundias deemed productive, will not be subjected to the new norms of the constitution. Even so, through a legal category known as the "agrarian business" (*empresa agricola*), a kind of corporative latifundia will be permitted, such that in theory, new latifundias may emerge despite the putative limits on property. This portion of the negotiated text was written in such a technicist language that it almost appears to be an esoteric scripture:

> The state recognizes property in land of all those juridical persons legally constituted in national territory as long as this [land] is utilized to fulfill the object of creation of an economic agent, the generation of jobs and the production and commercialization of goods and services [Art. 315.I].
>
> The juridical persons described in the prior paragraph that are constituted after the present Constitution will have a societal structure with a number of partners [socios] no less than the division of the total land surface by 5,000 hectares, rounding the result to the immediate superior whole number [Art 315.II].

This article, which has been given little attention in public commentaries on the constitution, means that one can skirt the upper limit of 5,000 hectares per landholding that was established in the referendum. For example, by creating a kind of corporation, a business with one hundred small stake-holders and one large could come to hold at least 505,000 hectares of land (CENDA 2009). The putative socialism and the supposed assault on private property often ascribed to the MAS are fallacies.

Conclusion: Domesticated Plurinationalism and the Minoritization of Indigenous Autonomies

The ongoing tensions over the remapping and remaking of the Bolivian state reflect a wider global situation in which *nation* as a unitary, totalizing, all-encompassing term is in crisis. Volatility, polysemy, and dispersion in relation to the concept of nation—reflecting the complex global and local social and political-economic webs into which nations are embedded in reality—are part of the so-called crisis of the nation-state and the emergence of post-national political forms (Negri and Hardt 2001). This crisis is also a reflection of the limitations of the nation-state's conventional pretensions to maintaining internal cultural and political hegemony. Scholars of Latin America have long emphasized that the state and the nation are cultural, social, symbolic, and political constructions, forms appropriated by both powerful and subaltern sectors to construct tools of domination, resistance, struggle, or change. There is certainly a clear historical imprint of a state constituted by elites according to their interests, but there are also state forms constructed and contested from positions of subalternity in distinct historical moments (Lagos and Calla 2007; A. Smith 2003), such as the participation of peasants in the making of the nation, as a kind of popular or communitarian nationalism (Mallon 1995).

In what I describe here, in the Bolivia of today, we also see that the indigenous peoples were and also are participating in national construction. Yet, distinct from the communitarian nationalism of the past, the pursuit now is of a plurinational state that has some consonance with the polysemic character of the term *plural* described above. In this sense, the indigenous and originary peoples, in their constitutional proposal, were and are pushing for their own form of state making, a significant point because this is a departure from the classical sense of the struggle against the state, or the struggle to take or capture state power. The issues are *which* kind of state the people will make and whether and how it might be constructed—whether they can construct an Other kind of state that resolves the historical discrimination and exclusion to which they have been subjected since the creation of the colonial republic.

The proposal of the organizations of the Unity Pact was that the Constitutional Assembly have the characteristic of a sovereign, participatory, and foundational entity (Pacto de Unidad 2004, n.d.). However, through the process described here, the outcome as reflected in the official constitutional text created by Congress advanced a moderate or domesticated plurinationality that puts into place forms of containment to assuage the fears of a de-structuring of the nation and of liberal institutionalism. This is, then, a kind of plurinationalism that establishes the limits of self-determination of indigenous peoples and sanctions only what is allowed. The plurinational seal of the new state remains, but it is a plurinationalism tamed and controlled by the already constituted powers, not determined by the originary, foundational powers of indigenous peoples. I have described how the assembly was marked by its derivative character and subjected to political games that allowed the rearticulation of a party-ocracy (*partidocracia*), a system of political parties that was in crisis after the insurrectionary mobilizations of 2000, 2003, and 2005 (Garcés 2008a, 2008b). This explains the reinsertion of the concept of the Bolivian nation (Art. 3), of Bolivian nationality (Arts. 142–143), and the reinsertion of the concept of the "Republic of Bolivia," none of which were in the original text of Oruro (Art. 11). These are the limits and the stubborn effects of state multiculturalism of the neoliberal era, a sign of the desperate attempt to retain the template of the nation-state.

In this context it is worth asking, Can the state be changed? Can it be decolonized, as is often said in certain circles of the MAS government? Can its practices and routines and its subjection to the constitutive efforts of the powerful be changed? Even if it is true that the recent constitutional labors in Ecuador and Bolivia have entailed attempts to transcend the multiculturalist gaze (Walsh 2009), the risk we now confront is that the proposal of the plurinational state will be converted into an arrangement within, among, and for the political classes to avoid social conflict, to achieve what is so often a triumphalist clucking and cackling about "governance" and "governability." This is how proposals of autonomous reordering are often viewed by the powerful, as a means of institutional arrangement that allows states to surpass crises of legitimacy (Safran 2002).

In this sense, the risk is that the proposal of territorial ordering—the remapping of Bolivia—and of indigenous autonomies becomes simply what the eminent Bolivian social theorist and historian René Zavaleta (1989) termed "state matter." That is to say, the remapping is transformed into a state reform that deepens the mechanisms of indigenous participation in the state but does so through their subordination, without changing the structures of the state itself, as was done with the politics of difference during the neoliberal multiculturalism of the 1990s (Garcés 2009a). The same thing can happen that happened with neoliberal multiculturalism: a domesticated plurinationalism emerges in which the state and that deemed politically correct dictate the themes to be dealt with, the allowable margins and limits, and so forth. Such a proposal remains functional to state management and not to transformative possibilities (Hale 2002). Transforming the density and complexity of demands for indigenous self-determination (auto-determinación) and self-government (*autogobierno*) into a primarily managerial problem allows the subtle re-establishment of mechanisms of state coloniality that continue to show signs of vigor and creativity.

For these reasons, one must insist again on the words of Zavaleta expressed in the chapter epigraph, that there is little to be gained with indigenous autonomies and the proposal of the plurinational state if made as a condescending offer based on a negotiated arrangement to maintain political institutionalism. The alternative has yet to be achieved: that it no longer be the indigenous peoples who should seek forms of accommodating themselves more or less independently to the modernization efforts of the state but that the state should have to accommodate itself to support forms of self-determination of the indigenous peoples without engulfing them. Given that the constitutional process has been gradually appropriated by the (elite) political class, it is necessary now to begin working again for an autonomous construction from below.[9]

The Unity Pact's proposal for a plurinational state and indigenous autonomies coincided with the idea of a republican democracy of a self-governed society that offers principles related to the limits of political rep-resentation, as Máiz (2008:36) suggests: "effective popular sovereignty, political equality, equality of opportunities, equality over resources, control (that is, accountability) over those elected, and a more active and informed citizenry." With indigenous autonomy understood as the "devolution of sovereignty to the originary peoples" (Regalsky 2009), the emphasis is on the sovereign rights of the peoples rather than on the sovereign right of the nation-state.

> [W]hat the indigenous peoples in fact propose is not simply the devolution of territory but the transformation of the concept of sovereignty, they are proposing in other words the devolution of sovereignty to the peoples, what is nothing less than the putting into practice of a more general democratic principle that one supposes was established by humanity in the 18th and 19th centuries. And we all believe that democracy supposes the exercises of sovereignty by the people. [Regalsky 2009:76]

It is clear that the plurinational state will be achieved not through the means consigned by the Constitution, but to the extent that the social mobilization that put the constitutional process into motion is maintained, and to the extent that the potentiality of this constitutive power can be maintained.

On the other hand, it should also be clear that what I have discussed is not a simple plea in favor of the purity of indigenous proposals for plurinationality. We know that, as with any political project proposed from positions of subalternity, these move in a continuous game of resistance and domination (Chatterjee 1993; Guha 1997). Nonetheless, it is important to make clear and visible our efforts of support for the recovery of power for the popular and indio civil society, rather than for the salvation of the state. This is so that, properly speaking, we can say that for the indios, "it is their time to rule" and that "the present is another time," as was said of the insurrections of 1780 and 1781 (Thomson 2003).

Colcapirhua, June 7, 2009

Notes

1. I was a member of the technical team of the Unity Pact during the process of the Constitutional Assembly (2006–2007), experiences on which this chapter is based.

2. On the 2002 march, see Romero 2005; on the Gas War, see Gordon and Luoma 2008.

3. These ideas draw on previous work: Garcés 2008a, 2008b, 2009a.

4. From the nationalist left, there has been a small but vocal critique of plurinationalism, indigenous rights, and the notion of indigenous autonomy, all seen as threatening Bolivian natural resource sovereignty, part of a conspiracy of American- and European-backed indigenous rights NGOs (Solíz Rada 2007). From the neoliberal right, the argument against plurinationalism is less about sovereignty than about "modernity" and "governance," assuming that legal and territorial pluralism is impossible, inefficient, and inherently unstable and that a nonethnic, decentralized federalism is ideal (Mayorga 2007). Both positions share a colonial view of indigeneity as pre- or nonmodern and an assumption that its robust recognition is inherently divisive and dangerous. —Eds.

5. On the departmental "autonomy" project, see Kirshner chapter 5, and Fabricant, chapter 7, this volume; Gustafson 2006.

6. In Bolivian Spanish, negociado (negotiated) has the connotation not of mutual consensus, but of questionable business-like malfeasance, something akin to "selling out." —Eds.

7. The original text of the constitution was approved by the popularly elected Constitutional Assembly in Oruro (November 2007) and is referred to here as the Oruro version. For the "official" version, which modified the Oruro text through the congressional pact (October 2008) and was later approved by referendum in January 2009, see Nueva Constitución Política del Estado, or NCPE, 2009. References herein are to the official version unless otherwise specified. For a rich archive of documents, including various documents of the Pacto de Unidad, see http://constituyentesoberana.org/.—Eds.

8. MAS (Movement to Socialism, the ruling party); PODEMOS (Democratic and Social Power, right wing); UN (National Unity, right wing); MNR (National Revolutionary Movement, right wing).

9. Albó and Barrios (2006) speak of two forms of territorial construction: one from above and another from below. In the first case, we encounter the formal, juridical, and administrative

version of state territorial ordering based on the interests of the managers responding to what are perceived as political, economic, social, and cultural variables. In the second, we refer to the concrete social groups that control, manage, and make decisions about their appropriated space, beyond the presence (or not) of effective state plans for territorial control. See also García Linera 2005.

Photo Essay
Envisioning Bolivia

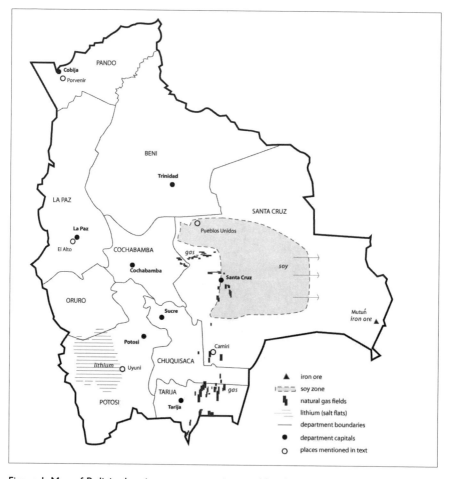

Figure 1. Map of Bolivia showing resource regions and key locations mentioned in the text. Map by Patricia Heyda.

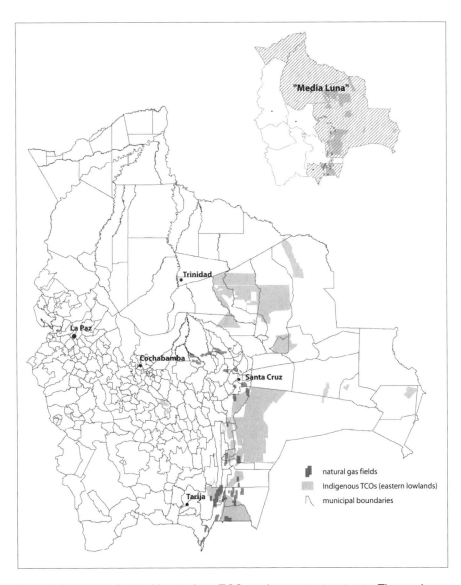

Figure 2. Remapping Bolivia: Municipalities, TCOs, and separatist imaginaries. The overlapping jurisdictions of municipalities, departments, and indigenous collective lands (TCOs) sets the stage for the conflictive rethinking of territoriality, rights, and citizenship. The shaded area of the inset map shows the four main departments of the Media Luna (halfmoon), where there is significant support for departmental autonomy in the model of radical federalism and, for a time, the creation of a distinct "Camba Nation." The gas fields of the southeast are complicated by indigenous, municipal, and departmental claims, especially around the geopolitical flashpoint where Chuquisaca intersects Tarija and Santa Cruz, with the wider region disputed between pro-MAS and anti-MAS sectors. Map by Patricia Heyda.

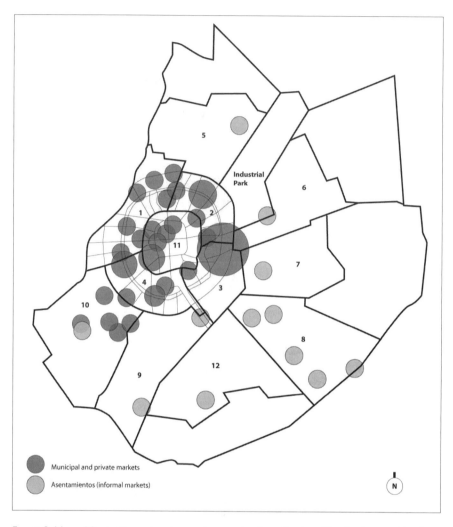

Figure 3. Map of Santa Cruz showing markets and urban districts. Map by Patricia Heyda based on original by Shannon Stone.

Figure 4. "100 Percent Camba." By 2006, in support of departmental autonomy and against the measures of the MAS government, especially agrarian reform, the ideology of the "camba" identity took on new forms in the city of Santa Cruz. Being a pure—or 100 percent—Camba meant embracing an identity of Santa Cruz and regionalist purism. This was a defense of Cruceño "culture" against perceived threats of the "militant" (Andean) highlanders. T-shirts, bumper stickers, flags, bracelets, and other symbols spread in this era, making of human bodies a site where loyalties to the region and opposition to the "Andean" MAS were to be expressed on a daily basis. Photo by Nicole Fabricant.

Figure 5. "Yes to Autonomy." The Santa Cruz–based conservative regionalist movement emphasized simple symbols (flags, the Christ statue, the cross potent), colors (green and white), and slogans—such as *¡Autonomía Sí!*—in its mobilization of upper- and middle-class citizens, a pattern that echoed the urban and also largely middle-class "color" revolutions of eastern Europe. Photo by Bret Gustafson.

Figure 6. Autonomy supporters. The spectacular forms of urban regionalist demonstrations added a carnival-like atmosphere to the conservative political stance, with bodies turned into billboards and carnival fraternities (*comparsas*, as seen here) mobilizing as collective "defenders" of the region. Photo by Nicole Fabricant.

Figure 7. Autonomy and racism. "Autonomy, Yes. Collas of the MAS Get Out [of Santa Cruz]." After the inauguration of Evo Morales in 2006, anti-Andean sentiments went from quiet grumbling to a very public racism, often equating Andeans or Collas in Santa Cruz to filth, pigs, or foreigners. These messages were also often voiced in public demonstrations and in violent attacks against rural farmers. Photo by Nicole Fabricant.

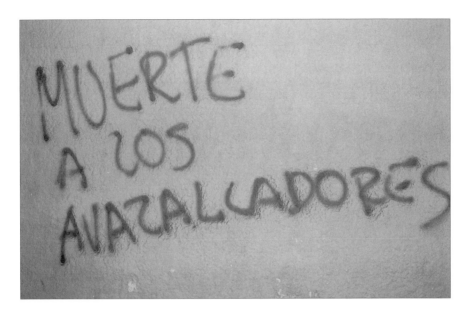

Figure 8. "Death to the Invaders." Graffiti in the city of Santa Cruz (2009) portrayed Andean migrants, both rural and urban, as colonial-like usurpers (avasalladores), in effect, noncitizens. Photo by Nicole Fabricant.

Figure 9. An asentamiento market, Santa Cruz. A typical vendor's stall in one of the asentamientos, nonformal markets that dot the urban landscape in Santa Cruz. Note the occupation of sidewalk space in front of other storefronts, an illustration of the micropolitics of territory and the struggle for urban livelihoods, seen as a threat to order, hygiene, and "public" space by many city planners. Photo by Joshua Kirshner.

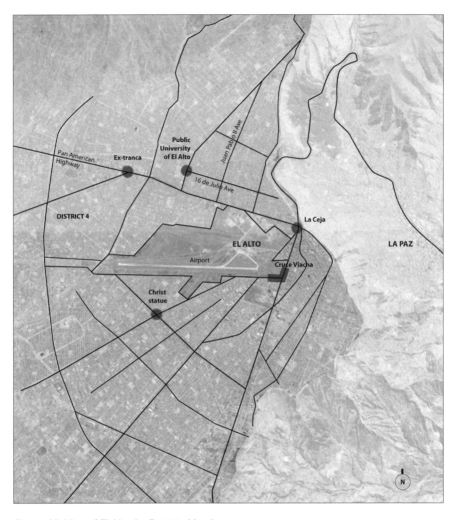

Figure 10. Map of El Alto by Patricia Heyda.

Figure 11. La Ceja, El Alto. La Ceja (The Eyebrow) is the passageway between El Alto and its sister city, La Paz. It is a microcosm of the city (with vendors, traffic jams, people waiting for buses, and a lack of city services) and a metaphor for the intensity of city life, informality, and spatialized inequality. It was also a key blockade point during the Gas War of 2003, which shut off movement in and out of La Paz. Photo by Nicole Fabricant.

Figure 12. El Alto, the solution for Bolivia. While people of La Paz (and of much of the country) blame El Alto for urban problems and plagues, people of El Alto (Alteños) resist these declarations by demanding that Bolivia take their proposals seriously. Photo by Nicole Fabricant.

Figure 13. MST (Movimiento Sin Tierra) production in the Gran Chaco. Women and men in a Landless Movement community in southeastern Bolivia harvest chile peppers, part of new community-based strategies of income generation and land redistribution in rural regions of eastern Bolivia. Photo by Kara Panowitz.

Figure 14. MST health post in Pueblos Unidos. Part of the Landless Movement agenda involves seeking new strategies for accessing services like health care—here provided by a community health worker based in the community—as a response to lack of access to the largely urban-centered or private health services that marginalize many rural people. Photo by Nicole Fabricant.

Figure 15. MST meeting in Pueblos Unidos. Men gather and chew coca at a community assembly in the Pueblos Unidos Landless Movement settlement, where local conflicts and wider national struggles over land are discussed. Photo by Nicole Fabricant.

Figure 16. Nationalism, beyond the MAS (Movimiento al Socialismo). Although conservative observers have attacked Bolivia's resource nationalization policies, the state did not, in fact, take ownership of multinational property, nor even exclusive control of gas operations, which are largely carried out by multinational firms. Critics from the left, such as the Revolutionary Workers Party (POR), have attacked this "nationalization" process as incomplete, a "sellout," and demand "expropriation of private property of gas" and the "expulsion of transnational companies." Photo by Bret Gustafson.

Figure 17. YPFB, coming back? The entry gate of the now decrepit, once thriving installations of the Bolivian national oil company known as Public Oilfields of Bolivia (YPFB, Yacimientos Petrolíferos Fiscales de Bolivia) in Camiri. There is a lingering hope among many that the golden days of oil—now gas—will return. YPFB has been reconstituted after its privatization in the 1990s. However, it has yet to take on a significant direct role in oil operations, working primarily through contracts with foreign firms. Photo by Bret Gustafson.

Figure 18. Explosive gas. The pipelines running out of Bolivia's southeastern gas region serve the domestic market but are primarily flow lines running south to Argentina and east to Brazil, where the vast majority (more than 80 percent) of Bolivian gas is consumed. The explosive potential of natural gas has, to date, been largely political. Photo by Bret Gustafson.

Figure 19. Oil dreams. In the offices of the retired oil workers in Camiri, a mural illustrates the once dominant vision of the heroic oilman, the nurturing mother, and the allegorical link between the worker—and the nation—benefiting from oil development. Photo by Bret Gustafson.

Figure 20. Nationalism, old and new? In an old oil-workers' trailer, a new poster proclaiming the "Democratic and Cultural Revolution" of the MAS is tacked up alongside older clippings that reflect an earlier era of oil nationalism—the pinup and cartoons calling for worker solidarity. It remains to be seen whether and how the new era of nationalism will confront the gendered and raced exclusions and contradictions of oil and gas development of the past. Photo by Bret Gustafson.

4 El Porvenir, the Future That Is No Longer Possible

Conquest and Autonomy in the Bolivian Oriente

Ximena Soruco Sologuren

On September 11, 2008, the thirty-fifth anniversary of the overthrow of democratically elected Chilean president Salvador Allende, the Bolivian right wing staged its most spectacular event. Indigenous and nonindigenous campesinos (small-scale farmers) from across the northern Pando department were converging on the town of Filadelfia, where they planned to hold *un ampliado* (a meeting) to bring together members of all the local unions. The meeting was perceived by local right-wing elites as a pro-government gathering of farmers' unions. In response, these antigovernment authorities of the region, who were intent on preventing the gathering, sent road crews to dig a huge trench across the dirt highway. The authorities also organized trucks to transport groups of armed men to confront the peasant caravan. These local authorities and their backers were claimants on regional power against the MAS and its peasant (campesino) supporters.

Like the elite-led civic movement of the city of Santa Cruz (see Kirshner, chapter 5, Fabricant, chapter 7, and Gustafson, chapter 8, this volume), they called themselves "autonomists" (*autonomistas*), as a marker of their claims for departmental autonomy against the MAS-led central government. By noon, in the center of a small town called El Porvenir—aptly named The Future—the confrontation between autonomistas and campesinos escalated into a massacre as the elites' armed men opened fire. Desperate campesinos fleeing the violence jumped into a neighboring river. Others fled into the jungle. Of the peasants who bore the brunt of the attack, eleven were left dead and more than fifty injured. Wounded peasants later transported to hospitals for treatment were dragged from ambulances and beaten. The local authorities and their supporters seized other campesinos and took them to the main plaza of Cobija, where they were tortured with whips and lashed with barbed wire, an exercise of public, plantation-style punishment aimed at humiliation and submission (Gustafson 2009b).

This event took place scarcely three weeks after Evo Morales had easily survived a national referendum to recall all of the country's major elected officials. As he would in elections the following year, Morales captured more than 67 percent of public support, far exceeding the 54 percent he garnered in the 2005 presidential elections. The right-wing opposition in Santa Cruz wasted little time reacting: it organized what many observers have referred to as a "civic coup" attempt, taking over government buildings, tax offices, the Agricultural Reform office, and the national telecommunications company, setting fire to nongovernmental human rights buildings in Santa Cruz, and attacking indigenous peoples and union leaders deemed sympathetic to the MAS government. The massacre in Pando followed on the heels of this urban-based putsch, marking the culmination of several years of right-wing–instigated violence that sought to destabilize, frustrate, and eventually collapse the MAS government.

The popular interpretations that followed in the wake of the horrific incident in Pando emphasized one name in particular: that of the then prefect (a departmental governor) of Pando, Leopoldo Fernández, who is now jailed and awaiting trial. The campesinos and their supporters saw in Fernández a symbol of the region's old landed elite, an elite whose logic of control culminated in the institutional planning of the assassinations of indigenous leaders and peasants, an exercise of the regionalist vision of hegemonic control over bodies and space. On the other hand, for the right-wing antigovernment (and anti-peasant) autonomists, the former prefect Fernández came to stand as the victim of a broader political-cultural clash on two fronts: Indians against landed elites and the national government against a decentralized form of governance based on departmental "autonomies."[1]

If Fernández's name represents one side of this conflict, another name, one that has been hidden from memory, represents the other side: that of Bernardino Racua. Racua, an indigenous Bolivian of the Tacana Nation and a leader of the Federation of Pando Peasants, was among those murdered that day. The United Nations commission reported:

> *Some peasant leaders appear to have been individually followed and executed. It is in these circumstances that Mr. Bernadino Racua, among others, may have been murdered. He died a block away from the Cocama Bridge [in Porvenir], hours after the shootings, with a bullet to his heart.... Bernadino Racua, from the Irak community [Municipality of Puerto Rico], was a well-known community leader in the department and the Executive Secretary of the Peasant Local Union of Conquista. Moreover, he promoted the measuring and certification of legal ownership of the land in the Department of Pando and fought for the Pando peasant communities' right to legal ownership of the land. [United Nations 2009:12]*

His name, or rather his anonymity in the public sphere, leads us to another story, one that dates back many years: the story of one of his forebears, Bruno Racua, a Tacana employed at a rubber estate in the same region, a peon or serf who was nonetheless honored in 1902 as a national hero for his defense of Bolivian sovereignty against Brazilian attacks, events that unfolded in the same locality of El Porvenir.

In contrast with Leopoldo Fernández, how can the names of Bruno and Bernardino Racua tell us a more nuanced story about September 11, 2008? How do these two names point toward a *longue durée* of uneven development associated with resource extraction and the exploitation of indigenous Bolivians? The organization of rubber extraction in Bruno Racua's time, the settlement of the Bolivian east, or Oriente, by *Cruceños* and European immigrants in search of El Dorado, and the absence of the state from the region until 1952—all point toward thematic and historic continuity with the present. To this day, the extraction of raw materials, the exploitation of native inhabitants, and the occupation of the land as private property and a source of accumulation shapes a vision of European conquest and dominance over the low-lying plains of the Oriente. Bernardino Racua's death brought to the fore the footprints of this logic of territorial occupation and its broader political scope, a vision now ensconced in the claim for *autonomy*, imagined as a mode through which Cruceños—those of the eastern city of Santa Cruz and their allies of the east, like Leopoldo Fernández—might defend unrestricted rule over the Oriente through claims justified by the right of conquest. A prominent Cruceño historian voiced the following:

> *It took Cruceños three and a half centuries to complete the occupation*

and territorial domination of the Oriente. They started with Chiquitos, then arrived at Moxos, where in search of rubber they established themselves on the Madera River.... From 1561, the year Santa Cruz de la Sierra was founded, until the first decades [of the twentieth] century, when ownership was definitely taken *over the eastern plains, this wandering and audacious people shaped a* sui generis *mestizo culture, with strong Hispanic traces: the Camba culture. [Roca 2001:17; emphasis added]*

In this chapter, I examine these protagonists as symbols of this much deeper trail of territorial and political expansion, a trajectory now couched in the language of autonomy as a legitimate form of rule over conquered territory. This political configuration explains why the massacre at Porvenir, unlike the ones previously committed by dictatorial and Republican governments, has not been concealed from popular view. Yet, despite common knowledge of this event nationally, there has been little if any critical reflection on, or public denunciation of, the massacre in the urban areas of eastern Bolivia such as Santa Cruz. This was evident in the way the event was covered by the media, which chose to frame the event as a "confrontation" rather than a "massacre" and, in most cases, established itself on the side of the autonomists. Even in the elite-controlled media of La Paz, where there was widespread outrage against the killings, *La Razón* (2009), for example, reported on the United Nations investigation by openly challenging it, emphasizing the legal language of "might have" (*se habría*), as did its eastern Bolivian media counterparts, rarely questioning the role of autonomists or autonomy claims and tacitly justifying the crime. Moreover, in Santa Cruz and the east, the protagonists and the killings have become a symbolic platform for extending and expanding the autonomist claims. Leopoldo Fernández himself, from his jail cell, was even chosen as the vice-presidential candidate for the National Convergence Party in the December 2009 elections, taking an astounding second, still from his jail cell, with nearly 27 percent of the vote. Yet, as I argue in this chapter, creating an epic legend out of a crime against humanity is not an act without consequences. It forms us as a society, makes us complicit, and converts a legitimate attempt to revindicate autonomy as a stance of political opposition into a defense to the death of a colonial right of conquest.

In order to understand the logic of the massacre and its popular interpretation in eastern Bolivia, we must conceptualize the event as a crucial hinge that articulates a hegemonic memory and past—the conquest of the Oriente—with a future to which these hegemons aspire, autonomy over the conquered lands. In eastern Bolivia, where self-ascribed Cambas see themselves threatened by an Andean onslaught, this colonial optic offers the same historical lens that produces and rationalizes a reading of Quechua and Aymara migration to the eastern lowlands as an act of "Colla conquest,"[2] an invasive onslaught and subjugation (*avasallamiento*), the planned occupation and dispossession of "our lands," and a threat to "our identity" and culture, which is "mestiza, with strong Hispanic traits" (see figure 8).[3]

The key word here, *subjugation* (avasallamiento), thus becomes a frightening image, not because it represents the Other, the Colla, or their actions but because it reflects the image of the colonial self projected onto the Other. The conqueror sees the world as a war of conquest in which the strongest prevails. For eastern Bolivian autonomists—although not indigenous themselves—the perception of "the Colla Other" is also constructed through this logic, as if easterners were now the conquered peoples, like the indigenous peoples of the eastern lowlands who rebelled against the occupation of the Oriente and were defeated by the Cruceños themselves toward the end of the nineteenth century (in the rebellion led by Andrés Guayocho in Moxos in 1887 and the battle of Kuruyuki fought by the Guaraní people in 1892). These former victors imagine themselves today as the victims of new conquerors, the indigenous Colla who have been migrating east since the second half of the twentieth century in search of better life opportunities. The conqueror now fears a new conquest. The fear rapidly turns into hatred, and it is a hatred that appears to exude from every pore of eastern Bolivian society, bringing into gestation a generation whose fear and loathing may destroy any possibility of coexistence with indigenous people and, consequently, with Bolivia as a nation.

El Porvenir of Bruno Racua

The past to which the future (El Porvenir) takes us begins with its name. El Porvenir is characteristic of names given to towns founded in Latin America during the nineteenth and twentieth centuries. These were invocations of faith in the progress that would gradually arrive at such isolated frontier regions. In the Bolivian Oriente, villages arose because of the extraction of *cascarilla*, a quinine-yielding bark, and rubber; both were processed in private extractive installations or large warehousing sheds known as *barracas*. Cobija, the current capital of the Department of Pando, used to be Bahía Barraca (Barraca Bay), which, like the Barraca El Porvenir, belonged to the rubber baron Nicolás Suárez. By 1916, Suárez, known as the "Rockefeller of the rubber trade," had created an empire (Fifer 1970, 1982). His import-export house, the Casa Suárez, became a highly integrated extractive enterprise. At the height of its power, it claimed 6.4 million hectares of land, or 75 percent of the Bolivian Amazon, and controlled 60 percent of the rubber production (Pacheco 2007; Sanabria 1999). That is to say, dreams of nineteenth-century "progress" went hand in hand with the subjugation of rural laborers and the extraction and export of raw materials, namely rubber. This also expanded the so-called conquest of the Oriente led by businessmen from Santa Cruz, European immigrants, and the Bolivian state, which, until this era, had not had a significant presence in the region. The rubber boom led the government to send delegations to the region—then still known as the National Territory of Northwestern Colonies—and in 1938 it became officially known as the Department of Pando (Soruco, Plata, and Medeiros 2008).

José Luis Roca, the Cruceño historian cited above, compares the occupation of the northwestern corner of eastern Bolivia with the settling of the United States by European pioneers, imagining it as a civilizing vanguard or advance ordained by Providence:

> The occupation of the Northwest was a sort of fulfillment of Santa Cruz's "manifest destiny," like the settlement of California and the Far West for the United States. If Cruceños had not arrived there [the northwest], their historical task as a people, with the efforts that had marked them as a vigorous society, would not have been fully completed. This was fulfilled in 1938, when the Department of Pando was created, shaping the definitive outline of the Bolivian Oriente, a neo-historic region forged by the Cruceños. [Roca 2001:53]

Among eastern Bolivian autonomist intellectuals, such interpretations of a glorious past and future continue to use this analogy. Mosqueira writes in one of the secessionist websites of Santa Cruz: "The Camba Cruceño people conquered [conquistó] and settled with much effort, courage and bravery all the territory that we know today as the Bolivian Oriente, from the Chaco to the Amazon. This feat [hazaña], as more than one honest scholar has acknowledged, was similar to the conquest of the West by Americans or the conquest of the Pampas by Argentine gauchos. All other characterizations are simply capricious and stingy (Mosqueira n.d.; emphasis added)."

The sublimation of Cruceño past and present centralizes protagonism around the city of Santa Cruz, borrowing not only from American myth but also from the gendered racializations and anxieties of the Spanish conquest. Roca continues, "The history of the territorial occupation of Bolivian Oriente is the history of Santa Cruz de la Sierra."[4] In other words, Beni, Pando, and the Chaco regions of the Department of Santa Cruz were all a product of the Cruceños' expansion, of their manifest destiny. Thus, by the end of the nineteenth century, the Oriente had come to be imagined as a "neo-historic region forged by the Cruceños." In the words of the late nineteenth-century Cruceño writer Gabriel René Moreno, the Cruceño conquerors saw themselves as part of a pure race, "descendants through the lines of females (*hembras*) and males (*machos*) of the Spanish concubines and soldiers who had founded Santa Cruz de la Sierra" (René Moreno 1989[1885]:137). However, the conquerors' purity was threatened with turbidity on two levels:

> In this region we find, for the first time in history, two floods [turbiones] invading the pure spring: one that comes from the [Andes] mountains, and another one that flows from the frontier and the indigenous zones of the department; on one side, the mestizo of Alto Peru; and on the other, the Guaraní Indian. [René Moreno 1989(1885):125]

René Moreno went on to argue that the force of law and progress would make both of these floods disappear, because those races simply could not coexist with modern civilization and would inevitably vanish. Invoking the spirit of the subject of his writings, another historian, Nicómedes Antelo, he asked:

> Will the poor Indian become extinct due to the drive of our race, as the dodo, the dinornis, the platypus became extinct? If extinction of the inferior is one of the conditions of universal progress,... the consequence, Sirs, is irrevocable, as painful as it may be. It is like a painful amputation that cures gangrene and saves one from death.... It was a common topic for Antelo, [the idea] that the indio and mestizo in Bolivia would disappear once and for all. He understood that this event would bring extraordinary consequences of greatness and prosperity for the predominant white race and for the nation. [René Moreno 1989 (1885):117]

Thus, progress, which came hand in hand with the conquest of the Oriente, also represented a racial interpretation of the world: those genetically stronger prevailed and bequeathed to their children "the famous repugnance of three centuries, repugnance at ever mixing their blood with that of the nearby Guaraní and Quechua" (René Moreno 1989[1885]:137).

The Cruceño identity was also built around the image of economic activity: the private extraction of raw materials, ostensibly opposed to any kind of state intervention and strongly linked to the international market. The rubber, chestnut, and wood barracas coexisted with sugarcane, cotton, soy, and cattle plantations (*haciendas*) as symbols of civilization and progress, the furtherance of the territorial occupation of the Oriente. Therefore, and until the present day, land represents for the Oriental elites what the mines represented to the elites from the Andean highlands of western Bolivia: their source of accumulation and their vital space of reproduction.

This hegemonic discourse about a "neo-historic region," the Oriente, consolidated during the nineteenth and twentieth centuries, would make a deep and lasting impression on the provincial elite of Santa Cruz. Thus, since the year 2000, the spatial configuration of a regionalist and autonomist territorial imaginary of a "half moon" (media luna), grouped together the previously "occupied" territories of Beni and Pando with the departments of Tarija and Chuquisaca (and especially their Chaco regions) into the manifest destiny of Santa Cruz (see figure 2). For these reasons, the autonomist demands were and still are dominated by Santa Cruz under a Cruceño form of leadership: the civic committee and, since 2003, the prefectural administration.

Yet, if the barraca and later the hacienda represented the dream of conquering and controlling virgin nature for Cruceño private investors, then these also symbolized a labor regime that, through debt peonage and violence, led to the annihilation and collapse of the region's indigenous population: Mojeños, Chiquitanos, Tacanas, Lecos, Guarayos, Guaraníes, and other indigenous laborers enlisted through debt and exploited by the estates. At the beginning of the twentieth century, Erland Nordenskiöld, a Swedish anthropologist and explorer, described the regime of *enganche*, the hook of debt, in the following way:

> During the good times, what was most needed in the rubber forests were men. Naturally, many of them went of their own free will to look for work; however, most of them were tricked with false promises or taken by force. Many people made a living from the sale of workers to the rubber forests, where they were bought by large commercial houses. Savage natives were captured to work in the collection of rubber. Many of these laborers died due to hardships and fever. [Nordenskiöld 2001:340]

To speak about primitive accumulation through the export of raw materials always implies a discussion of labor, most often of irrational labor regimes that acquire much wealth from the super-exploitation and destruction of human laborers, putting at risk the reproduction of the economic activity itself. In these cases, because raw materials do not appear out of thin air, money grows not from money but from exploitation of labor. Such super-exploitation is not new. It was enacted in the Andes through practices such as the *mit'a*[5] in the mines and in the Amazon through the enganche system, first used during the rubber era and still used for chestnut collection in the Amazonian north, the harvesting of sugarcane in Santa Cruz, and cattle farming in the ranches of the southeastern Chaco.

If, around 1900, Nordenskiöld (2001:341) tells us that "the Indians always owed great sums of money, and thus were actually slaves," then contemporary research confirms the reproduction of those labor relations in the Pando estates:

> The patrón [boss]...depends to a great degree on cheap manual labor. He needs to give the laborers incentives to stay in the barracas or to prevent them from leaving in another way, for example, by causing them to be indebted to him. The system of advancing [debt] for labor (called habilitación) still works well for that purpose, because the remote barraca remains almost completely isolated from urban centers and the patrón can largely control the transport of outgoing extractive products and incoming food products. The whole system is based on making the laborers indebted to him, or making them think they are [without other possibilities]. As long as this is the case, many workers do not dare leave. [Bedoya and Bedoya 2005:24]

Both the enganche system (the subjugation of the worker to the boss through a debt-bondage system) and the habilitación (a credit system established by the rubber industry, in which the employer supplies in advance utensils, food products, or cash in exchange for a future supply of forest products) depopulated indigenous communities and obliterated older ways of life that had remained intact since the colonial period and persist in distinct forms today (Assies 2002).

In this context, the El Porvenir barraca entered into the public sphere in 1902. The initial profits from its heyday (1880–1920) and the decision of the state to control its economic activity by building a customs post in Puerto Alonso (later Puerto Arce) created conflict between settlers and Bolivian and Brazilian businessmen, who had been able to export rubber freely prior to this governmental intervention. The conflict eventually led the business elite to declare the region the Independent Republic of Acre. Because of the struggle over the control of such highly priced resources, in 1902 the Brazilian army occupied the Bahía Barraca (today Cobija), which belonged to Nicolás Suárez. In turn, Suárez organized a small resistance army in another of his barracas, calling it the Column of El Porvenir, and won the battle against the Brazilian troops. The hero of this battle was a man named Bruno Racua, an indigenous Tacana who worked *enganchado*, by the hook of debt, in the Porvenir estate.

Nicolás Suárez himself later referred to Racua as a "nobody," a nameless person who nevertheless achieved the feat of protecting national sovereignty:

> An Ixiameño Indian, whose name I do not remember, was called and was given a bow and a kerosene-dampened arrow; he shot it into the

palm-leaf roofs, parched under the sun. Two minutes later, the sight of buildings and trenches at the mercy of the flames drove away, terrified in defeat, those [Brazilians] who days earlier had violated national sovereignty. [Cingolani 2008]

The Tacana native whose name the rubber baron did not remember, probably because he was one among the many indios bought by the rubber barracas, was recognized as a national hero by the Bolivian state in 2003. In the wake of the Gas War of October that year, Law 2557, passed in November 2003, declared Bruno Racua a national hero "in recognition of the heroism shown in the Battle of Bahía on 11 October 1902; because of his decisive action in the epic action of the Porvenir column, he contributed to consolidating national sovereignty in the Northwest of Bolivia, which now constitutes the Department of Pando." Five years later, on September 11, 2008, Bernardino Racua, a Tacana indigenous man identified as Bruno's descendant in local memory, was murdered in the landlord-backed Massacre of Porvenir. It is at this point that the two stories converge: the massacre was an event that signals the limits of the all-encompassing vision of total conquest of the Oriente and of autonomy as the legitimate claim to government over conquered lands. At the beginning of the twentieth century, Bruno Racua died as an enganchado worker in the barraca of the rubber baron. His descendant Bernardino Racua would die in 2008, selectively targeted and assassinated as a victim of the new army of elites who had exerted political and economic control of the Amazonian north throughout the twentieth century.

"El Porvenir" of Bernardino Racua

The elites' main discursive device, constructed since 2000 when the current political crisis emerged, has been *autonomy*. Autonomy is not a new political banner. It has been crucial in the lowland indigenous demand for territorial and cultural self-determination, made explicit during the March for Land and Dignity in 1990. Calls for autonomy in other forms have been heard for many years, including the push for administrative and political decentralization and a more equitable distribution of income from the centralized state (a centralized state in which elites from the Oriente had played a formative part, at least since Banzer's dictatorship in the early 1970s). But during the first decade of the 21st century, autonomy began to have a different meaning, representing a "modern" Bolivia, based on the sovereignty of the individual, a neoliberal economic model, and a representative and decentralized form of democracy—in short, a state of development consistent with neoliberal globalization and, in fact, consistent with what Bolivia had been before

2000, before the indigenous and popular challenge to the political system and Evo Morales's electoral victory.

Given that the neoliberal regime had been challenged by the central and western regions of the country—autonomy became a slogan used to fight for the preservation of the status quo in the eastern region. If Bolivia as a whole could not be modern, or made "modern" in its elite image, the reasoning went, at least some territories could be made so. The so-called Media Luna and its vision for the future, modern Bolivia, has been contrasted with an "archaic" Bolivia. Eastern autonomists see this archaic Bolivia as an indigenous utopia that speaks of overcoming racism—when racism, they argue, was invented by Evo Morales! This so-called archaic project is further hindered by nationalizing resources and installing state capitalism, all of which, eastern Bolivian autonomists argue, contradicts the common-sense notion that foreign investment creates jobs and development. Against what they see as a "dictatorship of the collective," the dichotomous interpretation of the elite argues that the civilized world (from which they exclude the MAS and much of "archaic" Bolivia) has come to agreement about the superiority of individual freedom. These views have become adopted as common sense in much of the country. Recent electoral results do show that support for the MAS-led government has increased at the national level (54 percent in 2005, 67 percent in 2008, and 61 percent in the referendum to ratify the Constitution in 2009). Even so, and although support for the MAS has increased even in the Media Luna of the east, in these four departments (Pando, Beni, Santa Cruz, and Tarija), all the autonomist prefects were also ratified, which means that their project of "autonomy" was seen as legitimate by at least a third of the country's population.

However, this self-labeled "modern" Bolivia bears the burdens of a colonial modernity because it bases its vision of territory on the conquest of the Oriente, from the Amazonian north to the Chaco in the south. It grounds its political project, the "autonomies," on the right to rule by conquest. It imagines its political opponent as an oppressive potential counter-conqueror. Behind this interpretation of the conquest of the Oriente as a foundational epic of Cruceña identity—its manifest destiny—lies an ethnocentric racialist logic, a colonial subjectivity.

The modern definition of the nation-state is of a collectivity of individuals who share a territory, a language, and a culture. This definition presupposes a fiction of cultural homogeneity and seeks to impose it upon regional space. The eastern regionalist critique of the Andes-centric Bolivian state is thus legitimate to the extent that it challenges a failed national project of cultural homogenization and modernization. Thus, if during Bolivian republican history, the state sought to impose one national identity on the population, whether through the discourse of racial purity and *criollo* (white) superiority until the 1930s or through the nationalist discourse of mestizaje later on, then the emergence of both the indigenous challenge and the regionalist challenge demonstrates the impossibility of this putative homogeneity.

In this sense, one must acknowledge that both indigenous populations and regions peripheral to La Paz suffered the violent imposition of the nation-state. The imposition of homogeneity has led to the appearance of opposing political projects, such as the Nación Camba (Camba Nation)—a group of intellectuals who speak of secession of the east and of themselves, the Cambas, not as a regionalist movement but as a subordinate nationalism (Gustafson 2006; Lowrey 2006; Pruden 2003). However, this movement is trapped within the same logic it criticizes, one that pursues the reproduction of ethnocentrism and the defense of the supremacy of a single culture that must be imposed upon the entire society. Therefore, its members present their organization as an emancipatory project to fragment the nation-state into other nation-states, a project that in turn will repeat the fiction of internal cultural homogeneity. They respond to domination with the same type of hegemonic control, the only difference being that it is territorially fragmented (balkanized); thus, these resistant cultural identities end up masking differences of class, ethnicity, and gender within each region, reproducing on a smaller scale what they had previously contested. It explains the appearance of definitions of Cruceño identity that are linked to birth, lineage, or cultural assimilation, which are as ethnocentric as the ones utilized by the centralist and republican Bolivian nation-state:

> Cruceño citizen *means an individual whose mother and/or father are Cruceños, whether born in Santa Cruz or not; individuals with a Cruceño spouse; as well as the peoples that have historically lived in the region of Chaco-Beni-Pando. Immigrants' children and adopted Cruceños are also considered citizens, whatever their origins, as long as they express the will to belong to the Camba-Cruceña culture.* Immigrants who strongly preserve their original cultural practices (such as dress or endogamy) are not *Cruceño* citizens. [Lacombes n.d.; emphasis added]

Remarkably, the writer collapses indigenous Bolivians into the same category as foreign immigrants, defining immigrants together as "Japanese, Chinese, Aymara, and Quechua communities" (Lacombes n.d.).

The discourse of Spanish conquest and European supremacy—which elites from Chuquisaca and La Paz and regional intellectuals such as Gabriel René Moreno developed in order to consolidate their national hegemony through the exclusion of the indigenous population—is now reproduced in eastern historiography from a new territorial place of enunciation: the city of Santa Cruz. Thus, eastern elites respond to the narrated history of the conquest and occupation of the Bolivian territory from the viceroyalty of Lima with their own narrated story of conquest, emanating not from the Andes but from the region of La Plata. Against the conqueror Andrés Manso (sent from Lima), they pose Ñuflo de Chávez (who had come from Asunción), arguing that eastern and western Bolivia are for these reasons two historically different territories (Plata 2008).

If, like the Cruceño autonomist elite, we ignore the critical vision that the indigenous movement brings to bear on the colonial state (and on its own project of colonial domination of the Indian), it then appears reasonable to agree with the regionalist argument that there is continuity between a longer history of Andean-centric colonialism and state centralism adopted by a long lineage of Bolivian presidents and the cultural performance of Andeanness enacted by Evo Morales. But this equates to a dispute among colonial elites, not a decolonizing project. However, if we consider the critique of the nation-state from the position of the indigenous movement, we see a more critical stance toward the nation-state and its coloniality. This is not simply part of the struggle for power among elites, but a challenge to the racialized relations of domination across the entirety of Bolivian society. Therefore, the indigenous movement has the potential for a more universal liberatory process, not just for the indigenous peoples but also for the mestizo populations that clamor for regional identities, because these have also been subjected to colonial domination as the periphery of the political power of the Republic. Nonetheless, if the indigenous project evolves into its own ethnocentrisms, then it should also be profoundly challenged, because the assumption of the superiority of a cultural or ethnic group over the others will inevitably lead to new relations of domination. In the words of Dionisio Inca Yupanqui, a South American representative before the Cádiz Cortes in 1809, "a people that oppresses another people cannot be free" (Solíz Rada 2004).

The arguments regarding the legitimacy and potential of the indigenous and autonomist political projects belong to the quotidian reality of the realm of political time—the space of public debates over these agendas in which the "political" implies recognition of the other, identified as an opponent but with whom one enters into dialogue. But what happens when political conflict turns into war or the massacre of people? What happens when the adversary becomes an enemy or worse, a faceless enemy, a dehumanized being, a body riddled with bullets in the back? It seems that in moments of crisis, colonial subjectivity based on the right to conquer and the right of conquest combines with modern individualism to become extremely solipsist.

The sense that "only I exist," that expresses a will of autonomy, of self-determination without any frame of reference, without the Other, without even the colonial, indigenous Other, privileges a subjectivity for which the individual's absolute sovereignty is the measure of all things. Samanamud recently noted:

> "I am the law" is the ultimate justification of the autonomists' legitimacy, which implies an identity with no frame of reference, with no "Other," an exacerbated autism, the void of the subject who has nobody with whom to dialogue, with no cultural grounding, the void that embraces the arbitrariness of the empire of the "I am." Only then is it possible to understand the autonomists' ultimate justification and their auto-referentiality, which entails simply the right to rule over oneself, conceiving freedom as the exclusion of others. [Samanamud 2008:3]

What is this abstraction, according to which racist, colonial reason frees itself from its counterpart in the relation of domination, from the indigenous, to imagine itself as completely alone and autonomous?

Viewed from the present perspective, the elites' strategy after 2006 was to blockade the discussion and approval of the new constitution, a text that entails, at least symbolically, the acknowledgment of indigenous people's full citizenship and equality under the law and, in practical terms, the construction of a decolonized state (see Garcés, chapter 3, Fabricant, chapter 7, and Gustafson, chapter 8, this volume). The strategy of elite resistance that evolved during the constitutional process implied pushing as far as possible for departmental autonomies. Therefore, the best-case scenario could be the creation of many ministates within the Bolivian nation-state, leading to a central government without the capacity to control half its territory and, in consequence, the exhaustion of the government and the possibility that the elite political parties survive until the next elections with some chance of victory. If the central government persisted, departmental governments would at least be able to preserve the elites' private interests and their sources of accumulation (the control of land, the freedom to export, the control over taxation) and the maintenance within their territory of their source of political power: the naturalized inferiority of the indigenous people.

It is interesting to note that one of the obsessions of the autonomist leaders is the tally of patronage money spent by the MAS to mobilize people. How much money, they ask, is paid to the people who march or who attend rallies in support of the MAS? How many people were mobilized by these funds, and who covers the cost? Thus, autonomists reduce every social protest to the instrumental logic of supply and demand, even redefining the demonstrators' bodies, which are exposed to threats, punches, and bullets, as a monetary yield. Given that elite political logic is based on prebendal patronage, they measure others by using the criteria of the self: How much I pay to the street thug or mercenary depends on how much you pay to the indigenous marcher. And if political participation is reduced to a commodity or, in a more paternalistic interpretation, to the result of manipulative marketing to exert influence over the ignorance of the masses, then the opponent is reduced to an object with which political strategies are devised and executed. But who, exactly, is being paid to expose their unarmed bodies to violence and death? Because this tactical calculus does not add up and this political strategy of "who pays more wins" did not work, Morales's second electoral victory in August 2008 and the approval of the constitution in January 2009 ushered in a feeling of bafflement: the elites' aristocratic subjectivity had been shattered.

By subjectivity I refer here simply to one's way of placing oneself in the world, of understanding it, of comprehending oneself and one's allies and opponents. Understanding subjectivity is critical for the analysis of the will to power, political projects, strategies, and potential alliances. It is a way of seeing oneself from the past and in the future, one's profound constitution, what one is and what one might become in a particular moment. By suggesting that elite subjectivity was shattered, resulting in bafflement and insecurity, I am suggesting what unfolds when these political actors are faced with a world that used to be "mine," in the sense that it was familiar, manageable, and logical because even in the midst of political struggle, opponents shared a frame of meaning. Among elites—whether Andean or Cruceño—political contest and strategy implied a basis of minimal calculability: the pieces on the board are moved according to the calculation of my opponent's moves; my strategy consists of anticipating my opponent's strategy and preempting it, unsettling my opponent and using his confusion to gain an advantage. With the indigenous resurgence and the recurring victories of the MAS—the outsider now in power—comes bafflement in the face of the world that one knew and valued and which has suddenly come tumbling down. By the same token, the self that one knew comes crashing down because suddenly things feel alien and unknown, leading to either paralysis or erratic violence. This violence is also a form of paralysis because it is expressed in outrageous actions with no aim, with no strategy, because there is no calculability, because the frame of shared meaning has been lost.[6]

The Bolivian elite, though based in Santa Cruz, wield influence that reaches the other cities in the country. The basis of their shared subjectivity was and is the conviction that they are masters—criollos, bureaucrats, bosses—in a world of Indians who owe them obedience, filial compliance, and respectful deference. In the worst-case scenario, through this lens, the master will wait for the dominated Indian to seek vengeance, to seek status, to rebel, because deep down, all Indians want to be masters. This serf's envy, this yearning to be the master, is part of the political calculation of the master: the expectation that one's opponent will act as one would, in a world shared by masters and serfs. If the master is willing to use weapons, violence, and death to defend his position, then he is sure that the rebellious serf would do the same, because that is the world in which his domination has been built.

When the serf, the Indian, the colonized, does not answer to his master and, even worse, does not act as the master would, trying to emulate him, this causes bewilderment and confusion. What happens, the master asks, when my being master does not make any sense, when we masters have lost our power to signify, stratify, and legitimize the world? What happens when I lose not only my source of power, my position as master, but also the foundation of this power, the master–Indian relationship? Without this frame of reference that fundamentally constitutes my relationship with the world, my subjectivity crumbles, and I do not attempt to articulate anything more than naked violence, panic, decadence, and defeat.

Actors in bewilderment need to search for certainties, and, given that they can no longer find certainties in the world, the certainties that emerge are those they create about themselves, about their fundamental identities. The elites now rebel and assert that the only thing they have—and that they will defend with their lives—is their land, because the land stands for the barraca and the hacienda, the relationship they have had historically with indigenous populations, the political control of the people by the law of the whip and the pistol. They also cry out their hatred of the Other, the Indian, because the Indian no longer obeys, the Indian is no longer afraid of the master, but, above all, because the Indian does not want to be like the master. In refusing to emulate the master, the rebellious Indian has unhinged and destroyed the elites' world.

The Novelty of Horror

The MAS government's decision to advance its own proposals for departmental autonomy in a completely different context and form, as well as the government's clear electoral legitimacy, contributed to this state of bewilderment. Thus, as described above, during that September in late 2008 the elite opposition in Santa Cruz mobilized supporters in every department of the eastern "half moon" to occupy state institutions through the force of violence. Through physical violence, these protestors intended to gain total control over territory—including taking control, by occupying offices and institutions, of the indigenous and peasant organizations and the non-aligned neighborhoods and municipalities. Their putsch moved against any coherent reading of the electoral results.

These actions were undertaken by members of the Unión Juvenil Cruceñista (UJC, Cruceñist Youth Union), an organized group of shock troops deployed for street violence and intimidation in support of autonomy. These mobilized youth groups had been prepared to intimidate supporters of the MAS government, as well as others deemed to be critical of regional autonomy and thus "traitors" to the region. The street thugs traveled in cars provided by the department authorities, brandishing clubs, flags, helmets, and shields emblazoned with the symbols of the departmental government. The UJC thus became an institutionally organized, repressive force set loose with the prefect's blessing. In the city of Santa Cruz, the violence led to the assault on state and civil society institutions, threatening calls and attacks on indigenous and peasant leaders, and a public ban on entering the main square of the city for those who looked "Colla" or "indigenous" or were deemed "traitors" to the cause. On the Amazon frontier far north in Pando, in the small village of El Porvenir, however, these crusades turned into something more sinister: cold-blooded murder.

Although the judicial investigation is not complete, reports by the United Nations, the Union of South American Nations (UNASUR), and Bolivian national institutions have described the event as follows. In weeks prior to the killings, there were a series of attempts by the landed elite to prevent the national land reform agency (INRA) from carrying out its legally certified task of measuring plots and assessing and verifying legal ownership of lands so as to make public lands available for redistribution. Days prior, the autonomist elites seized the national INRA office in Cobija and named their own local director—in effect, denying national sovereignty over public land and reproducing a deeper and unresolved contest over territory between autonomists and indigenous peoples. In this case, both indigenous and small farmer (campesino, or peasant) lands were at stake. Peasant and indigenous organizations from Pando, given the prefects' actions to gain political control of the region, called a meeting in the village of Cobija to analyze the situation and define courses of action. As one group traveled from El Porvenir toward Cobija, it was intercepted and ambushed by armed autonomists organized by the regional authorities. Once the assailants had cornered the farmers, they began firing. The next day, the autonomists returned to the area and to other villages to continue the persecution. In the images disseminated by the media, it is possible to see the sequence of confrontations in El Porvenir, the attack by the autonomists, the shootings, and the peasants' escape.[7] At this writing, the body count indicates that eleven were killed and fifty wounded. It is important to highlight that many of the victims were indigenous and peasant leaders or members of their families (United Nations 2009).

What happened in El Porvenir? Was this chaos produced by the collapse of the masters' authority? I think not. El Porvenir represents a transformation of colonial reasoning as the foundation of elite subjectivity. The Massacre of El Porvenir embodied the intensification of the modern logic of individualism, the absolute sovereignty of the "I," and the spread of that logic as solipsistic self-determination in a colonial and peripheral context. Although the autonomists lost control of events at El Porvenir, I argue that this episode took their political logic to its more radical and spectacular consequences. In that sense, it was not an irrational event, but rather the evolution of a particular logic. On this occasion, murder was not hidden or silenced. The authorities (in this case, the departmental prefects) did not distance themselves from the massacre out of fear of public backlash, as had happened in earlier massacres. Even so, the murders were not justified as the defense of a military state against an "internal enemy" (identified as communists, miners, indigenous groups, or organized labor), as had happened during the military dictatorships of the past. Nor even were they justified in the defense of private property, nor as actions to preserve the masters' domination over Collas and Indians, although these reasons were somewhat present. The justification I suggest—and there is always a justification, even if implicit, because murder is a social act—was built on the will of self-determination against anyone, campesino, indigenous, government, law, or human being, who opposed "my" absolute freedom to be what "I" want to be or to obtain what "my" rights of conquest grant.

Testimonies of witnesses and survivors allow a glimpse at the novelty of this horror in Bolivia:

> "They massacred the peasants, they hunted them down like wild pigs." (Ana María)

> "They shouted, 'Long live autonomy, death to these worthless peasants!'" (Esther)

> "I was abducted in El Porvenir, brought to Cobija, and hit against a coffin while they yelled, 'We will exterminate you, look at what we have for you!' while showing me a box of .22 caliber bullets." (A peasant farmer) [Stefanoni 2008]

Killing a human being requires complete objectification and dehumanization of the Other. In war, the opponent becomes the enemy because his ideology or his national, racial, or religious identity represents a threat to one's values, beliefs, and way of life. But even in war, the enemy is faced, man to man, weapon against weapon. In El Porvenir, there were no confrontations, not even an enemy to fight. There were only unarmed bodies, obstacles to "my" right of self-determination, human beings dehumanized as soon as they interfered with "my" absolute will. As one reads the world of meaning for these participants, the massacre was deemed legitimate because through their actions, individualism became the law, the criterion to judge truth and falsehood, life and death. Those obstacles, those bodies, belonged merely to peasants and unassimilated indigenous peoples—the objectified Other—who did not participate in this solipsistic reasoning.

Can this logic be completely understood as part of a colonial subjectivity of conquest? As brutal as a racist regime may be, the Other's naturalized inferiority, which justifies domination, requires the existence of the dominated. Being a master implies having Indians over whom to exert power. Colonial domination was based on this relationship, known during the times of Viceroy Toledo as Leyes de Indias, which implied separate jurisdictions for the Spanish settlers and the Indians, and in republican and liberal times as "the Indian question," which implied the violent assimilation of indigenous peoples. But what sort of master annihilates his Others, bringing us so dangerously close to the Nazi extermination of the Jews? It appears that racism, cultural difference naturalized as biological and inevitable, and the vision of territory as a conquest, when combined with modern notions of the absolute sovereignty of the individual, together become a death machine, a technology of horror that annihilates human beings who have ceased to be human because they have been left out of the intersubjective relationship with the self.

Zavaleta (1986) contended that Bolivian elites never had a sense of self-determination based on nationality or class, and, thus, their only understanding of territory was as property. Perhaps the novel element introduced by these elites was their deep sense of regional self-determination, their will to be, which reproduced the vision of conquest from a different locus of enunciation: the isolated, modern, auto-referential self. This explains their will to stateness, their conviction that this would be impossible on the national stage, and thus their separatist urge. It is clearly stated by Ronald Larsen, an American cattle rancher—and a sympathetic ally of the autonomist project:

> Why is it considered a crime to have various properties? In the United
> States, we are able to do this without a problem. They say that…we
> are vigilantes…. [But] this is a frontier, and the government doesn't

understand this. They impose a kind of state-based order where there really is no state. The state forgets about Santa Cruz—we live here the way we want to live, because we built this city with our own hands. What is happening in Bolivia has been happening for decades, actually for centuries, and now, it is becoming crystal clear. The main theme, the primary battle is land.… It is about Santa Cruz and this is going to determine where the entire country is headed. [Rudovsky 2009]

The Impunity of Death

Finally, when violence and the impunity of murder define subjectivity, how can this subjectivity with no other reference than itself constitute us as a society? We have been told that the massacre at El Porvenir was conducted by hired killers and directed by the prefect Leopoldo Fernández and his followers. Nonetheless, the ongoing persecution and intimidation endured by peasant and indigenous communities indicate that the perpetrators of the Pando massacre were not only paid killers but also neighbors, average people. At present, the ex-prefect of Pando is in jail and awaiting trial. It is not clear whether he should be tried as a public authority or in a regular trial, and this could lead to eventual impunity. The other prefects and opposition politicians have not publicly condemned Fernández or his participation in the massacre and, as stated above, invited him to be a candidate to vice presidency in the national election of December 2009. Still more troubling are the media, who frame the event as a clash between political factions and, in some cases, appear to be complicit with the violence itself. The United Nations report indicated the following:

> [We] were also informed that several peasants were forced by the Prefects' supporters to "confess" on camera that they had been sent by authorities or leaders linked with the Government. The form of forcing these confessions was, according to testimonies, with abuse, including shootings to the legs or threatened shootings. These scenes of violence, in an intentional way, were not recorded by some journalists who witnessed the procedures. However, they did record the "confessions." The violent extraction of these confessions, if proven, constitutes an act of torture. [United Nations 2009:13]

The peasants were made to confess that they were MAS supporters, and this constituted proof enough to warrant their "sentencing" by the perpetrators of the massacre. Thus, potential witnesses, people from the Oriente and the rest of the country, could watch the visual records of these "confessions" and thus interpret the event as a political confrontation rather than as a massacre. In effect, the media discourse and the lack of a speedy trial for the ex-prefect is turning the man accused of the massacre into a hero of the autonomy movement, someone who can obtain votes by invoking victimization.

What is going on in Bolivia if this massacre is understood in the public sphere as merely part of a political confrontation and thus an event that, if not normal, is at least tolerable? Why are the eastern territories interpreted as a land conquered by Cruceños and mestizo Bolivians, whereas the indigenous peoples of the lowlands are seen as conquered peoples and the Colla settlers as potential conquerors? Are these the visions that together justify a massacre according to urban common sense? And in this way, is the autonomist demand for self-government and cultural identity becoming an authoritarian demand, wherein "my" will to self-determination imposes itself on the lives of others, on those who do not agree?

In the past decade, autonomist assemblies and other demonstrations have been portrayed as public celebrations in which families walk, bearing flags and playing traditional music, down streets lined with cafés, restaurants, and luxury hotels to the main square in order to demand their right of self-determination and to celebrate their cultural identity, their *cruceñidad* (see figures 4–8). This cultural and political autonomy can tolerate difference only when the different one, the Other, does not challenge political dominion over territory. Thus, the prefects have incorporated indigenous symbols and traditional indigenous motifs into their dress and speech, as part of their official paraphernalia. They have even resignified the word *camba*, which a few decades ago was an ethnic slur against indigenous people who had migrated to the cities and were thus distinct from the racially pure Cruceño, or decent [whiter] people of European descent. "Camba" now refers to this regional subject, a blend of white and mestizo. These gestures indicate that multiculturalism is useful for re-creating identity as long as it does not challenge the structure of power. Once it does, however, freedom is suspended in the name of freedom, and difference becomes a threat to sovereignty, to be eliminated by a claim to autonomy.

The violent side of elite cultural identity was always present but seemed marginal. But today, in the east, according to autonomist logic, ownership of immense extensions of land and intense inequality, the beatings of opponents, the creation of lists of "traitors," the destruction of public institutions and neighborhoods that support the MAS, and the Massacre of El Porvenir, can all be tolerated as the price to pay for autonomy. Regional historiography, the media, and school curricula are now presenting an image of the Colla migrant as the cause of evil, the source of the *avasallamiento*, the subjugation that threatens the self-determination of the Oriente (Kirshner, chapter 5 this volume).

I want to emphasize that this chapter does not pretend to condemn an entire population. This is not a matter of individual conscience, good or bad, but rather the product of a subjectivity without Others and of the inevitable forces that this logic unleashes. This logic provides grounding for hatred and tolerance of impunity among regular people like you and me. In the name of what identity might we tolerate the massacre of Porvenir? And if I celebrate myself as the possessor of such an identity, a subject without Others, does this celebration not appear contradictory to the killings—and the ghosts—of Porvenir? Though many pressure groups work to demand justice for the massacre, our collective failure to issue a public, massive, and national condemnation of the massacre at El Porvenir, to construe it as an event tied to the elitist logic of the right of autonomy, turns us into accomplices and makes us part of the hatred and the violence. Meanwhile, Ana María, a survivor from El Porvenir, the place of those who could not be born, reminds us (in Stefanoni 2008): "As small as it is, in this village, there was a war between brothers. Now the military is here, but what will happen when they leave?"

Notes

1. Although the right-wing opposition sought to define the event as an orchestrated confrontation of political bands, a report of a UNASUR commission (UNASUR 2008:58) and that of the UN Commission on Human Rights (United Nations 2009:12) referred to the killings of the farmers as a "massacre." Both reports indicated that, nonetheless those who had taken part in this massacre were not given due process. The UN report (2009) emphasized the lack of police action to prevent the event or protect the victims. The UNASUR report, though critical of the autonomists' role in the killings, observed that "the matter suggests the [government's] intention to concentrate responsibility on those higher up…was unfair to Leopoldo Fernández himself, who is presented as the sole responsible scapegoat" (UNASUR 2008:51).

2. *Colla* (also *qulla*, *kolla*), in contrast to the lowland Bolivian, or *Camba*, is a derogatory term used to describe Andeans or Andean Indians in lowland cities such as Santa Cruz, Beni, and Pando (see Kirshner, chapter 5 this volume).

3. Sergio Antelo (n.d.), an autonomist intellectual of Santa Cruz, writes that "the INRA [Instituto Nacional de Reforma Agraria, National Land Reform Insitute] has two goals: to create TCOs [indigenous territorial entities] and to open up space for the 'recolonization of the lowlands' [read: 'Santa Cruz'] with the goal of 're-localizing' the undesirable populations of the Bolivian Andes."

4. This attempt to separate Santa Cruz from the wider geography and history of Bolivia involves an ongoing assertion that Cruceño ascendance is of a different kind of *criollaje* (the expression of locally born Spanish colonials) and mestizaje (mixing between Spanish and Indian) from that of the Andean of Upper Peru. Yet, Cruceño ascendance also derives from European migration at the end of the nineteenth century and the settling of the area by businessmen who came from elsewhere in Bolivia, both during the rubber age and along with rising

state investment after 1952. Against their claims, the Cruceño elite constitute, geohistorically speaking, a national elite settled in this region (Soruco, Plata, and Medeiros 2008).

5. Mit'a or mita was a form of mandatory labor during the Inca Empire that was reproduced during the Spanish colonial era and, in other forms, well into the republican period, as a means of assuring forced Indian labor in the mines.

6. For a parallel analysis of the surplus of meaning—or its inverse, the absence of reason—in certain expressions of political violence, see Aretxaga 2005.

7. For links to a video of the events, see Gustafson 2009c.

Visions from the Ground
Urban Spaces in El Alto and Santa Cruz

The cities of El Alto, outside La Paz in the high Andes, and Santa Cruz, in the tropical lowlands of the east, represent in many ways two extremes of Bolivian urban realities (see figures 3 and 9). As discussed in the following two chapters, they also reflect in different ways the formation of new political subjectivities—the sense of who we are and to what we aspire—that are tied to contested claims to territory, resources, and identity-based rights. These processes, shaped by local histories and by racial, gender, and class ideologies, are remapping politics and the exercise of citizenship in the country. In El Alto, a population of predominantly Aymara Bolivians is imagined by some to be a potential pool of cheap labor for *maquila*-style globalization of low-wage factories and assembly lines. Yet, threatened by water scarcity and deep inequalities alongside wealthier La Paz, it is frequently referred to by its leaders and by observers—at times, in an exaggerated way—as a national vanguard of political militance. For instance, El Alto's citizens (Alteños), put into practice a particularly Bolivian form of highly disciplined collective mobilization within nationalist idioms of grassroots democracy, providing an epicenter for the ideological resurgence that gave rise to the Gas War of 2003, the ouster of Gonzalo Sánchez de Lozada, and the eventual nationalization of gas in the country (Lazar 2008; Mamani Ramirez, chapter 2, this volume). Yet, El Alto's economy, marked by a vibrant range of small-scale commercial enterprises and craft industries, also reflects a popular entrepreneurialism alongside large and small-scale manufacturing (Gill 2000). It is a city where informality in the streets is accepted as the normal mode of survival and economic practice in the city (quite distinct from Santa Cruz, where informality is viewed by many as a threat to "civil" city life). El Alto thus encapsulates the complexities of contemporary Bolivian political and cultural economies, yielding poverty, inequality, and political militance alongside a grassroots Andean economic vibrancy (Arbona and Kohl 2004).

Santa Cruz is the center of the so-called "autonomy" movements that pursue a more radical federalism and an intensely regionalist set of political sentiments against the nationalist and state-led development approach of Evo Morales. The city (like the country as a whole) is the epicenter of a "narrow-based" political economy of natural resource extraction (Gray Molina 2005). Though often said to be the modern, wealthy economic engine of the country, its economic and political model is contradictory, reliant on re-emergent racism to hide its internal instability (Gustafson 2006). Regionalist elites seek to maintain stability by imagining that the MAS government and *Colla* [Andean] migrants are waging an onslaught against their city and region, an area that, in fact, has a long history of cultural mixing and pluralism, as well as its own internal causes of poverty and inequalities. The voices in this— the first from editorialist supporters of the regional "autonomist" and even "separatist" turn in Santa Cruz, the others from a series of El Alto activists— rise from these urban spaces and outline political subjectivities that have come to define the public identities of these two Bolivian cities, framing, in a wider sense, the national struggles over the future of the country.

"Santa Cruz Is Beautiful, But..."

> *Oh, how you have changed, Santa Cruz, how we have changed, and how much pain others have caused us!.... And with much pride, we say that we prefer to fight and die for your liberty before we become dominated by Others. We fight in order to defend these lands from invaders.... Santa Cruz, even though it was ignored by various governments, is a city of constant progress that has risen with the efforts of the people. But don't be fooled.... The real problem that we have that impedes our progress is migration. These collas do not respect our customs. They believe that they will be able to do whatever they want, whenever they want. They rob and kill us. They are the ones who convert our city into a marketplace cluttering the sidewalks. They close the streets without our consent to celebrate their festivities. [T]hey invade our lands. And what is their excuse? That they do it because they do not have anything to eat. Santa Cruz is not a garbage can, nor is it a*

Kleenex for the tears of anyone. It is not to be sacrificed. They think that they have the right to invade our lands because they are Bolivianos. Then, they ask for lands in Bolivia because this is Santa Cruz and it is as if [the land] doesn't belong to anyone. These people are violent and do not even respect the right to life. If we are willing to fight in order to bring our pueblo forward, why are we letting these collas debilitate our strength? Don't you realize it? These people do not like us, they only benefit from us. It is not sufficient to talk about your love for Santa Cruz or to get angry by the things that happen to us— this should convert itself into actions. Let us not be afraid to say and do what we feel, let us please stop being two-faced, let us leave our differences and personal interests behind us…. Let us unite, because dividing ourselves, we will not achieve anything, but if we are united, we are able to convert this continuous "invasion" into something that we all dream of! Our Liberty! [García Paz n.d.]

The Clean City (Santa Cruz)

Today, the city is not clean, not in the ethical sense or in the aesthetic sense. Today, the city is not clean, not in the physical sense or the mental one. Today, the city is not clean. Today, the city is dirty. Today, the city is descuidada [not taken care of]. Today, the city is a disaster…. We have some of the worst sanitary conditions in the world, with all sorts of festering diseases and spreading contagions. We are now faced with [the most horrible] epidemic of dengue in our history, mosquitoes that grow and multiply in the creeks and canals, and all over the marginal barrios. The dengue epidemic is the result of unsanitary conditions of our city. It is like the body of a homeless person who does not shower or bathe…collapses, and gets sick. This is Santa Cruz: it is sick and collapsing…. The markets are and will be spaces of filth and sick people if we don't do anything about it. The comerciantes [market vendors] throw their garbage in any part of the market. There is no order or discipline…. With deep pain, we watched the images unfold on television as street vendors from the Ramada market threw rocks and stones at the municipal agents who were trying to enforce the municipal clean-up orders. It is not up to the merchants to install their tolderíos in any which way, or any place that they so desire.[1] There should be an order to this city…. Cleaning the city is also about getting rid of the national police force. Control of transit should be at the municipal level, and we must put capable people in these positions…. Santa Cruz de la Sierra, the first city in Bolivia to grow in terms of population and expansion, has a very serious problem that is taking away Cruceña life.... We must eliminate the central foci of infection in the markets.... We must take serious measures to better the health and hygiene of the city. [Arias Castro 2009][2]

The Gas War, from the Rebellious Streets of El Alto

Pedro Huanaco is 42 years old. He was born in the province of Inquisivi [Department of La Paz]. He is the president of the Committee of Vigilance for the municipality of El Alto, District 8, situated on the Oruro highway. This is one of the urban, marginal communities with a population of 38,000 and it is one of the poorest areas. District 8 was one of the most active municipal zones during the Gas Wars.

"We begin to realize that the gas is not something we should sell, but instead we should industrialize it. The other thing is the poverty: we have about a 75 [percent] poverty rate, and the central government really doesn't pay much attention to this. We, the city of El Alto, have a growth that is reaching 7 [percent] annually. This signifies that there is a lack of attention to basic needs like potable water, sanitation services, electricity, health, and education; urban infrastructure is minimal. Even though the municipal government intends to take external resources from international sources, this is not sufficient. It is from this point of view that the people of El Alto come together...and we demand that the central government listen to this pueblo. The worst part of all of this is that the government, before listening to us, they started to repress people. With many dead, we were unable to sit down and dialogue with the central government because we have experienced this horrible repression unlike that even during the dictatorship of the '80s. It was a persecution of leaders, and has really broken and crippled this democratic process." [Cabezas 2006]

The following words come from Monica Beltrán, the director of an NGO called the Gregoria Apaza Center for the Promotion of Women. The organization also maintains a radio station, called Radio Pacha Mama. Community radios were a key means of communication during the conflicts that came to be called the Gas War (Cabezas 2006).

El Alto is the excluded city. It is here that the first causes of the conflict emerged, and these first and foremost were structural. The people live in conditions of permanent poverty, suffering from the false offers and

*the constant lies of the central government. El Alto consists of rural
Aymara people and middle-class and poor people of La Paz. But the
hope of a better life has never been fulfilled. This permanent poverty
made [the streets of] El Alto a dynamic social and political space, and
not in a bad way. The permanent theme of redistribution of wealth
expressed itself, in this occasion, as a specific category: the exploitation
of gas. Still, in El Alto and in Bolivia, there are women who cook with
the fire [with wood], yet we are a country rich in gas. El Alto is incredibly cold. When will households have gas to warm themselves? Why
can't we have access to gas, first and foremost, the Pueblo, the People?*

Notes

1. *Tolderío*, referring to the stalls of street vendors, also invokes the colloquial idea of the "huts" of indigenous peoples.

2. Both the market vendors (comerciantes) and the national police are implicitly identified as Collas, Andean Bolivians who have moved to Santa Cruz.

5 Migrants and Citizens

Hygiene Panic and Urban Space in Santa Cruz

Joshua Kirshner

Public space can be viewed as something of a Rorschach because various groups and constituencies can project onto it their vision of what the city is or what it should be. At the same time, public space is vital for urban livelihoods of the poor, particularly newcomers to the city who lack formal employment and have no alternative but to create their own jobs. This chapter looks at contests over urban public space as a window into deeper understandings of demographic change, informalization, and struggles for social integration in the eastern Bolivian city of Santa Cruz. Santa Cruz, like El Alto in the Andes, is a central—and highly contested—urban space that reflects the wider remappings of power, identity, and resources underway in contemporary Bolivia (see figures 1 and 3).

Once an isolated frontier, Santa Cruz benefited from state investment policies beginning in the 1950s with the MNR government's March to the East program, backed in part by the United States. The program sought to incorporate the eastern lowlands into the national economy (Gill 1987). By the 1990s, Santa Cruz had largely overtaken La Paz as Bolivia's financial capital and most important economic pole, and its political influence continues to grow. Regional economic growth has attracted—and resulted from—labor migration from poorer Andean regions over the past four decades. Santa Cruz is also the flashpoint of a growing regionalist movement, expressed in claims for "departmental autonomy" as a means for regional governments to play a greater role in public decision-making, a political agenda bolstered by the recent intensification of a strong, place-based, regionalist identity politics (Fabricant 2009; Gustafson 2006).

This chapter considers how migrant insertion into the local economy, in particular the informal economy, has led to conflicts over public space in Santa Cruz. Santa Cruz (in the eastern lowlands) provides a contrasting urban case to El Alto (in the Andes). El Alto is another booming city of migrants whose politics are shaped by the restructuring of the global economy, a city in which mass migration and hyper-urbanization are leading to new forms of political organizing and negotiation with the state (Revilla, chapter 6, this volume). If El Alto illustrates Bolivia's dynamics of labor surplus, political militance, and small-scale industrialization in the maquila model, then Santa Cruz expresses Bolivia's frontier agro-industrial and resource politics, one in which the city brings into relief the inequality-producing effects of a "narrow-based" regional export-oriented economy (Gray 2005). Recent shifts in the Santa Cruz local economy stemming from in-migration and the growing informal economy are producing specific patterns of urban growth and altering the built landscape. After examining these dynamics, I turn to growing conflicts over public space and, in reaction, local planning policies to reorganize market networks. The aim is to explore how overlapping and competing understandings of public space reflect unresolved tensions over urban expansion and demographic change.

In cities as diverse as Mexico City, Bogotá, Quito, Mumbai, and Durban, urban managers and elites view informal commerce in public space as unwelcome and harmful for attracting investment, tourism, and global capital (Bromley 1997; L. Fernandes 2004; Hunt 2009; Popke and Ballard 2004; Sanyal 1991; Swanson 2007). In particular, the visible presence of informal street vendors calls attention to the fact that not everyone can find employment in neoliberalized economies (Cross 1998). Public authorities in developing cities are also increasingly concerned about the alienation of elite and middle-class consumers who feel that informal trading results in the "privatization" of public space (Brown 2006). On this basis, informal vendors are often banished from gathering in public places, in an effort to reclaim the space for a segment of "the public" (Springer 2009). In many cases, informal vendors are seen as a threat to urban public health and hygiene, and their existence points to the need for local officials to reclaim control of civic spaces. Their removal and relocation suggests the exclusionary way in which the "public" is often defined and imagined.

In Santa Cruz, similar forces are at work. Yet, unlike cities where social class is the primary division related to struggles for public space, here the conflict—and issues of class inequality—is entangled with processes of internal migration from the Andean highlands to the eastern lowlands and the ethnic and racial meanings given to these processes in a city whose elite traditionally consider themselves more "European" than Andean, and especially indigenous, Bolivians. Minor disputes involving competing pressures for urban space are inflamed by racialized tensions over the migrant influx and regional polarization. The ongoing relations between migrants and prior residents serve to circulate ideas about ethnicity, region, and "us" versus "them" in Bolivia. In this context, urban space is more than a neutral background; rather, it plays a central role in the interaction, integration, and segregation of urban society (Massey 1994; Ruddick 1996).

Informality, Social Exclusion, and Contested Urban Space in Santa Cruz

Informal work in Santa Cruz includes a diverse range of economic activities spanning small-scale production, home-based industrial work, construction, and services such as car washing, shoe shining, watch mending, provision of phone or Internet access, public transport, and a wide array of commerce in food and produce, cosmetics and clothing, and herbs and medicines. Informality is perhaps most visibly and controversially reflected in the expansion of open-air markets and street vending that has spread onto adjacent sidewalks, in some cases engulfing any nearby available space. Established and high-status local residents have referred to the *mercadización* (marketization, or uncontrolled expansion of markets) of the city while using terms like *invasión* (invasion), *avasallamiento* (usurpation), and "illegal occupation of public space" in the local media and public discourse (Andia 2002:23; Ruíz 2009). Through such terms, informal vendors—many of whom are of Andean indigenous origin—are portrayed as a racial threat to the social/spatial order in Santa Cruz and to regional traditions. As in the interlude preceding this chapter, such visions are rife on the website of Nación Camba, a right-wing civic-regionalist group.

Such views suggest that hostility toward Andean migrants by some residents of Santa Cruz has to do with cultural or socioeconomic differences but also has a spatial manifestation. These claims in defense of the Cruceño (Cruceños or Cambas, those who define themselves in ethnic and social distinction to the "other" Andean Bolivians) are set against the image of an encroaching market and mass of Andean Collas that might envelop the city. Collas (or kollas, an epithet used in lowland Bolivia for people of Andean origin) are associated with unruly markets and incongruous festivities. Furthermore, the claiming of urban space, with Collas imagined to be "crushing onto the sidewalks" and "closing streets," is implicitly linked to the specter of their invasion of *"nuestras tierras"* [our lands] in rural areas of Santa Cruz through informal settlement and colonization, a process and discourse with longer historical origins that has intensified with overt racism in recent years (Painter 1985; Stearman 1985; Urioste and Kay 2005).

The idea that ethnic identity is, as Barth (1969) suggested, more about boundaries between groups than the cultural content within the boundaries, points to the importance of relations between migrants and their hosts in processes of self-definition and social reproduction. Cruceños' claim to a distinct regional history and identity that predate Bolivian independence has strengthened amid waves of interregional migration (Peña et al. 2003; Stearman 1985). The notion of "lowland exceptionalism"—of the East as a socioculturally and regionally separate space—is interwoven with questions of race, ethnicity, and geographic distance from centers of political power during earlier periods of Bolivia's history (Lowrey 2006).

Moreover, lowland Bolivia lacks the tradition of market exchange that is highly developed in Andean parts of the country. As the director of Santa Cruz's Office of Consumer Protection expressed it to me in a 2007 interview, Quechua and Aymara migrants are widely considered to be retail specialists in food products and other domestic goods. The forming of the city's largest markets, including La Ramada and Mercado Mutualista, coincided with the influx of highland migrants in the 1970s and 1980s (Limpias 2003). Cruceños have also expressed concern about the risk of contamination, perceived filth, and unhygienic conditions caused by the expansion of the markets onto surrounding streets and open spaces (for example, Arias 2009; Pérez 2009). Their unease is often couched in the language of orderly, rational urban development, such as advocating redesigning the municipal markets and removing ambulant vendors.

An important part of the construction of the discursive threat to local order posed by migrant vendors is the issue of public hygiene. As in other Latin American cities, Santa Cruz's public discourse of modernity tends to connect cleanliness and hygiene with progress (Swanson 2007). In this case, the current hygiene panic has roots in late nineteenth-century and early twentieth-century rhetoric surrounding eugenics, biology, and disease that was influential in the Andes, where a colonial logic that perceives indigenous people as dirty and contaminated—and the association of indigenous people with rural and "backward" spaces within the national territory—remains influential (Goldstein 2004; Radcliffe and Westwood 1996; Wilson 2004; Zulawski 2007). Accordingly, street vendors of highland and indigenous origin in Santa Cruz are often blamed for a range of urban problems, including congestion, overcrowding, physical deterioration, and hygiene concerns (Blanchard 2006; Salek 2007).

Many Cruceños have responded to the reshaping of the city through migration and urban growth by recalling a nostalgic image of Santa Cruz's past in which life was simpler, quieter, and seemingly more refined. As the pace of urbanization sped up during the past thirty years, Cruceño observers intensified the "remembering" of Santa Cruz as a genteel community composed mostly of criollo (white) residents (for example, Archondo 2000; Fernández 1984). The changes disrupting the city's social, economic, and spatial order have unsettled the traditional criollo elite, whose families had dominated Santa Cruz for centuries (Soruco 2008). In the 1980s, many of these elite families rallied around the Comite Cívico Pro Santa Cruz (Pro–Santa Cruz Civic Committee), calling it the "moral government of the Cruceños" and evoking the 1950s "civic struggles" when this business-led entity had spearheaded a push to receive a greater regional share of petroleum royalties (Flores et al. 2002; Peña et al. 2003). More recently, tensions between President Evo Morales's program of a strong centralized state with redistributive reforms and the intensified opposition support for departmental autonomy in the lowlands have reignited regionalist sentiments in Santa Cruz. In this charged context, the streets, sidewalks, and open spaces surrounding large urban markets have become sites where "traditional Santa Cruz" and newer "migrant Santa Cruz" meet and collide, a clash with deeper political meanings linked to the reterritorialization and transformation of the state itself.

Santa Cruz: Urban and Regional Growth and Migrant Attraction

The city and department of Santa Cruz began a process of rapid economic growth in the mid-1950s, when a state-sponsored project paved the road to the highland cities of Cochabamba and La Paz, improving the linkage between the city and region to the rest of the country (Prado et al. 2005). The city recorded 43,000 inhabitants in 1950, and by 1960 it had 70,000 spread across 5,700 hectares. In the 1970s the state further strengthened connections to Santa Cruz through transport and communications infrastructure, including constructing railroads to Puerto Suárez and Yacuiba on the borders of Brazil and Argentina, the continent's foremost economies. These events occurred amid national policies of import substitution in lowland commodities of sugar, rice, and timber, as well as expansion of the agricultural frontier, following a developmental approach then prevalent across Latin America. The city subsequently diversified its economy along the lines of agribusiness and petroleum extraction, as well as commerce and financial services. It received waves of migrants both from rural Santa Cruz and from poorer Andean regions, contributing by 2001 to a population of more than one million, extending more than 25,000 hectares (GMSC 2004a, 2004b).

Santa Cruz emerged as the principal motor of the Bolivian economy following state-led neoliberal reforms of the mid-1980s. Bolivia's participation in regional trade pacts such as the CAN (the Andean Community of Nations) and MERCOSUR (Southern Common Market) favored export sectors based in Santa Cruz, particularly soy and natural gas (Prado et al. 2005). By 2004 the city and its immediate environs produced 42 percent of the nation's marketed agricultural output and 34 percent of its industrial gross national product (PNUD 2004). From 1992 through 2007, Santa Cruz Department contributed 30 percent on average to Bolivia's GDP, with growth rates consistently higher than those of the national GDP (INE 2007). Santa Cruz now houses the Bolivian headquarters of multinational agricultural and petroleum firms including Archer Daniels Midland, British Gas, Spain's Repsol, and Brazil's Petrobras. Wealthy compared with the Bolivian Andes, Santa Cruz leads the country in gross domestic product (GDP), exports, and living standards.

In parallel with its economic growth, by 2001 Santa Cruz Department was receiving Bolivia's highest level of net migration, 428,000 (up from 74,000 in 1976). According to the most recent census, roughly 25 percent of the department's 2 million inhabitants and 38 percent of the city's 1.1 million were born outside the department, with the majority coming from Cochabamba, Chuquisaca, and Potosí (INE 2001a). Highland migrants—those whose communities of origin lie in the Andean valleys and *altiplano* (high plateau)—have formed enclaves in rural parts of the department such as Yapacaní and San Julian and in peripheral areas of the city of Santa Cruz. During the post-WWII expansion to the east, the state originally promoted migration to Santa Cruz through official programs to supply labor and reinforce agro-industrial expansion, efforts later surpassed by "spontaneous" settlement (Gill 1987; Stearman 1985; Urioste and Kay 2005). Yet, in the past two decades, the impetus of regional economic growth—combined with push factors of economic crisis and structural adjustment, along with severe droughts in the altiplano in the 1980s—have continued to encourage migration flows to Santa Cruz (PNUD 2004). The city's projected 2010 population of 1.6 million (INE 2001b) shows growth continuing at a high rate.

Santa Cruz's Changing Spatial and Economic Structures

The city's physical structure has developed outward from the colonial center (*casco viejo*), which is surrounded by a series of ring roads (*anillos*) (see figure 3). As Santa Cruz abruptly changed from a sleepy Macondo to having its first inkling of rapid growth in the late 1950s, the Italian-Brazilian firm Techint won a bid to design its first comprehensive city plan. The Plan Techint, drawing on early twentieth-century European modernist design principles and a 1930s plan of São Paulo, Brazil, envisioned a series of four radio-centric rings, which would enclose self-contained residential units with ample green space while limiting spatial expansion (Palmer 1979). Although the experience of modernist planning left a distinct imprint on the city's urban form, it failed to meet the needs of the vast influx of migrants arriving in the city. By 1978 the city's population had surpassed Techint's prediction for the year 2000, and new settlements had overtaken the outer limit of the fourth ring (Limpias 2003). In this respect, Santa Cruz shows similarities to the Bolivian city of Cochabamba, where modernist planning principles applied to urban design in the 1940s and 1950s ultimately proved incompatible with the massive urban migration that began in the 1970s and 1980s (Goldstein 2004).

Many of the communities that developed outside the fourth ring fit the UN-Habitat criteria for informal settlements, characterized by insecure tenure, overcrowding, and lack of basic services such as improved water and sanitation systems (UN-Habitat 2006:19). Attempting to confront and manage growth, recent planning efforts include the 1995 Plan Regulador (regulatory or comprehensive plan), which divided the city into twelve districts (see figure 3), with neighborhood units—*unidades vecinales*—within each district. In 2004 the municipality added four districts for future growth that are designated as rural and are largely unpopulated. Yet, the pace of demographic growth has exceeded the capacity of urban planners, municipal authorities, and civil society to respond adequately to meeting basic needs. Though architect Victor Hugo Limpias, of Santa Cruz's Private University (Universidad Privada de Santa Cruz) suggested to me that local officials have not intentionally excluded peripheral areas but instead were overwhelmed by the rate of growth, the result has been increasing segregation, primarily by income, in the absence of planning and acceptable basic service provision in outer urban areas.

In the past decade, the construction of several national highways opened up new axes for housing and private-sector investment on the edges of the city of Santa Cruz, signaling wider shifts in land usage in the metropolitan area. These areas are expanding into the secondary cities of Warnes,

La Guardia, and Cotoca, in some cases blurring the boundaries of Santa Cruz proper (PNUD 2004). Heightened demand for security has spurred the growth of gated communities and high-rise condominiums, which are now set apart and far from the city center, as one might find in São Paulo (Caldeira 2000) or Mexico City (Cabrales Barajas 2006), reversing a historical linkage between center-city habitation and elite status. Subdivisions and condominiums designed for elites feature recreational spaces such as swimming pools, sports grounds, golf courses, and horseback riding. New theme parks, such as Aqualand and Playland located on the edge of the urbanized area, outside the municipal jurisdiction, also aim to attract affluent residents and tourists (Prado et al. 2005). These changes to the city's spatial configuration have resulted in a process referred to as *metropolización*, heightening social and spatial inequality and demands for new and more decentralized forms of urban governance (GMSC 2004a).

The commodity booms of the 1970s in Santa Cruz supported a growing urban service economy, and since then, commerce, tourism, and financial activities have outpaced other sectors (CAINCO 2004). Many of the multinational firms operating in Bolivia are establishing their headquarters in Santa Cruz, often relocating offices from La Paz. These offices, as with petroleum firms such as Petrobras, Repsol, and British Gas, tend to locate near the fourth ring along major axial roads. Financial and producer services, such as banking, insurance, and advertising, are concentrated in the casco viejo, within the first ring. Here, newly erected shopping centers and sleek apartment complexes edge out decrepit colonial-era buildings.

Reflecting national-level conditions, official data suggest that informal forms of employment, including microenterprises, domestic service, and self-employment, accounted for roughly two-thirds of the employed population by 2001 in the city of Santa Cruz (GMSC 2004a). Self-employment is concentrated in the peripheral areas, but it is prevalent across the city (INE 2001a). Despite the stereotype that highland migrants are confined to the most degraded and informalized parts of the economy, a UN report found that, compared in relative terms with the total population of Santa Cruz, a higher percentage of recent migrants—those arriving between 1996 and 2001—are employed as formal wage workers (Blanchard 2006; PNUD 2004:75).

Writing on the Santa Cruz economy in the 1980s, Rojas (1988) observed that in commerce and small-scale manufacturing, informal arrangements predominated over formal ones. The author noted that informal employment involved productive units that were minimally capitalized and used labor without contracts, often through unpaid family arrangements. Furthermore, from a policy perspective, Rojas argued that it is misleading to artificially separate informal, small-scale activities from larger, more formal ones. They do not operate in different economic circuits; in fact, they often have complex economic linkages. Based on these observations and echoing theoretical perspectives on informalization (Benería 2003; Benería and Roldán 1987; Castells and Portes 1989), Rojas concluded that informal workers were not merely "leftover" parts of the local urban labor market. Rather, they provided vital services for the city and subsidized portions of the formal, capitalist sector.

In the period since, processes of labor informalization and urban expansion have deepened in Santa Cruz. Drawing on evidence from Delhi and Ahmedabad in India, Kudva (2006) has suggested that urban growth is being supported by informalization of labor markets in these cities. A similar relationship affects Santa Cruz because the enlarging informal economy has led to changes in the urban landscape. As with Kudva's discussion, here the shifting of production from centralized places of employment to smaller, decentralized sites, including microenterprises, workshops in residential areas, and home-based work, produced a form of urban growth that reflects rising social segregation. This process also involves the conversion of public spaces, such as parks, plazas, and streets, into market places and sites of informal commerce.

Informal Commerce in Santa Cruz and the Gremio Associations

Although informal vendors have long faced social and political marginalization, they have gained political influence in the city of Santa Cruz during the past two decades. This influence reflects their growing numbers, strong forms of organization, and opportunities for capital accumulation in the local economy (Rojas 1988). Replicating forms linked to the rise of the corporatist state and the trade union movement in the Andes (Albro 2006; Lazar 2008), urban Andean merchants in Santa Cruz have organized self-governing associations, or gremios (guilds), to defend their collective interests vis-à-vis the municipality. Rojas (1988:108) noted their appearance in Santa Cruz shortly after the 1952 revolution, most likely brought by highland migrants.

Although comprising migrants *and* nonmigrants, the gremios and the large urban markets they occupy are often viewed in the popular imagination as "Colla" or Andean spaces in the city. Even so, and despite their heavily indigenous Quechua and Aymara memberships, gremios do not generally frame their demands in ethnic terms but do so around working conditions, citizenship rights, and class solidarity. On the other hand, as

Andia (2002) observed, labor migration flows, particularly those from the Andean highlands, have sparked a regionalist and at times racist stance by urban elites and civic leaders. He linked this stance with political and social exclusion of highland migrants, especially those involved in small-scale commerce, in many cases self-employed. Self-employed workers in the expanding small-scale commerce sector also posed a threat because of their capacity to organize politically. This "racialization" of the migrant contrasts with the gremios' self-representation, which highlights class and citizenship over ethnic, cultural, or racial differentiation. These workers became visible targets for anti-migrant sentiment, as shown in the interlude preceding this chapter, from intellectuals of the Nación Camba. Despite the organizing efforts of the gremios, as citizens they were excluded from social expression and participation in local politics, experiencing what Andia (2002:25) calls a "postponed citizenship" as "second-class members of society."

By the 1990s, the gremios had gained a niche in local representative politics through holding a city council seat. Representing swelling ranks, the gremios solidified their organizations to become recognized local political actors. These dynamics were tied, in part, to shifts in urban politics. With the election of Percy Fernández as mayor in 1991, the city saw overtures to "newcomers" as citizens and voters, even though few concrete efforts were made to address issues of public markets and conflicts over space. In 1995 Johnny Fernández (no relation to Percy) unexpectedly took office as mayor after his father, the Cochabamba beer magnate and populist political figure Max Fernández (founder of the UCS party), was killed in a plane crash. The son was catapulted to the office by a sympathy vote and because of his connections with popular organizations, many of which had long been excluded from traditional local political parties. Among these was the federation that articulated most of the gremios in the city, an organization then led by Jesus Cahuana. Cahuana, a migrant himself who came from the Andean highland city of Oruro, was appointed to the city council in 1996, after which the gremios began to play a direct role in local politics.

By the 2000s, in Santa Cruz's largest market, La Ramada, there were sixty gremios representing 94 percent of the vendors in the huge market, all of whom were organized in distinct organizations with elected leaders and functioning statutes (Andia 2002). As a representative structure organized into regional federations, the gremios have become a bastion in the fight by informal vendors against municipal control of public space. They also represent vendors in negotiations with local residents and mediate conflicts between affiliates. Several observers stressed their organizational capacity and gremio leaders' *capacidad de convocatoria* (ability to convene members for meetings or public demonstrations). By 2000 there were twenty-two formal markets in the city, as well as numerous informal markets (*asentamientos*) outside municipal regulatory control, together representing around 35,000 market vendors (*gremialistas*) in the city. In 2007 the municipal planning office identified thirty-four municipal (publicly regulated) markets, with thirty-six private markets and eighteen asentamientos (Andia 2002; Salek 2007). Reflecting a highly organized informal economy, against a legacy of marginalization and racialization, the gremios illustrate the potency of Andean forms of social and political mobilization—even when expressed in the form of urban populism rather than Andean indigeneity—here in this megacity of the Bolivian East.

Large Public Markets: Problematics and Reactions

Municipal markets are located on public property, owned by the city government, and serve as hubs for the entire city. They are both prominent landmarks and anchors for dozens of local minibus companies that organize their routes around these critical spaces (see figure 3). The municipal markets include a range of economic activity, with formal merchants, self-employed merchants and vendors, and waged and unpaid family work, as well as fixed and ambulatory vendors who circulate around the markets' edges. Private supermarkets are owned by private firms, mostly based in Santa Cruz, and are similar to North American supermarkets; thus, they are not typically considered "informal." The asentamientos have little or no municipal oversight and are often nameless and spontaneous. Asentamientos include self-employment and some waged and unpaid family work that is unregistered and "informal." The range of employment in the three types of markets reflects the increasingly unclear boundaries between formal and informal activities (see Benería 2003; Pérez Sáinz 2003).

In keeping with rising income inequality and socioeconomic segregation in Santa Cruz, the three types of markets are not evenly distributed across the city (see figure 3). The vast majority of municipal and private markets are located in the centralized and more prosperous areas (districts 1–4 and 11, with a smaller number in intermediate districts 5 and 6). District 11, in the city center, has the largest number of private markets. In sharp contrast, the asentamientos are concentrated in outer districts 7–10 and 12, indicating poor market infrastructure in the urban periphery. The poorest districts, 8 and 12, have only asentamientos. District 12, the most recently established, has only two asentamientos. District 5, which is far from the center but home to newer, affluent, gated communities, lacks municipal markets but has several private ones. The most well-known municipal markets, La Ramada, Los Pozos, Abasto, and Mutualista, are located in central zones within the fourth ring.

Several of these markets were formed in the early 1970s when planners implemented Plan Techint, which advocated a decentralized supply system and self-contained neighborhoods enclosed by ring roads and a green belt (Palmer 1979). Although the ring roads continue to shape Cruceño urbanization, the decentralized supply system never materialized, and the central markets expanded along with rapid urban growth in the 1980s and 1990s. Because the municipality did not act when the central markets began to grow, the problems have compounded. The large municipal markets experience multifaceted problems related to overcrowding: lack of cleanliness, conflicts between established vendors and the newly arrived, competing pressures for land, and encroachment of vendors onto areas officially designated as public space. Absent effective intervention, expanding informal commerce in public spaces is generating social conflict in the opinion of many residents. As reflected in comments to me by personnel in the Municipal Planning Agency, pedestrians often find sidewalks filled with vendors' wares impassible. Disputes erupt between shopkeepers and informal merchants selling similar items from the front sidewalk. Another set of problems relates to hygiene and contamination, such as food vendors cooking on the street and disposing of cooking oil on the sidewalks or median strips. Public transport, also largely informal and unregulated by the municipality, converges around the central markets and their main transport arteries, exacerbating congestion and air and noise pollution (Salek 2007).

By the late 1990s, in the face of insufficient public funds, administrative policy, and both implicit and explicit municipal negligence, the gremios themselves began to play a role in municipal planning politics. Gremio leader and, by then, city council member Jesus Cahuana sought to rectify this situation by heading up the Comisión de Industria y Comercio, a commission of the city council. In 1998 the commission developed a municipal "macropolicy" for the markets, which proposed constructing district-level markets and wholesale produce markets at three of the city's main entry points. The proposal built on an achievement of several years earlier, when the municipality had passed an ordinance allowing usufruct ownership of market premises by the vendors for thirty years, at which point ownership would revert to the city (GMSC 1990). Cahuana, in interviews, noted that the usufruct system had enabled some US$50 million of investment in market infrastructure while, in effect, improving working conditions for merchants and vendors. Critics faulted the plan and the gremios for weakening municipal control over markets and adjacent spaces (Salek 2007:15), noting that it enabled the re-selling of usufruct rights, creating what another Cruceño city planner referred to as a "disorganized and chaotic situation." Others saw Cahuana as acting only "in the interest of the gremios—and even worse, a specific sector of gremios—rather than for the general interest of the city" (Andia 2002:32).

This expression of gremialista citizenship reflects and provokes the wider dynamics and meanings of the politics of public space in Santa Cruz. As Andia suggested, the municipal government recognizes that it has a physical and social problem: expanding markets occupy space, annex neighboring areas, worsen congestion, and thwart efforts to promote rational, orderly urban growth. This recognition articulates with an ideological stance, that of the elite civic powers in the city who spark public denunciations about "unhygienic" and "informal" uses of public space, in many ways a code for underlying fears of the rising political muscle of the gremios and other informal workers associations. As reflected by the eminent Cruceño architect and urban planning guru Fernando Prado, the former populist mayor Johnny Fernández had sparked these dilemmas by promoting the growing urban informal economy, including the gremios and the transport sector, and leading their representatives to create alliances with political parties "to support the interests of markets, street commerce, and illegal occupation of public land." The alliances are seen not as expressions of citizenship but as "patronage politics" in which "electoral votes are exchanged for favors in the use of public space that benefit the interested parties, while creating conflicts for the city at large" (Prado et al. 2005:164). The result is that while gremios exert political pressure and mobilize mass demonstrations, they are, in the words of another Cruceña interviewee, conflictive sources of disorder.

From Cahuana's perspective and that of the gremios, the municipal government has lacked the will to make concrete improvements in the city's markets. Cahuana noted that the municipal budget relies, in part, on fines levied on street vendors and that the current administration deliberately keeps the rules murky to extract higher rents. Moreover, the new municipal market plan does not appear to recognize gremio leaders' authority and has rarely sought their input, thereby suppressing their political influence. "When we organize marches and mobilizations, we do it to remind the municipality of its obligation to improve market infrastructure," explained Cahuana. Amid public sector retrenchment and the state's diminished role in social provisions, informal commerce not only offers a viable source of livelihood for many urban residents but also, as in the Andes, reflects a popular push for the state to assume responsibilities for citizens working within the discourse of citizenship rights and law (compare Goldstein 2004).

The Municipal Plan to Reorganize Markets and Market Networks

In recent years, as the country entered into a phase of instability and conflict tied to regionalist assaults against what was seen as a threatening "indigenous" government of the MAS, the city—a distinct if embedded political sphere within the wider region—continued to take steps to address the issue of the markets, interpreted by many as the presence of threatening Andean "indigenes" within the confines of the city "walls" (or rings). The city government, which again has Percy Fernández in the mayor's office, has retaken the initiative on limiting the growth of urban markets and curtailing informal economic activities in public spaces. With support from the Japanese International Cooperation Agency (JICA), the Municipal Planning Office has begun to implement a Municipal Plan for a New Supply Network, Markets, Ambulatory Vendors, and Commerce in Public Spaces, which aims to reorganize the city's market and supply system.

Though maintaining the dominant ideological view of migrants as sometimes "invasive" and "illegal," the plan and corresponding diagnostic research recognized that the vendors pursue livelihoods and dignity. The plan entails decentralizing the largest public markets, creating new municipally controlled markets in the outlying districts, and relocating ambulatory vendors—all to achieve the decongestion of existing markets, rotundas, and avenues. By upgrading the functioning and administration of markets with periodic, officially sponsored fairs for specific products and dedicated sites for food sale, the proposal hopes to enhance the wider urban market infrastructure. Finally, the plan aspires to redesign the food distribution network, create a wholesale produce market, and provide technical assistance to vendors and gremios in areas of health and hygiene. The overarching view is one of formalizing the informal, decongesting the urban core by relocating vendors and activities, and bringing these activities more firmly under the city's regulatory structure. Underlying these concerns, the anxiety many established Cruceños feel about the reshaping of the city through migration and urban expansion is expressed in heightened and racialized concerns about "hygiene"—the discourse through which wider anxieties about political change and demographic shifts are expressed—a "crisis" that can be met through rational urban planning.

Yet, these technical solutions suggest a spatialized and racialized effort at depoliticizing—or politically weakening—the gremialistas as a segment of the urban populace. Much of the municipal plan—including the proposed wholesale and district markets—draws on the unimplemented policy developed when Cahuana headed the commission on public markets. Yet according to Cahuana, the main difference is that the new plan "does not recognize the gremio leadership." He added that rather than use usufruct ownership rights for vendors, private firms will be encouraged to invest in infrastructure development through a bidding process. Vendors must accept "whatever price, whatever location, and whatever dimensions" the developers demand. In the context of rising political activism of the gremios, the rise of racialized hygiene panic and a more general anxiety about the indigenous turn, elites tactically choose to address the issue of urban markets with a classically liberal approach to private investment. This enhances the municipality's and civic groups' rationale in reordering the city's markets—and remapping urban territorial space—invoking yet exceeding aesthetic concerns and the promotion of a development ethos of private investment, entrepreneurship, and market values.

Reactions to the unfolding municipal plan reveal the stakes of these conceptions of urban public space and the dilemmas posed by expanding informal commerce in Santa Cruz. In what follows, I describe some of the reactions from those affected, based on interviews in 2007. Many of the vendors did not inherently oppose the municipal plan and would consider moving to new sanctioned locations under certain conditions. They were often critical, however, of the program's nonparticipatory structure and the manner in which they felt that "relocation" was being imposed on them, a practice that echoes the neoliberal reforms of the 1990s, which similarly displaced and relocated miners in the name of technocratic modernization. A woman of the Asociación 8 de Enero, a gremio based at the central Los Pozos market with 360 members, stated:

> We have unified five federations of gremios. Only the head of the federation attends the meetings [with the municipal government]. The membership base is not informed. They don't consult with us about the project. We don't know very much about it.

Other gremialistas worried that relocating away from the city center, away from its pedestrian flow, would hurt their sales. A woman of the Asociación 8 de Marzo gremio, also based at Los Pozos with four hundred members, responded:

> We won't be able to sell anything, so what will we live on? They should accommodate us well. If not, we cannot move.

A man of the same gremio added:

> They are going to build a new municipal market. We don't think we'll

stay here forever. Mayor Percy Fernández has offered us a place [in the new market], and we are waiting for it. But I hope they don't relocate us too far away, in the middle of nowhere. We have trained ourselves [acquired administrative skills], and they can't just send us away, just like that. Now, if they give us a place near the third or fourth ring, yes, we'd accept it. But only if there is transport available on the main road. If not, we'll fight until who knows when.

Underscoring this view, Jesus Cahuana, the gremio federation leader and former council member, noted:

Percy Fernández built a market called Miraflores in the zone of Villa Primero de Mayo for political reasons in the early 1990s. Right now, it is empty. It cost $400,000 in investment. Why? There is no vehicular or foot traffic. It's like new, but it's falling down. People who don't know the basics of commerce, they just do whatever they want.

These testimonies reveal an understandable concern about livelihood strategies among informal vendors. If forced to relocate far from the city center, they may sell less, and a long commute could cut into meager earnings. There is a spatial dimension to these livelihood concerns, as shown in the acceptability of relocating to the relatively central third or fourth ring or the infeasibility of a poorly situated new market. Yet, while prioritizing their survival strategies, many vendors, like civic leaders and planners, affirm the need for a system of rules regarding access to public space. Asked what happens when new arrivals, such as recent migrants, want to join a gremio in Los Pozos, another member of 8 de Enero commented:

Now there is no more space. Each association has its members, and there are nine associations here. There can no longer be disorder in the streets.

Currently, Griselda Muñoz, who serves as the Federación de Gremialistas director and, like Cahuana, became an elected city council member (though of a different party) under Mayor Percy Fernandez, suggested that the municipality was affecting vendor interests without having ever done much itself. Against the sense of migrants being dirty and disorderly threats to urban rationality and liberal progress, Muñoz suggested that vendors reflected precisely a kind of entrepreneurial, self-governed, and self-regulated subject:

The municipality has not constructed a single market in [twenty] years. It has not constructed any infrastructure. All of the markets exist because of the resources of the merchants.... What is missing is a

markets policy or a policy on the use of public space by the municipal-
ity that permits the decongesting of the older markets and the construc-
tion of new ones, that the new markets have defined spaces with set
schedules for work and guidelines on what should be sold, what you
can sell in the Casco Viejo [city center] and what things you cannot
sell. Now they sell anything, there is no order, and this stems precisely
from the political problems and from corruption.... The majority of us
have educated our children in the streets. If you go to La Ramada,
where my association is.... You'll see that we've educated our kids in
the streets, and I know from my own experience, this is not an ade-
quate place for them to do their homework and to learn. It would be a
good idea if a private company—because the mayor's office will never
be able to do this, they can't even provide security guards—or an NGO
or foundation could construct spaces near the markets where children
could do their homework seated on chairs, at desks, as they should be.

The position suggests that the "panic" approach to vendors—which proposes their containment and removal in the name of order and aesthetics—might better be served by gaining familiarity with local informal production and linkages between informal and formal production and markets. The municipality could support vendors in more effective and creative ways rather than see relocation as the only solution.

Parallel to the proposals to order through relocation, another municipal ordinance, Ordenanza Municipal 050/2004 (GMSC 2004a), which was reapproved in 2007, sheds light on the "official" views of public space. The ordinance specifies that the municipality must "guarantee equality of opportunities in accessing public space and the smooth functioning of activities in such spaces...without causing harm to pedestrians or vehicular traffic flow" (2004a:4). It states objectives on uses, including "protecting the environment...improving the quality of public space through rationalizing and designating compatible uses according to established zones...recuper-ating and preserving public spaces so that areas of circulation, green space, and public ornamentation perform their functions...[and] prioritizing the collective interests of citizens above individual interests" (GMSC 2004a). Legally, public space is a "public dominion" for "satisfying collective urban needs [that] transcend the individual interests of the city's inhabitants and are subject to regulation" (GMSC 2004a:5). Socioculturally, "public space has the role of enabling social interaction, communal expression, and the construction of citizen identity" (GMSC 2004a:6). "In this city in particular," it adds, "with its history of migrant reception, a diversity of people live together who leave their mark on the urban landscape" (2004a:6).

This recognition of the "migrant" population is echoed in a segmented conception of space and functionality—one that in turn echoes a segmented notion of urban society as divided ethnoracially and by class. Accordingly, the municipality explicitly recognizes that urban public space must encompass uses of diverse cultural and ethnic origins, such as selling a range of products and services that are implicitly marked in ethnoracial terms. It reserves the right, however, to set limitations on infringing green space, impeding traffic flows, and activities deemed unhygienic or unsanitary, including certain forms of food preparation. Such activities are frequently denounced in the local press (see Arias 2009; Pérez 2009). In several public places, such as the central Plaza 24 de Septiembre, informal commerce is barred, except for registered shoe shiners and coffee sellers.

Adopting a language of inclusiveness, the city ordinance prioritizes "collective" above "individual" interests in "preserving public spaces for all citizens to enjoy." But efforts to limit the popular-collective gremio organizations seem to contradict this position. Regarding the uses of urban public space, the municipality emphasizes notions of aesthetics, hygiene, and public order to promote a modernizing and cosmopolitan image. Both the public space ordinance and the municipal plan advocate for "collective urban needs" while condemning certain income-generating activities as based on "individual gain" (GMSC 2004a:5; Salek 2007). Paradoxically contradicting the sublimation of individual gain and entrepreneurship embedded in the various planning documents, this critique of individual gain is aimed directly at the vendors and gremios as somehow threatening to privatize space. Vendors of course demand the right to work and to a livelihood, part of their citizenship rights integral to the city's collective interest—as well as a potential alleviation of more generalized economic distress—rights asserted amid deteriorating labor market conditions and reduced social protections for the poor (Benería 2003; Pérez Sainz 2003). It is the *public* quality of public space that offers the possibility for excluded groups to gain visibility and demand inclusion (Springer 2009; Staeheli and Thompson 1997). Yet, collective concerns about the public and collective are, from the municipality's perspective, focused on concern for the "*patrimonio paisajístico*" (landscape patrimony) and "*imagen urbana*" (urban image)—said to be necessary to attract investment, tourism, and market-oriented growth while projecting symbolic qualities of civic life, stability, and "modernity" (GMSC 2004a:4). The municipal plan restricts informal trading in public space, and it refers to it in negative terms such as "avasallamiento" (usurpation) and "invasión" (invasion).

Conclusions and Ongoing Histories

Santa Cruz's primary newspaper, *El Deber* (2010a, 2010b), reported on the ongoing contestation of street space and the relocation of vendors in the name of "reordering" and retaking public space. By 2010 these conflicts had devolved into literal street battles, pitting fruit-throwing vendors against police who sought to move them to the outlying markets. With the vendors represented as violent and dangerous threats to order, the newspaper—a bastion of civic authority in the city—did its part to further question the gremialistas:

> *Santa Cruz, June 8. Fruit sellers who commercialize their wares in the public way [la vía pública] have for several days been refusing to leave their spaces, arguing that conditions do not exist for them to sell in another sector of the city. During the battle, the gremialistas attacked with fruits, sticks, and stones while nearly 100 uniformed police in groups responded with regulation night-sticks and teargas.*

> *Santa Cruz, June 21. The pressure of shouts, sticks, and stones was enough to convince the Municipal Council of Santa Cruz to declare a temporary hold [cuarto intermedio] on the question of reordering of the gremialistas who sell in the streets of the capital city. This morning, more than a hundred vendors were at the door of the Council to demand that they be allowed to sell in the public way. While the issue was being debated inside, outside there was aggression against the guards who sought to prevent the entry of the outraged merchants.*

Suspicious fires and gas explosions have also begun to occur in market selling areas, and there are nearly daily headlines decrying, for instance, the "Chaos That Has Installed Itself in La Ramada Market" (*El Deber* 2010c). Editorialists replicate the panic discourse that structures wider processes of struggle over democracy and citizenship, writing only somewhat facetiously that

> *foreign experts in urbanism have suggested converting the La Ramada market into a tourist attraction and recommended to the municipality that this be the means of reordering one of the largest and most chaotic centers of popular provisioning in the city. One of the experts who recently toured the markets for a couple of hours observed that it was a "question of Cambas and Collas understanding each other" so that there will be no more conflicts in the market. In order for tourists to go to La Ramada, surely there must be a minimum of order, cleanliness,*

and security. Otherwise tourist visitors will have to arrive accompanied by a corps of firemen, another of public health workers, and one more of infantry. [El Deber 2010c]

In this way, the relocation of vendors serves as a tool of exclusion by the municipality through its unwillingness to recognize them as legitimate petitioners of public interests. This spatial stigmatization and territorial control of unwanted groups constitute a normative ordering of the urban (and regional) landscape, one in which indigeneity is marked as a racialized, dirty migrant subject, much like matter "out of place," in Mary Douglas's words (1966). This matter out of place is targeted for control even as this same subject represents the emergence of a new subjectivity and citizen in a country undergoing a tense decolonizing turn (Harvey 2000; Mamani, chapter 2, this volume). Such a vision is not unique to Santa Cruz but is a predominant way of seeing public space in developing cities under neoliberal policies (L. Fernandes 2004; Holston 2008; Springer 2009; Swanson 2007). According to Cahuana—perhaps again evidencing a strategy of de-ethnicizing or de-racializing the self in a claim for citizenship—the municipal plan is merely a "political issue" rather than an outright effort to discriminate against highlanders as ethnic or racial others. Yet, these battles over territorial control of urban space are a key arena in which the racially charged remapping of Bolivia and the issue of "migrant" social integration play out in the heart of contemporary Santa Cruz. Whether implicitly or explicitly racialized, the battle over territorial control of urban space and the social integration of the "migrant" is a key arena in which the remapping of Bolivia unfolds, pitting a localized struggle between gremialista "insurgent" citizenship (Holston 2008) against tactics of relocation defended by a conservative "civic" aesthetics of hygiene and racial and social order.

6 Understanding the Mobilizations of Octubre 2003

Dynamic Pressures and Shifting Leadership Practices in El Alto

Carlos Revilla

In 2003 the city of El Alto was the epicenter of the national mobilizations and protests that ultimately led to the resignation of President Gonzalo "Goni" Sánchez de Lozada and to the legitimacy crisis of neoliberal governance. Popular and scholarly representations of this conflict and crisis—popularly referred to as La Guerra de Gas (The Gas War), Octubre Negro (Black October), or simply lo de Octubre 2003—have congealed, in part, around an explanation based on the idea that quotidian organizational practices tied to urban militance mechanically explain what happened. Another analytic frame emphasized—in an exaggerated way, I suggest—the role played by a homogenous Aymara communitarian form of democracy with no real leadership and with collective decision-making. Drawing on ethnographic observations of the buildup to the events of 2003 and from my long-term residence in El Alto and life as an Alteño, I argue here for a more complex understanding of these processes. The discussion focuses on the interweaving between macro- and micropolitical pressures and forms of leadership that were as much about rupture as they were about the exercise of existing—whether real or imagined in a romanticist way—modalities of organization, identity, and struggle.

In relationship to leadership, a conventional assumption about the Gas War is that we can project daily models of organizing in neighborhood groups from earlier years onto what happened in 2003, without understanding the intervening steps in the process. For example, Lazar (2008) and Albó (2006, 2007) argue that the event was predicated on well-established patterns of political behavior that created a normal democratic cycle of protest and negotiation with the government, broken only by the violent response of the state. I argue, however, that the event involved a critical questioning of the "normal" ways in which people related to the state through leadership on a day-to-day basis. This critical reflection on grassroots leadership led to a fundamental change, which I discuss below, in the relationship between the grassroots Alteños, their leaders, and the state.[1]

A second body of literature on Octubre refers to the idea that Alteño politics are determined by a static and isolated urban communitarian democracy based on highland indigenous (Aymara) culture. The implication—as suggested in works such as Patzi (2004), P. Mamani (2005; chapter 2, this volume), and Zibechi (2006)—is that there is an organic process of indigenous Aymara horizontal decision-making at work in this complex urban milieu. I assert, on the contrary, that this idea does not satisfactorily address the institutional structures and barriers that challenged the legitimacy of local leadership and ultimately prevented the realization of such ideal(ized) communitarian forms of democracy in the urban context of El Alto. Furthermore, leadership and decision-making of a different sort were actually critical to creating conditions for mass mobilization. There was an organizational and articulatory transformation underway, moving from a highly individualistic, pragmatic, and clientelistic form of leadership to a situation in which grassroots Alteños began to question quotidian forms of interaction with leaders and the role of their leaders in representing their needs to the state.[2] By putting pressure on leaders and electing new ones who were more accountable to peoples' needs, I suggest, new kinds of possibilities for vertical and horizontal articulation emerged.[3] As such, neither pre-existing organizational forms nor an idealized communitarian democracy are sufficient explanations for what was behind the upheaval of 2003 and for what continues to reshape and remap the cultural politics of citizenship and urban space in El Alto.

This misreading is due to the fact that much of the scholarly work on Octubre has focused only on outcomes rather than processes, without examining how such dynamic forms of mobilization emerged. In what follows, I draw on participant observation and political engagement with neighbor-hood organizations in a particular district in El Alto. I explore how leadership, when subjected to external and internal pressures, eventually changed in relationship to the daily work and practical content of organizing and led to the popular uprisings of 2003. This daily labor eventually moves into extraordinary forms of mobilization and articulation between social groups. This analysis will allow us to better understand how grassroots movements engage and modify political pressures in their favor on a day-to-day basis in order to transform the role and character of leadership and in turn pressure the state to address their needs.

El Alto and La Paz: Growth, Inequality, and the Rise of Urban Territorial Organizations

In order to understand the precariousness of everyday life and the forces that challenged people to explicitly confront the state in El Alto, it is useful to consider El Alto in relation to the neighboring city of La Paz. El Alto and La Paz compose part of the same metropolis but can be thought of as opposing urban environments (Albó 2006, 2007). El Alto, the younger and poorer sister city, sits 14,000 feet above the steep canyon that cradles the wealthier administrative capital of La Paz (see figure 10). La Paz, founded in 1548, is the seat of legislative and executive power in Bolivia. It historically served as a supply settlement for the caravans that traveled between the silver-producing colonial city of Potosí and the Pacific Ocean harbors (Escobari 2001). El Alto was part of the marginal rural area that extended alongside this important commercial center and comprised indigenous peasant communities and haciendas belonging to rich families from La Paz (Qayum, Soux, and Barragán 1997; Quispe 2004:9; Urzagasti 1986).

It was not until the mid-twentieth century that El Alto began to urbanize at a rapid rate. Between the 1940s and 1950s, El Alto solidified its subordinate functional role with respect to the needs of La Paz as a district of railway workshops, airport freight terminals, and specialized storage (PAR 2005:15–18). The second half of the twentieth century saw rapid growth of El Alto resulting from social and economic changes in the country. The agrarian and educational reforms that followed the Revolution of 1952, along with critical climatic events, created both change and crisis in the rural peasant economy, stimulating massive migration to urban areas (Calderón and Szmukler 1999; Poupeau 2009; Sandóval 1999). The city of El Alto expanded from 3,000 inhabitants in 1950 to a city of 1.4 million by the late 1990s. The rapid migration created new challenges in gaining access to services, resources, and employment and even obtaining decision-making spaces in the new urban environment (Gill 2000; Rivera 1993, 1996).

The development of neighborhood organizations in El Alto tracked the growth of the city as a whole. The first association of *vecinos* (neighbors), referring to city residents, which took the form of a Central Neighbors' Council, arose out of residents' recognition that their ability to obtain services would be improved by working as a collective. These early groups were strongly associated with the MNR (Nationalist Revolutionary Movement) party apparatus, the political party that led the National Revolution of 1952 (Malloy 1970). In 1963 these associations developed into a subfederation connected to affiliate umbrella organizations in the city of La Paz. Foreshadowing the later split between the two cities, by 1979 El Alto's neighborhood councils achieved independence from those of La Paz, taking on the form of the present-day Alteño federation, FEJUVE, The Federation of Neighborhood Boards of El Alto (Federación de Juntas Vecinales). The split reflected the recognition by Alteños that their organizations required independent governance because of the unequal distribution of resources in relation to La Paz. El Alto residents saw a larger share of municipal resources being spent in the city center and thus demanded access to and control over their own financial resources. Conversely, municipal leaders in La Paz recognized that the growing and impoverished population of El Alto would inevitably strain its resources as well. Finally, La Paz residents (*Paceños*) saw the growing population of El Alto as an electoral threat to their control over municipal politics. This paradoxical convergence of the pursuit of municipal autonomy and the detachment of that seen as an impoverished burden from the more wealthy La Paz led to the formal split between the two cities in 1988.

Amid the historic divisions and inequalities between the two cities, El Alto's situation was exacerbated by neoliberal policies introduced in 1985. For Bolivians, neoliberal free-market ideas were seen as imported northern economic prescriptions, from the "Chicago School" or the Chicago "Boys" associated with Milton Friedman.[4] With the country deep in debt as a result of a series of corrupt and profligate military dictatorships, then-president Victor Paz Estensorro signed Supreme Decree 21060, putatively to aid the ailing Bolivian economy but actually launching the opening salvo in a twenty-year assault on the poor called the New Economic Policy. As many scholars have noted, this was one of the most draconian economic and social engineering initiatives launched in any Latin American country, pursuing an adjustment of the economy and, by way of changes to the public sector, the state itself. The curtailment of state subsidies, the elimination of much public-sector employment, wage freezes, and the reconfiguration of state agencies dedicated to social welfare such as health, education, and housing into privatized forms, or the outsourcing of their activities to development agencies, exposed the urban and rural poor and the working class to much hardship (Conaghan, Malloy, and Abugattas 1990; Gill 2000; Nash 1992).

Neoliberal reforms also uprooted whole communities and remapped the ethnic and racial dynamics of the country, further contributing to the urbanization and growth of El Alto (Albó 2006, 2007). Supreme Decree 21060, for example, enabled the government to privatize state-operated tin mines and fire some thirty thousand workers during the mid- and late 1980s. Miners lost not only their jobs but also their entire way of life and were forced to find work elsewhere, many migrating to the city of El Alto (Sanabria 1999). Other migrants were ex-peasants from the rural areas of the altiplano, driven off their land as a result of both El Niño–related droughts between 1982 and 1984 and the liberalization of markets, which made it difficult for small-scale producers to compete with larger businesses. Another important but less commonly analyzed trend brought people from cities and townships of La Paz and the interior of the country to El Alto, the search for social mobility and cheaper housing. These distinct groups wound up in communities and neighborhoods of El Alto, sharing and exchanging sociocultural and political practices.

The neoliberal "adjustments" not only remapped the racial and ethnic landscape of the country through mass migrations but also substantially altered the availability of formal employment (Calderón and Szmukler 1999). There were radical shifts in the types and quality of work available to migrants. In the 1980s the largest part of the economically active population worked in manufacturing (38.9 percent), followed by small business (12.4 percent) and personal services (12.1 percent) (Urzagasti 1986). By 2001 more than 28 percent of the population was dedicated to wholesale and retail commerce, a rise of 10 percent compared with 1980. Another important shift was the increase in the transportation services sector, rising from 5.7 percent to 10.38 percent in the same period (INE 2005). Manufacturing, conversely, decreased to 23.08 percent. Although 57 percent of the industrial establishments in the metropolitan area of La Paz are still located in El Alto, this does not generate income for the municipal government, nor does it increase productive employment for families living there (Rossel and Rojas 2002). More significantly, between 1989 and 1995 the informal sector grew by a striking 1,120 percent, with a yearly rate of growth of 130 percent. The "informal sector" continues to employ the greatest part of the population of El Alto (Arbona 2006; CEDLA 2008). Added to this, there was a general increase in the labor force during this period, caused by the loss of fixed employment, forcing more members of families to enter the labor market (Domic 1999). In so doing, they faced precarious circumstances such as the absence of social security, the extension of working hours, and low wages.

Migration to El Alto exceeded the capacity and desire of a hollowed-out state to deal with the increasing needs of the expanding population. Urban space became politicized and territorialized as groups tried to gain access to material resources such as housing, employment, and basic services (Espósito and Arteaga 2007). Neoliberal reform was accompanied by compensatory measures such as the Social Emergency Fund (FSE), which sought to alleviate the effects of dislocation by creating temporary, small-scale employment and food-for-work programs (many furnished with surplus American food aid) through the building of infrastructural projects. But, these were palliative measures that did not address the deeper demands of residents and functioned as disciplinary and mystifying strategies that sought both to neutralize a possible explosion of demands and to further the debilitation of an already weakened labor movement, the COB (Central Obrera Boliviano, Bolivian Workers' Central) (Calderón and Szmukler 1999). The widespread informality of El Alto's workers—which excluded them from most formalized labor unions—as well as the intentional weakening of labor unions carried out by neoliberal reformers, left neighborhood organizations (*juntas*) positioned as the crucial and primary mode and vehicle of political-organizing struggle for urban citizens. This paralleled the rising protagonism of indigenous organizations that accompanied the decline of organized labor elsewhere in the country (Sanabria 1999). In El Alto, the Neighborhood Boards (Juntas Vecinales) thus became the most important grassroots social organizations. Neighborhoods organized the boards to plan, finance, and build basic infrastructure and provide services. The boards were the main instrument used for building the city and were also a tool of mediation, representation, and accountability in both public and private spaces (Sandóval and Sostres 1989).

Neoliberal economic reforms were also accompanied by later political reforms that contributed to the rise in place-based or territorial exercises of citizenship, as compared with formal organized labor unions. The 1994 Law of Popular Participation transferred responsibilities—and to a much lesser degree, resources—over infrastructure, education, and public health from the central government to the municipal level. In theory, the law was designed to facilitate grassroots involvement in decision-making and control over resources (Van Cott 2000). In reality, municipalities were forced to take over management of significant public needs with insufficient resources transferred from the state. Further, the privatization of public-sector responsibilities, for example, hydrocarbons, air and ground transportation, water, and electricity, made these more centralized, less open to participation, and less accountable to the grassroots. Thus, despite the high-sounding name of *Popular Participation*, the actual possibilities for participation were restricted, leading to a fragmentation of grassroots demands because the competition over access to resources for immediate needs superseded attention to wider political issues. Arguably, this was the depoliticizing thrust and intent of neoliberal decentralization strategy. This, along with the reduction in public-sector and formal private-sector employment, contributed to changing understandings of citizenship from being labor or class based to being exercised primarily through territorial—in this case, urban—organization.

Urban Heterogeneity

These broad-based macroeconomic shifts and their effects are useful for understanding and contextualizing the ethnic, racial, and economic heterogeneity that shapes the construction of grassroots social movements. Although scholars might generally view El Alto as solely an indigenous and poor city, there is a socioeconomic and racialized geography that cuts across this urban environment. Alteños see a basic difference between El Alto Norte (North) and El Alto Sur (South), with the airport cutting through the middle. El Alto Norte is 80 percent Aymara, whereas the districts and neighborhoods south of the airport have a larger share of Quechua and non-indigenous people (see figure 10). The southern neighborhoods are generally more socioculturally diverse and show higher levels of education and differentiated levels of consumption, but El Alto Sur is still approximately 60 percent Aymara (Albó 2006).

Aymara predominance should not be interpreted as reflecting a homogeneous and stable ethnic population and category that organically determines urban politics. For example, younger people are likely to abandon the Aymara language spoken by their parents in search of urban codes. On the other hand, this does not signify an all-out rejection of Aymara ethnicity. In El Alto, there is a creative mixing of rural and urban forms in various dimensions of social life, such as the hybridization of distinct musical styles that has created Aymara-Spanish hip-hop (Archondo 2001; Balboa 1993; Dangl 2007; Rodríguez 2003). Another example of the fluidity of ethnic–class relations is found in neighborhoods in the south, such as the one where I grew up. There, one can observe those who do not identify as indigenous and who try to distinguish themselves from the more indigenous Alteños, both culturally and socioeconomically. Yet, their heightened investment in obtaining social status through Western aesthetic cues and modes of consumption does not always signify economic superiority, given that the majority of Alteños live in precarious economic conditions.

Another complicating factor in urban politics is what Bolivian scholars have referred to as egocentric and exocentric networks attributed to Aymara migrants. *Egocentric* refers to the networks extending from the ego (spouse, children, cousins, and so forth), *exocentric* to those outside the ego or away from nuclear families (such as *compadrazgo* and *comadrazgo*, co-godparent relations) (Rivera 1984). Some scholars assumed that migrants directly transplanted these egocentric/exocentric networks and systems of cooperative and collective economic exchange from the rural environment to the urban. But these networks are often co-opted by capital through ubiquitous microcredit programs that ostensibly promote development and entrepreneurship through small-scale loans. The co-optation reduces the organizing potential of the networks by promoting competition that eventually weakens economic ties and modifies the logic of solidarity (Rivera 1996). Further, although familial networks extend access to labor, startup capital credit, and contacts to initiate or improve economic activities, capital, and profits rarely move beyond the nuclear family. These private ways of managing labor result from the pressures of market-oriented production and create a sphere subject to intense competition in economic and social dimensions.

It is within this context of heterogeneous class and ethnic relations and precarious economic circumstances—marked by informality, competition, and highly individualized family survival strategies—that I argue against mechanical conceptualizations of the events of 2003 as an explosion of communitarian Aymara resistance. More accurately, complex identities, new political and social alliances, and daily economic challenges set the stage for distinct forms of organizing and understandings of leadership at the grassroots level, which eventually forced people to move beyond everyday concerns to making more substantive claims, as expressed in the mobilizations of 2003.

District 4: The World in a Grain of Sand

District 4 is an ideal location to explore these questions because, in many ways, it is a microcosm of the broad-based processes discussed earlier. The district also played an important role in the mobilizations of October 2003. District 4 is located in the northwestern sector of the city (see figure 10). It is cut in half by the airport of El Alto in the east, Juan Pablo II Avenue in the north, and the road to Laja in the west and south. Both roads connect La Paz and El Alto with important rural towns and communities such as Desaguadero and Copacabana. In September and later in October 2003, Juan Pablo II Avenue, which crosses El Alto from east to west, was blockaded by residents who used their bodies to paralyze movement and make this key sector inaccessible, closing off the Public University of El Alto

(UPEA) and blocking the crossroads heading toward the town of Laja. The long lines of bodies were ultimately converted into ready-made targets by the army, which staged the mass killing of more than eighty civilian Alteños during the Gas War that ensued (Gomes 2004). District 4 was a microcosm of ongoing economic conditions and political strategies and would also become a memorialized epicenter of national change.

Economically, District 4 illustrates the combination of poverty, structural inequality, and lack of basic services that shapes daily life in El Alto more generally. According to municipal data (GMEA 2005), the percentage of poverty in District 4, based on the Index of Unsatisfied Basic Needs (NBI), is 77 percent, the fifth poorest in El Alto. Though unemployment is technically low, the conditions of paid or salaried employment are precarious and the wages minimal. About half of the district works in commerce and manufacturing, in equal portions, with 10 percent employed in transportation and communications and the remainder divided roughly evenly between construction, education, and food services. Much of this employment is "informal," that is, without social benefits, guaranteed income, or protection under labor laws. Access to education is low, with about half of the district having completed only primary education, a quarter completing high school, and only 3 percent at the university level. Some 10 percent have no formal education at all. In 2001 a quarter of the population had no drinking water, sewage reached only 30 percent of the residents or households, and the energy grid reached only 68 percent. Living in and seeking to transform these conditions characterizes the struggles of everyday life and also highlights the need for organizational forms of the neighborhood associations to negotiate for the most vulnerable.

Changing Notions of Leadership through Time

In District 4, as elsewhere, leadership within the neighborhood organizations is critical for securing access to basic services for vecinos and for creating articulatory spaces between the local grassroots and district level and the higher levels of the city-wide organization FEJUVE. Echoing the labor union or "syndical" model that characterized Bolivian politics more widely after 1952, local neighborhood leaders are elected at a subdistrict "zonal" level to represent each of the district's zones. The zonal representatives— usually the president and vice president of the zone—meet regularly, ideally once a month, at general district meetings (*ampliados distritales*). Other representatives are selected to meet at a higher level, with leaders from each district interacting and participating in the executive committee of FEJUVE, the city-wide council. During the crisis of neoliberalism's decline and in the context of the various macroeconomic and political processes described above, these pressures greatly affected the ability of leaders to represent the needs of their communities.

Residents in District 4 evaluate leaders in the present based upon an idealized understanding of the characteristics leaders took on in order to build critical services during the early formation of the city, in particular, the extent to which community representatives work for collective rather than individual interests. Leaders of the past are said to have worked for "the common good," whereas many leaders of the present have become "individualists," what I call the leader "who walks alone." The ideal notion of leadership is seen, in part, to relate to a person's long-term residence in a community —illustrating both individual stability and emotional commitment to space and place. Residents believe that this leads to a desire or willingness to build infrastructure and public works in the neighborhood. An outsider who attempts to get involved in neighborhood matters usually experiences harsh criticism and can be reprimanded. Compared with leaders of long-term residence, they are seen as temporary figures with "selfish" intentions who work against those of the neighborhood, or an ideal collective territorial identity. Home ownership—with residence there for a minimum of three years—is a formal requirement to demonstrate territorial commitment and trustworthiness, despite the fact that this tends to exclude women and younger Alteños (often renters) from formal leadership roles (Cottle and Ruiz 1993:142). Even so, the ideal does not always play out in practice because daily economic struggles force vecinos to move across urban space in search of jobs. Therefore, it is difficult to find leaders who remain rooted in a particular neighborhood for an extended period of time. Further, many acquire property in a zone as a form of speculative capital, which implies home ownership but not necessarily commitment to a community.

Beyond home ownership and residence, another characteristic relates to the perceived availability of a community resident to fulfill the demands of leadership. Because the grassroots believe that the work of a neighborhood board "takes time" (*es para tiempo*), those who identify as self-employed workers, such as handcrafters, traders, or pensioners, are more likely to obtain leadership roles. This tends to exclude those who might have to work two or three jobs or have less flexible employment.

Being "talkative" (*hablador*) or "knowing how to express" (*saber expresarse*) one's ideas clearly and fluidly constitutes an important basic requirement for being an authority at the grassroots level. Neighborhood meetings are the main stage where individuals gain access to spaces of power in the local arena and demonstrate their confidence in public speech. An effective discourse displays knowledge and moral virtues and suggests a willingness to act in behalf of the neighbors. This quality is evident in a discourse that is given with clarity and energy. For example, one neighborhood representative expressed:

> Leadership is important. A person should know, should be a leader.... Whoever more or less can represent, whoever has a good personality, that is what people are looking for...because the better the person was at it, the larger the number of people who knew him, then everyone preferred to vote for him, he has won. [Interview with Francisco Valencia, ex-president, Villa Tunari, Second Section, November 2002]

Part of demonstrating "knowing how to express oneself" is the ability to speak well in Spanish, which for many is a second language. Spanish is the institutional language and proves critical to operating in bureaucratic spheres that can often be authoritarian and discriminatory. Interactions with the political and administrative bureaucracy to achieve some outcome for the neighborhood are characterized in the following way:

> Each one of the steps, from getting an interview to the approval of the project, supposes begging, an excessive expenditure of money and time, and putting up with the authoritarian and disrespectful language of the authorities. This situation worsens if leaders speak poor Spanish or are women. They are scarcely recognized as social actors or interlocutors with the local power. [Cottle and Ruiz 1993:127]

Against such challenges, an ideal leader should "lose his fear" when speaking to authority figures. Serapio Mamani, a neighborhood president of the Villa Tunari neighborhood, told me in July of 2002:

> If one does not become a leader, then they are like that—quiet, closed up—that's why when there are troubles that involve the police, they are threatened like children. But if one is a leader, one already knows how to defend oneself, which is very important too, I think.

Along with both public performance and the ability to express oneself in Spanish, an ideal leader must be able to display experience and education useful to the improvement of the neighborhood, such as having been a public officer, a municipal officer, or a worker at one of the service providers. This is a relatively new phenomenon because most leaders of the recent past never finished high school. In addition, and echoing a shift to technocratic styles of discourse and knowledge described by Julia Paley (2001) in peri-urban Santiago, Chile, leaders are increasingly expected to speak with reference to technical, bureaucratic, or legal matters related to municipal management in a way that demonstrates greater possibilities for becoming "a good manager" of the works or projects in relation to the institutional arena. Further, this excludes recent migrants or women with less access to formal education and jobs, who do not have experience with technocratic discourse. Yet, because many aspirants to leadership positions are unknown newcomers, many are able to fake experience or education. For instance, Francisco Valencia, then president from Villa Tunari, recounted:

> [A person's] preparation, level of education, [is important, but] people look at who is talking and they might be nothing but a talker who may not be so well educated. People don't see, they don't notice, if it is a good person. Sometimes in the heat of politics, in a heated meeting, people are not like they seem to be.

Despite the fact that "building the city" was a collective effort, individual leaders also often sought to construct legitimacy by "showing off" or "claiming responsibility" for outcomes of collective action, for obtaining funds, or for achieving concrete results. For instance, in some cases, the creation of infrastructure such as public squares and parks or the improvement of streets serves as the symbolic or political capital that gives a leader legitimacy. This operates as a "symbol of advancement and progress [that] should be evident in the eyes of the whole community" (Cottle and Ruiz 1993:140). Physical projects are obviously visible and tangible and are also accompanied by material symbols such as plaques, which commemorate the name of neighborhood leaders and authorities who executed them. Other kinds of material symbols include photographs, videos, and certificates. When neighbors organize an important public event, such as an inauguration or a celebration, leaders will produce and distribute such "mementos" as a way of making visible their accomplishments (Revilla 2007:118).

All of these characteristics—territorial commitment, discursive ability, Spanish language facility, the performance of technical knowledge, and the visible demonstration of effort—indicate whether a leader has the ability and commitment to negotiate and facilitate solutions to problems of inequality and maintain collective solidarity. But, according to the testimonies of old leaders and neighbors, these practices of collective solidarity are disappearing because of the "lack of interest" of the new leaders or recently arrived neighbors, many of whom "don't have the [long-term] commitment to the zone." Many elections and decisions of the local board in District 4 are organized because of matters of urgency regarding scarce resources as a result of the allocation of participatory budget funds. These elections tend to be realized by direct acclamation of any resident who expresses interest in running, without considering his trajectory or previous experience. All of this, then, contributes to the difficulties or challenges of assessing the moral character of a person elected as president of the barrios.

In contrast to this imagined ideal leader, residents see current leadership as constrained by political and economic forces. One factor working against the leadership ideal is the re-shaping of leadership roles and deeper meanings of the state, citizenship, and rights that were pursued by The Law of Popular Participation and the process of decentralization. Neoliberal reforms, by trying to free the state from its responsibilities to provide housing, basic services, and jobs, reinforced a particular understanding of state management of urban development as focused on things external to basic household and social needs. That is to say, the Law of Popular Participa-tion forced leaders to focus more on large-scale infrastructural projects but inhibited their engagement with more intimate—and crucial—forms of what we call "integral" development involving social welfare and daily needs. This promoted a kind of development (and leadership) focused on a shallow dimension based primarily on the visible and tangible features of the city—plazas, parks, streets, and monuments—while masking the precariousness of daily life (Espósito and Arteaga 2007; Revilla 2007).

The introduction of new mechanisms of participation also fractured the overarching structure of the Neighborhood Boards (FEJUVE). The law, on the one hand, gave new forms of participation such as participatory budgets and accountability measures to the grassroots level. On the other hand, it displaced the superior executive committee of the FEJUVE. The introduction of new bodies such as the oversight committees (Comités de Vigilancia) and district deputy mayors (Sub Alcaldes), appointed by the mayor, created spaces of competition between neighborhood leaders and political appointees and disrupted existing modes of articulation between social organizations and the state. Though theoretically laudable, the oversight committees—which were to articulate neighborhood demands and ensure accountability and social control over budgets—tended to compete with the local neighborhood boards. The deputy mayors—appointed by the mayor to work at district levels on local projects—created a position that competed with existing district representatives.

This essentially fragmented the organizational structure of the city-wide federation, limiting communications between distinct levels. Decentralization also propelled internal divisions between districts and neighborhoods that, in turn, forced them to search for budgets for small projects, deepening competition for limited public resources from the government. Curiously, despite the fact that neoliberalism revolved around a mantra of efficiency and bureaucratic simplification, in District 4, the number of local neighborhood organizations (OTBs, *organizaciones territoriales de base*) that were formally recognized as bodies that formulated and controlled public budgets rose from forty-six to seventy-five between 2002 and 2009. The number of districts in El Alto rose from seven to fourteen between 1996 and 2010.

The law also came with new technical requirements for leadership, such as the ability to deal with paperwork, distribution of public budgets, project definitions, and accountability mechanisms. This tended to bureaucratize the role of leaders and transform their character from that of a moral authority seen as an articulator of collective demands and actions to a colder and more distant project manager closely linked to bureaucracies (Espósito and Arteaga 2007; Kohl and Farthing 2006).

Paradoxically, the supposed weakening of the state pursued by neoliberalism—and its discourse of local control and popular participation—did not contribute to the autonomy of grassroots organizations or the absence of the state itself. Despite the transfer of responsibilities from the state to civil society, the state continued to exercise its power and presence through the exploitation of unpaid social labor for public projects. For example, vecinos often used their family labor, income, and organizational capacity to lay pipes for water and plumbing even as they continued to pay formal taxes. Further, the state exercised power through the indirect control of the NGOs that came to provide services formerly delivered by the state and through the continuation of a political party system that worked through creating clientelistic relationships with vecinos to assure access to bud-gets, jobs, and resources (Albó 2006; 2007; Gill 2000; Kohl and Farthing 2006). Prior to the 2003 crisis, these kinds of relationships often went unquestioned.

Shifting Practices: Clientelism and Upheaval

The legacy, then, of the longer history of neighborhood boards and the more recent shifts associated with neoliberalism, is one in which discourses valuing leaders who work in the public collective interest are posed against the realities and pressures of party politics, technocratic managerialism, and top-down clientelism, a pattern that continues today in the era of the MAS and Evo Morales. The word *political* itself references this tension, because residents, vecinos, and leaders themselves often distinguish between "civic" leaders and "political" leaders. The civic is associated with collective interests, whereas the political represents what are called *particular* (private) or *externa* (external) interests of individual leaders or the parties. Vecinos see such leaders using them "as a ladder"—to climb up the hierarchy of the party—even though these leaders have not reciprocated with collective benefits for all. Another ex-president, Antonio Jarro, described it in this way:

> *The leaders sometimes are political leaders and only look after their*
> *own interests to get their jobs in the municipal office, and once they're*
> *in, they forget about us. They don't even call a meeting. They want to*
> *get a hold on power without getting us any public works, and because*
> *of this situation, the zone has fallen back.*

Some leaders may avoid politically compromising their ideals and betraying their bases, through various strategies, and still obtain collective benefits from their clientelistic relationships with the party structure. Often, however, there are less fortunate results for a leader who rejects party pressures. For instance, during the opening of one infrastructural project, a neighborhood leader who had adopted the ideological stance of leftist Marxism was asked by municipal leaders to "receive" the mayor, who was visiting his zone, by first covering the area with flags and paraphernalia of the mayor's party (emphatically not of the Marxist left). After the leader refused, party agents offered to pave a street and even went so far as to truck in and pile up the stone pavers that would be used. But the project would be finalized only if the leader agreed to support the mayoral campaign. The leader held firm, explaining that "giving in to party pressure" would not only betray his ideological principles but would also affect his reputation with other district leaders. This provoked anger among the residents, who demanded—against the discourse described above—that he act "civically" or according to "neighborhood politics." In the end, the leader sent his vice president to negotiate the conditions for completing the project, but he himself was later forced to resign.

As this illustrates, the clear positive valuation of the category of the civic over a political leader does not imply a rejection of the clientelist relationship between leaders and political parties. In order to benefit the grassroots, a "civic" leader might have to sacrifice his ideological stance and engage in party politics. In contrast, leaders "who walk alone" are not respected, because their individual desires take precedence over the needs of the neighborhood. From the perspective of neighbors, supporting a political party or leader requires collective agreement and control, not simply voicing an idealized critique of clientelism and patronage (see also Lazar 2008). The vecinos establish an important analytic distinction between forms of individual "approximation" or "getting close to" clientelist parties for individual gain and "clientelist pacts," which have the capacity to generate collective benefits.

In everyday life, the clientelistic relationship between the leader of the party and neighborhood organizations is neither as personal nor as close as during elections, and the more immediate experience of leadership revolves around district level actors who become intermediaries between residents and the state. It is at this district level that complex relationships form between the district municipal office, the oversight committees, and the representatives of the various zones, a space in which leaders compete for status and which is seen by residents as the central place where expectations about performance are measured. It is also this district intermediary space that is targeted for control by top-down party efforts, which offer "projects" to residents or try to capture leaders at this level so as to co-opt the intermediate scales and expand the party apparatus. The wider point is that organizing and transformation revolve heavily around an intermediary space—emerging neither wholly from grassroots organic characteristics or from simple top-down impositions or responses to these (Revilla 2007). As such, even when neighborhood authorities on the juntas have taken the position as "civic" leaders, the general consensus is that at least in recent years these posts are rapidly made "political"—or are at the risk of becoming so—and subsumed into the party structure. This contrasts paradoxically with the (false) idea that neoliberalism somehow reduced party and bureaucratic apparatuses.

The Pressure from the Grassroots and the Emergence of New Leaders

In the face of the possibility for leaders to use relationships for personal or "political" benefits, residents have formal and informal mechanisms to "control" leaders' activities and hold them accountable. One such mechanism is the policing of leaders' consumption habits—often an index of perceived corruption. Leaders such as Luis Cabrera, of the Barrio Municipal, point to the importance of not showing notable changes in their levels of consumption or making grandiose modifications to their houses:

> People think that one takes a lot of money and profits from it. Even if I just came in and just built my house, they would assume that I built it with money from the membership dues—but I built my house before becoming a leader—so they don't tell me anything. Then we have to be careful in everything. If you eat well, you took the money. If you dress well, you took the money. For instance, I always used a suit, but now I always use my sweater. I don't use a suit because they may still be watching…the leader is like a book. Every day he is being read.

But it is not enough to simply show humility. A leader must be in permanent communication with members of the board. If he fails to call meetings, provide accurate and full reports, or account for his actions, such "walking alone" could leave him open to criticism, suspicions, potential accusations, and possible defeat.

As in communities around the world, the proximity of these intermediaries to the residents makes verbal control a powerful weapon. Criticism, satire, or *comentarios* (commentary) against the leader are communicated informally and also publicly at formal meetings. Leaders often refer to these verbal sanctions as comparable to physical punishment, saying things like the following: "Many times, if we don't fulfill our roles, the neighbors will *huasquearnos* [whip us]," or "We're beaten with an *itapallu* [a thorny green stick used for communal punishment]." These metaphors refer to physical punishments that are, in fact, sometimes applied in rural communal settings to police the wrongdoings of authorities or criminals. In the same way, verbal instruments of control and sanction leave a "mark for life" on leaders.

Nevertheless, observation and control over the fulfillment of norms and ideals about leadership, exerted through commentaries, criticisms, public shaming, or even ostracism, seem to have lost part of their effectiveness in a more individualized, fragmented, and dynamic urban context where collective opinion fails to regulate individual behavior. At the risk of simplification, the years leading up to 2003 saw a distancing between residents' expectations and leaders' performance, marked by the temporal routines and rhythms of party politics and their pressures on leadership rather than the collective interests of the communities. My sense was that leaders had become those who "walk alone," who managed the technical discourse of the higher social classes and were able to evade social control and criticism from below. This responded to fluid clientelistic relationships that were effectively made invisible to the grassroots residents, with achievement demonstrated only through periodic monumental "projects." In this context before 2003—in which the traditional conservative parties still held sway over national politics—leaders seemed, ironically, to have gained more power (with influence over neighborhood boards, jobs, and so forth) even as they were increasingly less accountable to the grassroots.

Two alternative discourses of leadership emerged to counter this situation, discursive representations that were as much imagined in public reflection and critique as they were exercised by any specific figures. Both were seen as representing an earlier, more ideal time of struggle when the city was rising up. One was the leader from the left (Marxista); the other was the humble or Indianist leader (*dirigente humilde* or *indianista*). The Marxista leader from the left—whose traits derived from the history of mining and from union forms of organizing—spoke a more politicized discourse, based less on technical knowledge and more on political knowledge, that is, issues of exploitation, structural inequality, and consciousness. Having grown up in leftist political circles, he—and they were and are usually male—articulated a strong ideological position tied, for instance, to class-centric analysis and practice. The leftist leader tried to carry through on promises by seeking to build an image of honesty and transparency. He maintained a vertical, authoritarian relationship with the residents, although he discursively appealed to the grassroots through a mass or "base" (grassroots) discourse, what is called literally a *discurso basista*. The more authoritarian form tended to contradict the ideological content and limit political achievement of such a leader, and he tended to avoid settings of dialogue or negotiation. The stance sought to avoid co-optation by political parties by delegitimizing and questioning them, and such a leader was often critical of participation in state-sponsored initiatives. His reluctance to engage with the political system left him with few tangible achievements. He had no discernible influence on the grassroots, but his oppositional discourse was often a means of gaining credibility and clout at the district level and with the Executive Committee of FEJUVE, where such discourse and militance was useful to mobilize the bases and question authorities higher up.

The humble or Indianist leader came out of a more rural, communitarian tradition of ayllu systems in campesino communities. This leader tended to lack expressivity (at least in the expected forms) and the ability to make public speeches. Any speeches made were often not based on technical or ideologized normative concerns. The humble leader was perceived and self-represented as a simple man (and again, most were men). Obedience to grassroots demands was highly valued, leading to a substantial degree of loyalty from the territorial group. The position, less vertical than that of the "left" leader, was predicated on honesty, transparency, and egalitarian principles in relationships with the grassroots. Such a leader refused to be co-opted or to negotiate with parties or the government unless directed by the grassroots. By the same token, if so ordered, he would assume a role of representation and confrontation with the political system. His tenure would be successful as long as he followed the desires of the grassroots and was not blocked by party interests or bureaucratic procedures. Because he emerged from the grassroots, he had limited options for social ascent and would be more likely to make the group's needs his priority. Distinct from those who "walk alone" and from the "leader of the left," the humble "Indianist" leader lacked the basic skills and resources to move beyond the local level of the organization, and his effect on the larger organizational structure would be negligible. What I suggest was happening, then, was the emergence—both in discourse and in practice—of a counter-movement and concept of leadership that worked against the technocratic clientelism that had begun to capture the intermediate levels of organization.

This questioned the changing meanings of state and leadership that neoliberalism introduced. It moved to restore an ideal of accountability in different styles rooted in the idea of long-term residents and moral leadership that reflects what we might call a "sociological" or "strong" representation and allows for a grassroots (sociocultural) identification with a leader (Mayorga 1997:327; Tapia 2000:18; Vilas 1998:309–311). Contrary to this ideal, neoliberal pressures fostered a more "rational" or "intellectual" type of leadership based more on the practical requirements of the institutional context (Vilas 1998). The emergence, or re-emergence—or re-imagination —of the leftist and Indianist models of leadership in District 4 and elsewhere, again, imagined in discourse as much as reflected in any particular individual, served as the basis for a critical questioning and building of ideological consciousness regarding the role of the state as residents thought beyond the daily to critique local politics and articulate a broader focus for their movement. The successes of 2003—I suggest—were dependent not on existing forms of organization, but on the emergence of a dialectical relationship between a more politically conscious base and leaders judged against and nurtured through these models imagined from the past, leaders seen as better able to represent the needs of the bases to the state. Of course, the critique of leadership and the revival of older discourses of struggle coalesced into the massive upheaval only through a series of other conjunctures and conditions, to which I now turn.

Pressure and Tension: The Mobilizations of 2003

Building on the analysis above, in this final section, I consider how these ideal or alternative notions of leadership operated in practice and opened possibilities for the mass mobilizations that occurred between September and October of 2003. These events represented a watershed moment in the remapping of Bolivian politics through the ouster of President Gonzalo "Goni" Sánchez de Lozada and the virtual collapse of the traditional party system. Through the mobilizations of September 2003, Alteños expressed displeasure that had been fomenting for years over the role of local- and national-level government in responding to their needs and demands. Leaders played an important role in (re)directing the explosive discontent over taxes that ultimately led to wider political action. The key spaces for the multiscalar articulation between different levels of the organization brought together radically different ideological frames as leaders from the Indianist side and the Marxist left found points of commonality. A new expression of leadership marked by both traditions had taken a position within FEJUVE by 2002. Yet, this convergence surrounded concerns that had nothing to do with the nationalization of gas, which arose a year later. Returning to District 4, in what follows, I describe a series of events that illustrates this wider reshaping of urban mobilizing forms and relationships of authority and leadership, ultimately leading to the conflicts of bloody October.

At the beginning of May 2003, a group from District 4, including representatives to FEJUVE, pushed forward an agenda for change, proposing new representatives for the Oversight Committee, a position filled successively by leaders from better-off neighborhoods and, in this case, by one close to the municipal party. The group and its leaders denounced "irregularities, abuse, and lack of attention to residents" and proposed to retake control through an alternative program of "honesty, and a political position of contestation and knowledge related to public management" (Leaders Group Planning Meeting, May 4, 2003). This led to the candidacy of Sebastián Quispe, president of the Neighborhood Board in the 25 July Zone of District 4. The local movement was successful, and Quispe, an Aymara teacher and a school principal, was elected on June 9. The resistance of the incumbent to leave his position led to conflicts between the competing factions, but Quispe eventually took over on June 23, with the support of FEJUVE and other leaders from the district. Illustrating the microlevel war of position through which wider institutional shifts are facilitated and fought, at the beginning of August, a new series of meetings were initiated in order to take over another important decision-making space of the District Office, though with only partial success. Nevertheless, the same position would be later brought under control of the pro-change faction, albeit through less conventional methods tied to direct-action mobilizing (Leaders Group Planning Meeting, August 15, 2003).

That same month, the municipal government of El Alto launched an initiative to gather information (for taxation purposes) that involved the city population filling out two new forms, called Maya and Paya (in Aymara, literally, *one* and *two*). The Maya and Paya forms sought to collect detailed information about the condition of houses in the city, but with the expressed intention of increasing municipal tax collection. Soon, the FEJUVE began investigating the Maya-Paya issue after receiving multiple complaints about increased taxes that followed upon submission of this detailed household registry. (Indeed, a new tax announced by Gonzalo "Goni" Sánchez de Lozada in January of 2002 had already led to mass protests and violence, suggesting that readings of the "gas war" as an unmediated expression of antiglobalization or indigenous fervor must be matched by recognition of these more quotidian shifts in citizen–state relations). In this case, opposition to the tax was a reflection of the urban poor's disgust with conventional municipal politics and their resentment for having to pay to support ineffective local and national governments. Discontent soon collided with wider ideological upheaval.

On July 19, the representative of the Commission for the Defense of the Consumer of FEJUVE, Luis Flores—a small-scale craftsman and minibus driver—helped the District Oversight Committee organize a Forum for Alteño Dignity. Held in the public space of the Ceja de El Alto, the forum proposed to examine the issue of the Maya and Paya forms. Here information and debates about possible protest measures circulated, after which demands trickled up to a special meeting called by FEJUVE to address the problem. Meanwhile, negotiations with the mayor's office about the new forms and the increased taxes were tried and failed. After an extraordinary—as in nonroutine, though also remarkable—meeting took place in mid August, tensions between leadership blocks within FEJUVE, for and against the measures, were expressed with greater intensity. With the tax as mobilizing fuel, the insurgent factions were able to rally a deeper discontent and questioning of the entrenched style of party politics. Fights broke out between members of the FEJUVE Executive Committee who expressed neither traditional individual nor party disputes, nor even the pressures of grassroots, but a deeper ideological divide over objectives that pit the clients of the mayor against the emerging leaders of the Marxist left and Indianist style and discourse (Discussion Group Session, September 2004). Eventually, those opposing the municipal policy won out. They controlled the highest positions in the organization and had ample support from the grassroots. In this context, it had been decided that the protest measures would expand with a march, a traditional and often unremarkable event in the context of Bolivian urban politics.

Nevertheless, the march—on September 1—brought together the city's districts, which had been fragmented by years of daily clientelism and haggling. By then, wider articulatory processes were converging—bringing together local issues and discontent with national questions such as gas. Alliances emerged, for instance, between the leaders of FEJUVE and the Federation of Small-Scale Traders (gremialistas) and the meatpackers' union of FETUCRA, also significant in El Alto, where meat processing is centered.

The march would begin at two massive *concentraciones*—places where people gathered in central points. These followed the spatial ordering of El Alto Norte and El Alto Sur. The first group concentrated districts 4, 5, 6, 7, and 9 around the Papal Cross on Juan Pablo II Avenue. The second, districts 1, 2, 3, and 8, gathered around the so-called Cruce a Viacha—a highway intersection (see figure 10). After converging at this last point, both groups advanced toward the municipal building in Villa Calama in the southern part of the city. Immediately after the march, leaders of FEJUVE were admonished by grassroots leaders not to negotiate their demands to abrogate the Maya and Paya forms. Ultimately, at the municipal building, the marchers were violently attacked by the police. This was the first in a series of monumental clashes that led to the escalation of the movement.

Given the mayor's refusal to eliminate the forms—compounded by the suggestion that a third form, the Kimsa (yes, *three*, in Aymara) might be used to collect information on the small-scale traders' groups—the FEJUVE Executive Committee announced on September 9 plans for a city-wide blockade, starting the 15th of the month. Again illustrating the gradual coalition and alliance-building that mark the escalating protest, this measure received the support from the Central Obrera Regional (the COR, Regional Workers Union) and the Teachers Federation, both perennial opponents of the traditional party elites. FEJUVE had also issued public instructions about blockade points. With the geopolitically strategic positions closest to District 4, these blockade points would be set up at the so-called Ex-Tranca of the road to Copacabana, on the Bridge of Rio Seco, and in the sector known as the End of the Andes [Boulevard]. Such tactical decisions revolved around the most effective ways to shut down key circulatory avenues, as well as how to establish points that allowed a relatively small number of residents close proximity to blockade points, conditions that converged in District 4.

On Saturday the 13th—with formal decision-making rituals crucial to construct collective legitimacy for such actions that may have emerged through less formal means—the representatives of the Executive Committee of FEJUVE, the new insurgent representatives of the Oversight Committee, and the presidents of the zones of District 4 all resolved to support the general blockade. All presidents and members of the various juntas would control the operation, which was put under the responsibility of the "Grassroots" or "Base" Commission headed by an ex-miner named Florián Calcinas and Sebastian Quispe, the new Oversight Committee representative. Zones whose residents did not participate would be punished with the reduction of their yearly budget to projects. If residents did not march, they had to provide logistical support, such as food and drink.

At midnight on the 15th, the general blockade and strike began. In the streets around the Ex-Tranca of Rio Seco, districts 4, 5, and 7 called a general meeting in which they discussed the municipal measure. It was in such spaces that issues opposed by much of Bolivia began to filter into the discussions—including the question of exporting Bolivia's natural gas to the United

States through Chile, wider privatization policies, and the new law of Citizen Security and Public Order, which, rather than address criminality and insecurity in daily life, criminalized protest and converted the military into a repressive internal policing force. In the same meeting, the residents from districts 4 and 5 pressured their district municipal officers—the submayors who were former neighborhood leaders close to the municipal government—to join the mobilization by signing a document expressing their explicit rejection of the measure. This pressure from below was echoed in other places of the city, where FEJUVE Executive Committee leaders who visited the points of the blockade were pressured and warned by the grassroots to "not negotiate" with the mayor and to hold their positions. Meanwhile, the mayor continued forward with the legal prosecution of leaders and residents who had been arrested and jailed in relation to the initial march on September 1 riots (J. Mamani 2006).

Nonetheless, the strike, which paralyzed El Alto and seriously affected order in the city of La Paz (including shutting off supplies of diesel and gasoline to the city) during a highly volatile national juncture, led the national government to pressure the mayor to suspend the measures. By the second day, a plenary session of the Municipal Council decided to "abrogate *in extenso*" the laws that created the Maya and Paya forms (*La Razón* 2003). This victory provided the impetus for social and political actions against the hydrocarbon policies of Sánchez de Lozada less than a month later, when blockades and marches again emerged in El Alto to question the wider policies of gas exportation and demand nationalization. As is well known, the convergence of other events—a coca growers' march, the killing of Aymara protestors in the town of Warisata, and the rising anger of other movements—eventually coalesced into what we now know as "Bloody" or "Black" October.

Conclusion

What I hope to reveal in this discussion and description is that idealized representations of El Alto as a "rebel" city (Lazar 2008) or as an antiglobalization, "indigenous" or "Aymara" city characterized by utopianist political practices are flawed. The Maya-Paya protests—and the later events of Octubre—illustrated how grassroots political pressures and tactics such as strikes and urban blockades congealed around and through structures of leadership groups at intermediate levels and articulated with critique and decision-making that emerged from the grassroots, critiques tied both to mundane complaints (taxes) and to deeper ideological rifts about the role of the state and its relation to its citizens. Collectively, the pressures led to the emergence of neighborhood assemblies and a new discourse on leadership as a means of questioning individualistic forms of leadership. Conflict, struggle, and reflection generated, not emerged from, these political forms and practices.

This event, then, was not about the mechanical projection of everyday social relations, but a more complex construction of politics that contested leadership practices and led to a new kind of organizing. The leftist and the indigenist leaders, who were not successful in the day-to-day politics of clientelism, became very important figures in extraordinary moments like 2003. These leaders, with more advanced political knowledge, could establish critical links between the grassroots and the executive levels of the FEJUVE. At the same time, they connected to other groups that had previously been displaced and fragmented as a result of the Law of Popular Participation. This yielded—against the forms of top-down or managerial style linked to institutional practice—new spaces of authority and decision-making that, as Bolivians say, "relativized" power across levels. Under grassroots and insurgent group pressure, the intermediate district level, which was reshaped by decentralization and had for years contributed to the fragmentation of collective demands at the grassroots level, was re-construed as a space for cohesion and accountability. These spaces allowed for a closer relationship between neighborhood leaders and district authorities, facilitating their subjection to the decisions of the increasingly strengthened and radicalized social bases, who took control of the mobilization and neighborhood leadership as a whole in order to pressure local and national governments. Paradoxically, the neoliberal mantra of "local control" and "accountability" was put into practice, ultimately to question and bring down the neoliberal regime itself.

I have tried to provide a more complex picture of the events leading up to the mobilization of 2003 by illustrating connections between the daily practice of organizing and the seemingly spontaneous eruption of collective political will. If we conceptualize this event as some sort of spontaneous, horizontal uprising then we really have not learned the lessons of 2003. If we solely focus on the end point of social organizing, then we risk either romanticizing resistance or failing to recognize the challenges that these movements had to overcome to bridge ideological and practical differences. This mass mobilization stemmed from a long-term transformation in the relationship between leadership and the base, in which the grassroots were able to elect new leaders and hold them accountable for significant change. These movements did not reject leadership or the state but instead made specific demands moving beyond local, everyday struggles, demands that eventually articulated and converged with broader interests and national concerns. In turn, this process challenged the ways people relate to the state, forcing the grassroots to think differently about the present and future of Bolivia. Paradoxically, although El Alto and Octubre 2003 contributed greatly to bringing the MAS and Evo Morales to power, there are growing signs of criticism of the MAS in El Alto. Many feel that the proposals that emerged out of organizing and struggle have not been addressed. Others are now comparing the revolution of 1952—seen as a frustrated or incomplete revolution—to the election of Evo Morales in 2005, also frustrated and incomplete, co-opted by party politics and marked by high symbolism with little deep material or structural change. It remains to be seen whether the new Bolivia created by the election of Evo Morales will revert to an older style of party patronage and clientelism and again seek to routinize municipal politics into the logic of clientelism and "walking alone."

Notes

1. For this line of thought, see Arbona 2008.

2. On clientelistic leadership, see Calderón and Szmukler 1999; Cottle and Ruiz 1993; García et al. 2004; Lazar 2004; Quisbert 2003; Rivera (1993); Sandoval and Sostres (1989).

3. By *horizontal* I refer to connections within organizational structures and between social organizations in El Alto. By *vertical* I refer to new and effective organizational strategies that influenced the relationship between these organizations and the state.

4. Gill (2000) provides a detailed ethnographic portrait of the effects of neoliberal reform on various aspects of daily life in El Alto.

Visions from the Ground
Land Invasion or Agrarian Justice?

On August 8, 2004, several families from the Landless Movement (MST) occupied the hacienda known as Los Yuquises, located 170 miles northwest of Santa Cruz. They squatted for approximately nine months on 200 acres of unproductive land owned by Rafael Paz Hurtado, a businessman with old political links to Hugo Bánzer, the now deceased former dictator (1971–1978) and president (1997–2001) whose regimes oversaw the illicit distribution of some 10 million hectares of public land to wealthy supporters. In response and with the implicit support of the powerful Civic Committee of Santa Cruz, landowners hired armed thugs from marginal urban areas of Santa Cruz to attack the peasant occupation. The attackers entered the settlement, burned crops, physically abused MST members, and eventually sequestered and tortured MST leaders. At the same time, in the city of Santa Cruz, members of the Unión Juvenil Cruceñista beat MST leader Silvestre Saisari in the center of the city's main plaza. Saisari was traveling to a local human rights office to denounce the violations against landless peoples. Back in the conflictive rural region, MST campesinos retaliated by taking sixty of the hired thugs hostage in the nearby settlement of Pueblos Unidos. After negotiations, MST released the hostages, but the government—then led by interim president Carlos Mesa—responded by using the military to forcibly expel the settlers later that month. The land was transferred to military control, and MST occupants were given orders to stay away until the state could settle the matter. With no place to go, many of the farmers set up a tent settlement under a bridge in Chané, a small agricultural town located in the northern region of Obispo Santiesteban. Two years later, with Evo Morales in the presidency, the Yuquises land was officially titled to the movement as the agro-ecological community of Pueblos Unidos. Now under the auspices of agrarian reform, President Evo Morales visited with tractors, a gas-powered generator, and a pump for the community.

Land occupation and redistribution, which for the MAS (Movement to Socialism) and the MST was an action aimed at redistributing illegally held state lands to the rural poor, was seen by those who claim ownership over land and natural resources as a dangerous assault on private property and the law. For both lowland indigenous peoples and the rural farmers or campesinos who have settled in the eastern lowlands, the issue of land reform also generates questions of communal autonomy, political alliances, and internal disputes over whether the struggle should be for collective title and "territory" or individual title and "property." The following two inter-views—one with an indigenous leader-turned-government-official, the other with one of Santa Cruz's most powerful landowners—were held about a month before the official titling of the land to MST. They illustrate the deeper historical struggles behind land, as well as the very different relation-ships to land and territory held by those who claim to "own" it and by those who rely on it to survive.

Guarayu Leader and Government Official Bienvenido Sacú

I am an indigenous Guarayu from the Department of Santa Cruz.[1] Right now, I am the general director of TCOs [Communal Lands of Origin] in the Vice Ministry of Lands.... Around the year 2000, the landless movement had been struggling to acquire lands—I am talking about the peasant broth-ers and our own relatives...and I was an indigenous leader of the CIDOB [Confederation of Indigenous Peoples of Bolivia].[2] We had been coordinat-ing with them and we led a march on Montero. This was after the Massacre of Pananti,[3] where some of our landless brothers fell in the Chaco. From that point, we began to help one another, the indigenous organization, the union of colonists, and the wage laborers of Santa Cruz. From that point on, we began to have meetings, events, that sort of thing. By then, we had estab-lished a pact to struggle together, not only indigenous but also with the landless movement...and we have been supporting one another since, and now from this level where we are now—through the Vice Ministry—we have been helping them to consolidate their organization.

I can tell you about the case of Pueblos Unidos. That was one of the first experiences of our government that we achieved—though we did so after serious battles with the landlords who wanted to stay, even by acting above the law, in that area. But we said, as the government now, we cannot simply favor those who have resources—our communities, our people, also deserve to have [something] too. And so we are giving our assistance to the landless brothers.... So, through the Institute of Agrarian Reform [INRA], the measurements were done. And that is public land, with no owner—but there is always someone who has machinery, a tractor, who goes to take possession illegally.... So after measuring the lands and distributing them to the landless brothers, we could not just leave them there. We worked through INRA to give support, to establish a settlement...to eventually plant products like soy, rice...to expand their farming and [to eventually achieve] development for the brothers of the community of Pueblos Unidos.

For us, for the indigenous peoples, the first priority is the struggle—and I include myself in this struggle because I come from that family and have lived as such. And though I have this government post now, it does not mean I will be here permanently. We know from experience, the past governments were always people of the necktie, all karai people, as we say, white people, businessmen. It was that kind of bureaucracy, that kind of discrimination toward the peoples, toward the poor, that made us mobilize, to seek unity. And unity is important because alone we will never be able to confront such a massive economic and political power.... So we mobilized through peaceful struggle. What does that mean? Through marches. Because we are bothering no one, we gain more support. I remember arriving in Cocha-bamba [after walking] from Santa Cruz, making the just demand that the country had to change, that we had to refound the country through a Constitutional Assembly. We demanded a new country, a new refounding, a new construction, as if it were a house, building a new house, to rebuild this house that is broken down, destroyed, right?... And when we got to Cochabamba, people from the other working classes, of the health department, the pensioners, many other sectors, came out to meet us, and we pulled them into [our struggle], countering the campaign of defamation that the landlords had been waging against us in Santa Cruz. The landlords were saying, "These crazy Indians just want to walk to La Paz to see the city." But it is not about that. And now there is a positive result and the Constitutional Assembly is in place in Sucre, and it gives us pride because we didn't wear our feet out in vain, did we?

Prominent Landlord and Agro-industrial Businessman Rafael Paz Hurtado

So they did a cadastral survey of the lands, and in this process they would not give up.[4] Of my property, which was 24,000 or 25,000 hectares, they left me 7,800 hectares, supposedly measured, but the titles have not yet been emitted by this government. And when they intervened in the zone, these same landless movements [MST] went onto my land, my crops, my soy, and stuck in twelve little marijuana plants. And then they pronounced that I was a drug trafficker, that I was an extortionist, and they put it on the Internet, in the newspapers. I even went to the DEA [US Drug Enforcement Agency] and the FELCN [Bolivian Special Anti-narcotics Force] to ask them to investigate, and it turns out they found twelve little marijuana plants in more than 5,000 hectares of crops. And there, where soy is planted, we fumigate against weeds. There is no living plant except soy—so how incredible is it that they find marijuana there? The soy was a meter high, and these little plants about two feet tall. And so based on that, the social movements, the landless movements, the human rights people, all backed the cadastral process. These are all things managed by NGOs, which is what does the most damage to Bolivia—the incursion of NGOs in the country. They back all of this, all of these movements, right?...

It was all a show, to keep invading lands and to enter other lands like they are doing now. Do you have that clear? And they are taking other lands as well, like in my brother's section, which is Pueblo Unidos, with the help of the government itself. If you go there [to the settlement], you will see that they are not eating Bolivian food. They are eating Cuban and Venezuelan food. Those people are maintained by the government. They give them food, everything. And these are people from this area who have lands elsewhere. They are traffickers [of land], invaders of land.

Well, you see, the laws—you know if you have lived here—establish that land deforested without permits is illegal, but 90 percent of the land is illegally deforested. Because of bureaucracy, it is easier to deforest and then pay a fine...and the government knows this, and now they want to hand over all of the best lands to distribute them to their people. And that is the chaos, the judicial insecurity that exists. They do not take into account that those lands have been worked, that they generate employment, they generate the flow of money into the country. And people are afraid to invest, and thus comes the unemployment, the migration to Spain, to the United States, to Argentina.... I think this government will have to realize that without Santa Cruz and without [departmental] autonomy and juridical security, it will not be able to govern. The really poor people who do not support MAS are going to rise up against them and their own people as well. They are going to reap what they sow. They started with blockades and got into power, and if they continue with the confrontation, with division, without unifying the country, they are going to end up with the same, with blockades, with all of that. I hope God rehabilitates the president. I think he has some bad people around him that do not let him see things as they truly are.

Notes

1. Interviewed by Nicole Fabricant in La Paz, August 16, 2007.

2. *CIDOB* stands for Confederación de Pueblos Indígenas de Bolivia, or the Confederation of Indigenous Peoples of Bolivia.

3. The Massacre of Pananti in November of 2001 was the first organized attack against the MST. Hired paramilitaries attacked MST families squatting on land in the southern Chaco. Six MST members were killed and twenty-one wounded. A rancher was also killed in the exchange.

4. Interviewed by Nicole Fabricant in Santa Cruz, August 20, 2007.

7 *Ocupar, Resistir, Producir*

Reterritorializing Soyscapes in Santa Cruz

Nicole Fabricant

In a country in which 90 percent of the productive land is owned by 7 percent of the population, distinct groups of landless Bolivians have come together in the eastern region to build a political movement intent on reclaiming productive resources. El Movimiento Sin Tierra, the Landless Peasant Movement (MST-Bolivia), is a national-level indigenous-campesino movement of fifty thousand farm workers, displaced peasants, and urban informal laborers, many of whom initially migrated to the lowlands in the 1950s and 1960s in search of employment in the expansive sugar industry. Through state-based colonization programs,[1] recruiters encouraged highland indigenous people to migrate to the lowlands with the lure of monetary aid, food, tools, seeds, and access to land. Despite governmental promises, the majority of the migrants never received access to land, and many were forced to rent small plots as they eked out a living through mixed economic strategies of subsistence farming and wage labor. But as sugar rapidly turned to soy—which was less labor intensive—migrants in the northern region lost even their few hectares of land and joined the ranks of the unemployed and dispossessed, becoming what some scholars have referred to as "the refugees of neoliberalism" (Davis 2006; Harvey 2006). As their numbers swelled, these displaced peoples began to think about long-term, sustainable strategies to confront the problems of landlessness.

Borrowing from the more well-known Brazilian Landless Movement, MST-Bolivia has addressed this growing inequality through a political praxis of peacefully occupying or seizing haciendas (plantations) whose putative, oligarchic owners are well-known enemies of landless campesinos. Most of the productive land in this region remains in the hands of a few agrarian elite families who acquired hundreds of thousands of hectares from military dictators as gifts of political patronage in the 1970s and 1980s (Dunkerley 1984, 2006; H. Klein 1982, 2003). Class relations of inequality between those who own land and those who do not have thus increased as landless peasants are displaced and search for work in the informal sector. Much of this land is unproductive, speculative holdings and is also of questionable legal ownership—such that peasant occupiers base their claims in Bolivian law, which says that illegally held and socially unproductive land is subject to expropriation and redistribution. MST occupations have generally been peaceful, aimed at building collective farms, constructing houses and schools, and promoting indigenous culture and a healthy and sustainable environment (see figures 13–15). They are also part of a militant, radical strategy deeply situated in class relations, because a successful invasion of latifundio land by the MST is intended to lead to the conquest of the means of production and a re-creation of the peasantry.

Bernardo Mancano Fernandez (2001) argues that the struggle for land is a constant struggle against capital. The territorialization of capital means the deterritorialization of the peasantry and the creation, destruction, and re-creation of family labor. The occupation, then, represents a new form of resistance to what David Harvey (2003) calls "accumulation by dispossession." As such, after Harvey, many original features of Marx's notion of primitive accumulation have remained powerfully present within capitalism's historical geography. These include the commoditization and privatization of land and the forceful expulsion of peasant populations, the conversion of various forms of property rights (common, collective, state) into exclusive private property rights, and the suppression of rights to the commons. In eastern Bolivia, much of this process has been linked to the expansive soy industry. By occupying unproductive land, setting up encampments, and finally achieving title to land, campesinos both resist this process and seek solutions to new forms of displacement through the building of permanent and sustainable farming communities.

The first and most successful land occupation in the region against a large-scale soy producer was that of Yuquises, where movement members seized Rafael Paz Hurtado's 45,000 hectares (about 110,000 acres) of illegally owned land in the northern Obispo Santiesteban region of Santa Cruz. (See Paz Hurtado's comments in the section, "Visions from the Ground: Land Invasion or Agrarian Justice?" preceding chapter 7.) The Paz Hurtado family is typical of unproductive land-holding patterns of elite Cruceños, Bolivians of Santa Cruz. The family first acquired large extensions of agricultural land in the early twentieth century through the rubber industry. By 1954 Paz Hurtado's father owned 14,350 hectares of land yet cultivated only 1 percent of the entire plot (Gill 1987). Today, the exporter of sunflower and soy oil owns 76,000 hectares given to him in five separate *dotaciónes* (grants) in Obispo Santiesteban Province. Much of this has been sitting idle as a form of speculative capital. This history began to unravel when on August 8, 2004, five hundred campesinos occupied his hacienda, located 170 miles outside the city of Santa Cruz. On May 8, 2005, exactly nine months after the initial occupation, Paz Hurtado hired *sicarios* (contracted thugs, referred to in Bolivia as "hired killers") from urban, impoverished communities to violently displace the landless workers. Two days later, according to interviews with victims, these mercenaries looted homes, burned pineapple and rice fields, beat and reportedly raped women, and took several MST members hostage. The military later took control and claimed ownership of the settlement until the civilian arm of the national government resolved the dispute. Many landless, however, have consequently been displaced and rendered homeless for several months, living with their families in plazas, parks, and under a bridge. Despite their forced relocation, the landless continued to organize as a regional bloc and pressured the national government to survey this unproductive plot of land and re-title it to the movement (see "Visions from the Ground: Land Invasion or Agrarian Justice?" preceding chapter 7).

Over time, this hacienda came to be known as Pueblos Unidos (United Towns, or United Peoples). In September of 2007, it became the first official MST land reform settlement in Santa Cruz titled to the movement as part of Evo Morales's Agrarian Revolution, the Community Redirection of the Agrarian Reform Law.[2] I arrived to conduct ethnographic fieldwork with MST in January of 2006, in the aftermath of the Yuquises land occupation, as movement intellectuals began imagining the evolution of the settlement democratically, socially, and economically. This chapter draws on this fieldwork, during which time I lived with MST leaders and rank-and-file in the Obispo Santiesteban and Ichilo agricultural zones, participated in local, regional, and national meetings, joined protest marches, and observed spectacular agricultural festivals.

In this chapter, I draw on this research to discuss the MST phenomenon in relation to the production and export of soy, considering the ways in which shifts in the global economy have physically, politically, and environmentally redesigned a region. Landless workers who have historically lived and worked in what are now soy-producing areas struggle to survive in these towns and cities. Yet, despite their constant migration in search of new forms of employment, these workers have built a movement that relies on the creative and performative use of historical memories and tales of the ayllu—the fundamental social organization of ancient Andean communities, based on kinship groups and communally held territory—as a visual and spatial cartography for building farming collectives.[3] Over time, I became increasingly interested in the use of cultural performance and tale-telling as a political strategy to build worker consciousness and inspire the landless to participate in collective action. What is so striking about the contemporary use and appeal of the ayllu is that MST members, unlike their Andean forebears, do not share residence or descent. Some rank-and-file members never lived in an ayllu, nor do they understand what it represented historically, culturally, or socially. Nevertheless, the imagined ayllu, or what Mary Weismantel (2006) calls the "activist ayllu,"[4] serves as a powerful ideological construct for sculpting landscapes of meaning in the wake of much economic, social, and physical destruction. Originally, the concept was rooted in rural life and focused on questions of livelihood, but now it has become a mobile framework used by indigenous peoples, urban informal workers, and intellectuals to reclaim natural resources and promote redistributive legislation. In order to understand how the landless use such narratives to inform the creation of communities of meaning, we must first turn toward the ways in which their lives, their jobs, and even their physical landscapes have all been transformed by the increasing production of soy.

The Social and Political History of Soy

Soy was initially imported to Bolivia with the first Japanese and Mennonite settlers, who arrived in the east in the mid-1950s. In those days, the characteristics of soy production were quite different than they are today, because the crop was grown primarily for family use. Its expansion as a commercial and export crop began in the 1970s and 1980s as a result of state policies that favored large-scale agricultural expansion. As with the neoliberal "adjustments" of the 1990s, these earlier policies thought that the solution for debt-strapped nations was to liberalize markets, reduce trade barriers, and promote exports. As a result, today two zones of Santa Cruz (Chiquitania and the Integrated North, or Obispo Santiesteban) form the geographical base for soy production and related industries in Bolivia (see figure 1). Soy is the country's most important export crop (valued at $360 million in 2006), and Bolivia ranks among the world's top-ten soy exporters (Catacora 2007).

Increased Bolivian production of soy has been accompanied by ever greater international demand for this crop. In Asia, China's burgeoning demand for soy has everything to do with its growing appetite for pork, poultry, and beef, which requires higher volumes of soybeans as animal feed. More recent demand for soy comes from the emerging biodiesel market.[5] The high global prices of crude oil and the excessive use of fossil fuels by industrialized nations have led to a more urgent and aggressive search for new energy supplies. The soy sector within the Southern Cone promotes the idea that it should be a growing supplier of biodiesel and has promised to set new production records in the near future (Rulli 2007). The promotion of a biodiesel market, however, has been accompanied by further consolidation of unequal landownership, deforestation, expansion of monocultures, and production of alternative fuels at the expense of food crops.

This new global soyscape, created in and through increased production in secondary cities such as Santa Cruz, has redesigned political environments. The international demand for biodiesel has contributed to the tilling of an expansive political space by soy-producing elites in Santa Cruz to lay greater claim to regional politics, calling for autonomy from the western half of the country and staging spectacular theatrical "shows" in opposition to the democratically elected government of Evo Morales. The shows of autonomy have everything to do with the desire to monopolize natural resources, which are disproportionately located in the eastern region. Santa Cruz accounts for 42 percent of the nation's agricultural output, and neighboring lowland department, Tarija, accounts for 80 percent of the natural gas (Gustafson 2006). By forging political and economic ties across the east, civic leaders have been able to create a powerful oppositional countermovement against Morales and his administration's social democratic proposals. Although political power might have shifted at the national level, economic strength in the east is simultaneously being consolidated by a small group of agrarian elites with transnational and corporate connections.

One of the most vocal figures of the autonomy movement was Branko Marinkovic, son of the late Silvo Marinkovic, a Croatian immigrant who, as Gustafson (2008:20) argues, "built wealth the Cruceño way: by holding large tracts of productive and nonproductive lands through many titles acquired during [military] dictatorships." The senior Marinkovic, whom many in Bolivia's activist community allege had suspected links to the pro-Nazi Ustasche regime in the former Yugoslavia, migrated to Bolivia after World War II. Once there, he founded Industrias Oleaginosas Limitada

(IOL-SA). IOL-SA is now the largest domestically owned exporter of soy and sunflower oil. His son has followed in his footsteps, not only taking over the soy business but also leading the Cruceño countermovement against the MAS project of change. Marinkovic has been linked to violent groups, such as the Union Juvenil Cruceñista, a young men's paramilitary organization in Santa Cruz that has attacked leftist groups, laid siege to indigenous communities, looted NGO buildings, stolen critical documents, and destroyed files on land reform. More recently, Marinkovic was tied to an alleged plot to kill Morales, offering a Hungarian hit man $200,000 (£135,000) to buy weapons and, in his words, "finish the job we started" (Stapff 2009). Now on the run from the Bolivian government, Marinkovic's whereabouts are unknown, with activists speculating that he may have fled to Brazil, hidden in the jungles of eastern Bolivia, or gone to the United States, where he is imagined to be living in Chevy Chase, Maryland, with another once powerful Bolivian elite, the former president Gonzalo "Goni" Sanchez de Lozada. Increased militarization and elite recourse to extralegal violence, as in Marinkovic's case, is a critical theme that runs like a fault line through these new regional soy republics. Other cases of increased militarization are part of a soy trail from Bolivia to neighboring Paraguay, which is viewed as perhaps the most brutal face of agro-industrial wealth and power. Paraguayan journalist Javiera Rulli (2007:221) states, "The militarization and para-militarization of the countryside are linked to the increase of soy cultivation and the security systems of agribusiness elites. Soy does not only grow on large estates, but also on the lands of rural and indigenous people." As these farmers have organized to protect their land and natural resources, military forces have opened fire on them in an effort to preserve the interests of capital.

The increasing worldwide demand for this crop has displaced rural farmers, created high rates of unemployment, and produced an array of toxic chemicals. It is this commodification and privatization of land—turning environment and landscape into a sector of the globalized economy—that has paradoxically stimulated a new form of local political organizing to resist the encroachment of environmental degradation, which promotes ever thinner economic and social margins for survival and threatens campesinos' very existence. As Bebbington (2009:19) argues, social movements in the Andes "are moving away from these more conservationist currents; other environmentalisms in the region draw their energy from commitments that are more social in character." It seems to be the case that this social movement is not either/or, but rather a creative mixing of the economic, social, and environmental: something economist Joan Martinez-Alier (2002) called the "environmentalism of the poor," in which the protection of the environment is crucial for poor people to sustain their lives and livelihoods.

Creative Destruction of a Soy Town

In order to more fully conceptualize the human dimensions of these new soyscapes, we must journey through a soy-producing region in Santa Cruz: Obispo Santiesteban.[6] Thanks to a north-south highway, the city of Santa Cruz is linked to the provincial town of Montero and eventually to the northern agricultural region of Obispo Santiesteban. My research collaborator and friend Ademar Valda Vargas (an undergraduate at the University of San Simon in Cochabamba) and I traveled one day in early April of 2006 across the Grigotá, a zone with an important agricultural and cultural history. It was named the Grigotá by the Spaniards in the seventeenth century, after a "mythistoric" indigenous leader said to have fought against Guaraní incursions from the east. In the region, a small number of Spaniards gradually gained control over local populations and organized settlements in the jungle, which they cleared for sugar, rice, and cotton production and eventually cattle ranching. By the late twentieth century, a powerful new regional soy economy had come to exist in the area, the contours of which were marked by the tires of our microbus as my friend and I crossed the region. As we traveled, we headed backward through a commodity chain, from the site of packaging and exportation, to that of manufacturing, to the places of production. We passed a strip of factories along the Santa Cruz-Montero highway, Aceite Fino and Aceite Rico, which manufacture and export soy oils. Both are owned by IOL-SA.

Through our steamy windows, we observed the physical landscape shift from a highly industrial factory zone of soy processing plants to rural extensions of land. We passed several houses of *motacú*, named for the roofs made with dried leaves of the motacú, a palm tree of the tropical rainforest lowlands, with walls and foundations of sticks and slabs of wood piled one on top of the other to provide protection from the rain. Around 11 a.m., we arrived in Chané, a town of highland migrants from parts of Cochabamba and the outer regions of Potosí. Most of the women were dressed *de pollera* (in the Andean traditional layered skirt) with rubber flip-flops. One young boy shouted, "*Salteñas, salteñas, a un boliviano,*" in a squeaky voice, selling breakfast snacks common in the tropical east. As if mesmerized by the images in a Buñuel film, we watched the scene unfolding outside the bus.

Since soy relies on mono-cropping, an agricultural process that destroys land, forests, and soil—often taking over lands previously owned and cultivated by small-scale farmers—the agricultural elites constantly move farther north in search of new land. We can think of this as what Joseph Schumpeter (1975) called "creative destruction," in which outmoded industries such as textiles diverted workers to new endeavors. On the one hand, these enterprises create wealth and improve living standards, but on the other, as Schumpeter noted, the continuous process of creative destruction is attended by considerable stress, especially for laborers on the other side of the equation. A similar phenomenon of uneven geographic development and accumulation by dispossession occurs in the rural areas of Santa Cruz. Large-scale soy producers set up shop in a particular area, use mainly machines instead of human labor, and then, in rather short order, move to another plot of land farther north. Because of the intensity of this highly mechanized form of agriculture and its rapid exhaustion of fertile soil, large-scale soy production cannot remain in the same area for an extended period of time. Clearly, such forms of industrial agriculture not only disrupt human life but the natural habitat as well.

The center of Chané was ringed by a water tank and a few stores, Internet cafés, and family-owned restaurants. The hollowed-out city center was economically depressed, with run-down buildings and abandoned storefronts occupying the central rotunda. Perhaps the most vivid scenes were of displaced farmers sleeping in makeshift tents under a small bridge, with their belongings sprawled across a small space. From a distance, I saw several landless organizers in red baseball caps and t-shirts waiting at the bus stop. They jumped on the bus, and as our journey continued, many of the MST members told us of the devastation as we passed one small agricultural community after another on our way to San Pedro, the epicenter of MST organizing. Rafael Pozo, a middle-aged man dressed like an airplane pilot, with his red MST hat perched on his balding scalp, spoke in a deep, raspy voice, creating a blues-like cadence imbued with sadness as the scene below unfolded. I listened to his narration while covering my nose with a handkerchief, protecting myself from the smells of cow dung mixed with dangerous fertilizers. He turned to me and said:

> What you smell and feel tingling your nose are the heavy chemicals that we small-scale producers have been forced to use.[7] We were completely excluded from the review process for requests for approval of GMO soya, and only representatives from FUNDACRUZ [Agricultural Development Foundation of Santa Cruz] and ANAPO [National Association of Producers of Soy and Wheat Crops] made the decision.[8]

Pozo inspired me to think about a series of texts on the licensing and patenting of genetic material (Harvey 2003). The reliance on a single herbicide has allowed corporations such as Monsanto to gain monopolistic control over a single seed, such as Roundup Ready. This "roundup-ready" strain, a genetically modified organism designed to resist herbicides developed from glyphosate, has been used frequently in soy cultivation in Santa Cruz.

But before I had time to reflect on these new forms of corporate power and what David Harvey (2003) calls "biopiracy," Pozo supplemented my thoughts with the human costs of reliance on toxic chemicals:

> We see the consequences these chemicals had on our community. Every season, our animals become sick. Just when they start cultivating soy, our chickens and ducks die. When they spray, it affects not only the animals but the people too. Our children have diarrhea and stomach problems, men have liver problems, and women miscarry babies. Further, we have seen our children break out in all sorts of skin problems. Some develop rashes, others break out in hives. We know that this is a result of the chemicals seeping into our drinking water.

The devastating results of new soyscapes are similar to what Javier Auyero and Deborah Swinston (2008) describe as "flammable communities" in Buenos Aires, Argentina, where the toxic effects of industrial runoff mark the bodies and minds of the working classes and poor. They argue that children in these communities experience physical and biological damage, such as deformities and growths on their bodies, lead in their bloodstream, and a slew of other conditions. These are some of the embodied effects of the corporate quest for cheap land and resources. Additionally, the petrochemical Shell compound sits directly inside their community, and now their soil, air, and water streams are polluted with lead, chromium, benzene, and other chemicals (Auyero and Swinston 2008). These urban residents, along with the rural farmers of Chané, Mineros, and San Pedro, are the very disposable labor for environmental, economic, and political forces.

As our bus journey continued, I noticed that the soil had turned into a sand-like brown substance that covered my body, clinging to my hair, fingernails, and eyebrows as the northerly winds blew it up and into the bus. It was eroded soil. Pozo explained, "Niki, *sos más choca que antes* [you are even blonder than before]." He indicated that such *tierra muerta* (dead land) is the result of the intense mechanization of agriculture. As forests disappear because of the industrialization or corporatization of farming, the soil loses its dense vegetation cover and is left vulnerable to strong rains and the hot sun. Soybean cultivation has always led to erosion, especially in areas where it is not part of a long rotation. Large-scale soybean cultivation has rendered Amazonian soils unusable; in areas of poor soils, fertilizers and lime have to be applied heavily within two years. In parts of eastern Bolivia, hundreds of thousands of hectares of land have been abandoned and turned over to cattle grazing, which only further destroys the natural environment.

As we passed long stretches of dry, caked-over land, the horizon was lined with an endless stretch of farms, a kind of assembly line of agro-industry, many with foreign names: Cargill, Archer Daniels Midland, and Bunge SA. The bus sped past signs advertising fertilizing chemicals, leaving behind a blur of images. Then, Pozo spoke about new forms of displacement as a result of this industry:

> In the past ten to fifteen years, I have personally experienced the transformation of this landscape from cotton, to sugar, to soy. We used to all work on sugar plantations, but since the 1980s, this has really transformed into soy. The soy corporations no longer need our labor. They have machines to do most of the work. We can no longer grow our own crops because of soil erosion. And so we have few options. We either migrate to city centers or head farther north in search of land that has been untouched by these corporations. Nevertheless, we are left without land, livelihood, and a sufficient income to survive.

Through this bus ride to the Integrated North, Pozo told of new forms of agricultural expansion, extraction, and subsequent destruction and displacement. This regime of extraction, or what some have referred to as "soy republics,"[9] is simply the most recent manifestation of the global trend toward emphasizing one commodity and uneven economic development in particular regions. As Soruco, Plata, and Medeiros (2008) argue, the ghosts of highly unequal soy trade date back to the eighteenth- and nineteenth-century European rubber trade, which brought German immigrants to Bolivia and linked Santa Cruz to an earlier, more primitive, global economy. Despite the rubber industry collapsing in 1913 because of the fall in prices in the world market, this model of extractive capitalism and uneven development remained powerfully etched into the landscape of Santa Cruz through the sugar era, the cotton boom, and, more recently, the soybean explosion (see Soruco, chapter 4, this volume).

New Landless Politics in Bolivia

Displacement, or in Harvey's language "accumulation by dispossession," set the stage for the birth of new rural-based peasant movements such as MST, which began organizing in the early 2000s. Historically, in the lowlands, sindicatos (unions) were the only peasant organizational structure. The sindicatos directed and participated in a wide range of activities, including but not limited to organizing campesinos, distributing land, initiating infrastructural development, and resolving internal disputes at the village level (Gill 1987). Unions legitimized peasant land claims through an intricate process of petitioning land reform agencies to survey the unproductive land, expropriate plantations, and redistribute the land to the landless. Legal ownership of land was thus often contingent upon residency in a particular community and compliance with communal obligations maintained by syndicate structures. As market forces shifted toward investment in large-scale and export-oriented agriculture, however, peasants found a way to temporarily survive by mercantilizing their land. This process of buying and selling ruptured historic communal ties as some migrated out and others moved into the agricultural zones. Douglas Hertzler (2002), witnessed the problems incurred when poor peasants were offered money in exchange for titles by large landowners. Peasant unions repeatedly pressured members not to sell to buyers unapproved by the community, but they had little legal recourse to prevent land from being sold away and thus diminishing the community. Communities were often bought out piecemeal by neighboring large farms, and the fabric of the community was destroyed. This constant mobility led to the dissolution of unions in the lowlands.

With the peasantry fragmented and leaderless, new social movements like MST gained substantial momentum. The landless workers created a social and political structure that over time had a national reach. The first land occupation occurred in the Gran Chaco region of Bolivia in June of 2003; two hundred migrants occupied the hacienda owned by President Gonzalo Sanchez de Lozada s sister-in-law. This initial occupation impelled workers to develop a national-level platform for agrarian reform that included eliminating the latifundio, returning unproductive land to small-scale farmers, and building a sustainable model of agriculture. Each successful occupation led to the establishment of an asentamiento (land reform settlement), which provided the springboard for further occupations and new *acampamentos* (encampments), and hence the territorialization of a movement. Territorialization not only results in the spatial conquest of land but also leads to the dissemination of a national-level and global ambition or counter-hegemonic vision. This analysis does not suggest that territorialization is a straightforward process. Rather, occupations often face violent evictions, resulting in injury, arrest, or death, and occupiers may have to live in an encampment for years, facing harsh conditions before obtaining title to the land (Karriem 2009).

The external work of territorializing or claiming land for campesinos is joined to the critical internal praxis of building a movement organization that gets diffused in an acampamento. Once established, the movement organization becomes a space for building campesino power, political socialization, and solidarity and forging a larger national or global ambition. Based on the Ecclesiastical Base Community Model from the Brazilian Landless Movement, an MST-Bolivian acampamento of one hundred families would be divided into ten nucleos of ten families, with two coordinators, a man and a woman (the latter to encourage greater participation by women). For instance, the newly titled Pueblos Unidos settlement consists of approximately three hundred families, who are further divided into thirty nucleos of ten families, each with two coordinators. Other members of the nucleo participate in commissions responsible for education, health, communication, security, or political education. Instead of the hierarchical or vertical structure found in the sindicatos, MST relies on a horizontal form of leadership in which distinct leaders come together from the various commissions in order to make community-based decisions. This decentralized organizational structure and self-organization also maps onto the regional and national-level movement that has been central to the ideological and spatial growth of MST.

The movement's intention to territorialize space informs national-level land reform and new peasant politics of the 21st century, but what is perhaps most interesting is how the themes from that bus ride—the extractive and expansive model of soy production, loss of employment, environmental degradation, and eventual displacement—inform MST's reimagining of the intersects between cultural history, politics, and ideology at the local level. The movement's ideas regarding the reclaiming or reterritorialization of space, the struggle to rethink modes of production, and the need to build environmentally sustainable communities are the most critical points to explore. While camped out in Yuquises waiting for a governmental response to this unproductive plot of land, MST organizers experimented with the use and exchange of ancestor tales as a vehicle for political and community-based action. These stories, as relayed to me by organizers, formed the backbone of the occupation. Such historical memory of ancient Andean communities—whether or not everyone shared the same ancestral, ethnic, and racial background—proved critical to imagining what this settlement could look like in the future.

Social-Economic Reclamation

The MST model for community production is, in part, drawn from memories of labor conditions in the lowlands and a creative reimagining of a form of farming without exploitation. In the latter sense, MST describes the ayllu first and foremost as economic reclamation: members envision an alternative model based on collective landholding patterns and small-scale peasant production. One particular narrative illustrates the material appeal for reclaiming the means of production. Many people spoke of the use and appeal of these ancestor stories in the early days of the Yuquises occupation, especially as the community struggled to organize itself into communal work and production groups. Braulio, an MST member, asserted:

> I remember, in the first days of the occupation, everyone was really beaten down and tired. An encampment is not such an easy thing. There is no food, clean drinking water, or organizational structure. We have to create all of this from scratch. I remember a seasoned leader stood in front of all of us and said, "Compañeros [comrades], no one ever said this would be easy. We have braved difficult moments together. And now it is time to build a settlement on this land. And we must use our ancestors as a force. They lived in ayllus that functioned independently. They sustained a system of small-scale agriculture by organizing people into collective work groups, reciprocal forms of exchange, and an egalitarian structure of democratic decision-making. And this worked."

MST members discursively mobilize two aspects of the ayllu's economic organization inside encampments that are seen as critically important and antithetical to the profit motive.[10] The first is a system of exchange based upon the principles of *ayni*, which refers to reciprocity. Social relations in Andean rural communities are marked by rules specifying that the service rendered between equals in a symmetrical exchange should be returned at some later time with the same service, resulting in a completed cycle of exchanges that cancels debt (Mayer 2002:109). The second term, also critical to MST's productive model is *minka*, which is a form of economic exchange conducted among persons of differing socioeconomic or ritual status. Usually, a laborer provides work service in return for a meal or daily wage. Enrique Mayer (2002) investigated how small-scale peasants in an Andean highland community were always linked into a broader capitalist system while simultaneously buffered from major cultural and social transformation through the reproduction of norms of reciprocity and exchange. He carefully documented the ways in which barter and cash purchases coexisted in many highland villages, which relied on both reciprocal relations and market-based exchange for survival. Although a number of anthropologists noted the coexistence of these forces, MST leaders with whom I spoke in 2006 revived and politicized essentialized notions of Andean highland culture by labeling ayni and minka as "inherently resistant to Western trends of capitalist production." These ancient Andean notions of reciprocity and redistribution, then, became critical to reimagining community as a place where small-scale production relied upon social relations of exchange.

Collective Work and Labor

The radical shift from sugar to soy not only produced greater estrangement from the means of production but also created intensified competition between workers, all of whom were eager to find employment in the region. Many MST members indicated that this corporate power created an environment in which laborers were constantly suspicious of one another. It was within this context that in the Yuquises encampment (later renamed Pueblos Unidos), leaders mobilized concepts like ayni to stress the importance of collective work as central to rebuilding relations among workers. MST members imagined the ayni system as having economic implications, as, for example, when residents cultivated neighbors' plots to implement more communal modes of production. It also had social implications when the community collaborated or exchanged services to support the needy— orphans, widows, and the sick—with food and housing. In both instances, the translation of ayni into acts of solidarity and collective production helped campesinos resist the countervailing tendency to distrust co-workers after decades of intensified competition for jobs.

The tendency, however, toward individual rather than collective models of work and survival proved difficult to displace. For example, the model of communal plowing, preparing of land, and reaping the fruits of labor initially felt foreign to many laborers. Many rented individual plots of land in the agricultural provinces of Santa Cruz, struggled to survive on their own, and could not fully understand the benefits of communal work. MST members often wanted to care only for their own family, not an entire community. These were just some of the daily tugs-of-war inside MST communities, where most residents could not conceptualize the contemporary benefits of ancient Andean systems of exchange and where MST leaders struggled to re-socialize members to reach an understanding that struggle over land is not solely about acquiring a plot of property to advance self-interest. Leaders also insisted that the movement must have a commitment to the socialization of surplus value subsequent to the redistribution of land. For example, they must bring schools to rural communities, rethink the structure of healthcare delivery, and use ancient medicinal herbs for healing as preventative medicine.

Alternative Environmental Imaginary

The discussion regarding the re-socialization of social relationships was joined to dialogue on how farmers should work the land. Again, ayllu stories formed a cultural and historic basis for connecting themes on the sacredness

of the environment, the use of crops for subsistence farming, and the importance of natural fertilizers to contemporary struggles. One MST organizer
relayed to me in 2006 that during the Yuquises occupation, someone said to
the squatters:

> In the Andes, our ancestors used something called "raised fields," which
> provided drainage and improved soil conditions and temperatures for
> crops. It was an ecologically sound alternative to agricultural develop-
> ment based on expensive imported technology. We must be creative
> now in order to think about adapting such kinds of sustainable agricul-
> ture in MST areas.

Initially, environmental consciousness was not explicitly a part of MST's
organizational or productive model. However, environmental and economic
contradictions within the dominant agricultural paradigm forced MST communities like Pueblos Unidos to reimagine small-scale production and create long-term projects focused on issues of resource conservation and
sustainability. In the field of political ecology, the idea of an "environmental
imaginary" has emerged to describe the ways in which social groups recon-
ceptualize the environment. The environmental imaginary has physical
roots in the complex natural ecology of a location but is molded by social
perceptions of nature and its possibilities for human use and habitation.
Watts and Peet (1996) explain that although environmental imaginaries
stem from material and social practices in natural settings, they also guide
further practice. Referring to landscape production, Cosgrove (1998) argues
that landscapes are "ways of seeing," and MST's ways of seeing are directly
influenced by the destruction of their natural environment and their emergent politics. Questions regarding how to recuperate dead soil, limit the use
of chemicals, and reforest particular areas of the region have defined many
political and farming conversations.

Several of the MST encampments and settlements are experimenting
with alternative farming techniques and strategies. In one particular area of
the northern region, MST organizers are trying to plant half the area organically: organic matter improves the soil structure, increases its water-storage
capacity, enhances fertility, and promotes tilth, a characteristic of soil structure. The better the tilth, the more easily the soil can be cultivated, and the
easier it is for seedlings to emerge. Further, they have relied upon green
manure as a natural pesticide. Green manure helps to control weeds,
insects, pests, and soil erosion while also providing forage for livestock and
cover for wildlife. Controlling insects, diseases, and weeds without chemicals is a goal of their system of sustainable agriculture.

A socioecological perspective recognizes that landscapes are produced and contested through the interaction of biological, physical, and social features or with what people "see" and experience in terms of the built landscape. Much more work still needs to be done to more fully understand how small-scale farming communities are beginning to rely upon ancient knowledge in their struggle to reshape socioecological landscapes (Whittman 2005). Borrowing from a systems theory approach, the movement also understands the connections between socioeconomic, environmental, and political concerns. The land is quite literally a contested terrain between multinational corporations and small-scale farmers, as well as all sorts of actors in between who work for "Big Soy," the *grandes soyeros*. MST leaders and rank-and-file discuss the ways in which, during an occupation, people talk about the political struggle for greater control over the physical environment, but also about a broader community structure that evolves a practice for sustaining both physical survival and a collective consciousness. The soy model has only created displacement, relocation to city centers, and hunger. Although this might be the members' lived and personal experience, part of an occupation also entails rethinking the other end of the spectrum: the redistribution of surplus wealth.

Redistribution of Surplus Wealth

For MST activists, the settlement must be an enclave or an experiment in socialized capital accumulation. Organizers use the concept of *mit'a* to advocate redistribution of surplus wealth in the aftermath of cutbacks in education, healthcare, and other basic services. Mit'a was mandatory public service during the time of the Inca empire. It was effectively a form of tribute to the Inca government, in the form of labor, that is, a corvée (see Soruco, chapter 4, this volume). Here its meaning is reimagined and transformed into a kind of localized redistributive practice. One organizer suggested to me in 2006:

> In ancient Andean ayllus, they relied upon this idea of the mit'a, which we could translate as redistributive wealth. So I ask you: why redistributive wealth? We need to pool resources in order to create a better life for our children and grandchildren. In the past thirty years, we have seen the failure of market-based solutions to our problems of poverty: privatization of natural resources and drastic cutbacks in services like education and healthcare.

Mit'a literally comes from the Quechua word for "turn," but actually this translates loosely into "assigned tasks" in order to reclaim services. Activists asserted that in ancient Andean communities, men from each of the four communities of an ayllu would work one day a week for two years to provide a steady supply of rotating labor. MST organizers develop such historic-cultural frames of reference in an era in which collective social needs have been systematically dismantled with the restructuring of the economy. Not only the expansion of soy but also the retreat of the state has created an ever more difficult situation for campesinos struggling to receive adequate education, healthcare, and even protection in their communities.

For example, Don Braulio Cusipuma told me in 2006 that one of the first collective projects in the Yuquises settlement was the building of a school for the children:

> With our own hands, [together] we built a school. I actually took the proposal for a school to the municipality to get us a permit to teach the kids during the occupation. The mayor paid the salary of the teacher and also collaborated with the priest in Sagrado Corazon. We had a little library with books that they gave us, and the school functioned from kindergarten to 5 basico [grade 5]. Our goal was to eventually create a curriculum that taught the ideology of the movement. But just having a school in this remote rural area was a huge accomplishment. There were two rotations [of students], one in the morning and one in the afternoon. The contract that we had with the professor was that we would cover the expenses associated with schooling through a system of exchange. We gave her a substantial amount of food (vegetables, rice, and beans) and she taught our kids. The little school in Yuquises functioned for three months, from March until the displacement in May.

Around the same time, another organizer also described the educational situation to me:

> We would eventually love to have an alternative educational model, MST schools inside the encampments. In the Brazilian settlements, they propose that access to education and the organization of schools coincide with the critical goals of the movement. The encampment schools teach the values important to the members, which they describe as humanist values—development of the person as a whole rather than just particular aspects and skills. In the past, the classic vision of agrarian reform, the problem that limited advancement of campesinos, was the "mentality of dividing up the land." For us, the most important thing is "redistributing educational knowledge." These rural schools produce important thoughts and benefit the workers because they begin with a new vision, new understandings of rural life.

Along with education, inside the Yuquises encampment site, members experimented with alternative forms of healthcare, relying upon *naturalistas* (naturalists, healers) to provide services and ideas regarding preventative medicine. All of this, then, leads to the rebuilding of community (which envisions new ways of conserving and working the land and distinct socio-economic relations) in a post-neoliberal era. MST's ideas of community might be rather utopian, and their imaginings of the ayllu, through their illustrative discourse, certainly set a standard that can never be met through the lived practice of building an agro-ecological settlement. Yet, that tension is part of the ongoing struggle that defines much of the politics of MST. Critically, this political struggle is transported and reinvented for many members of MST alongside the constant movement of labor and capital. When I asked one MST organizer, Ponciano Sulca, about his home, he described it as follows:

> Oh, this is my temporary home. I set up shop here because there were jobs on sugarcane plantations. My real home, my real community, will be Pueblos Unidos. This is where I will set up a permanent home, and I will never leave until I die.

Although he has lived in San Pedro, Obispo Santiesteban, for fifteen years and raised his children and grandchildren there, he did not feel as though this residential area was *his* home. In part, this has to do with notions of renting versus owning land—he always understood the dialectical nature between place and home for a campesino. There is no permanent home for a migrant worker because no matter the comfort and length of time in a physical place, in a moment's notice you can be displaced and then must pick up and move to another location. One illustration of this form of temporary settlement is the predominance of houses made of motacú in the northern region. Instead of concrete or brick homes, which represent permanence, these houses can be easily assembled, disassembled, and reassembled in a new location. More importantly, the idea of a mobile community of workers has much to do with their laboring lives as farmers. Sulca said, "I set up shop here because there were jobs on sugarcane plantations." But as sugar production moved rapidly into export-oriented, large-scale soy production, laborers like Sulca moved their families in search of employment. He also distinguishes between working for others as inherently about temporary settlement, as compared with self-determination, in which the worker controls the means of production and thus has a more permanent residence or place. Gaining a plot of land that he can call his own was about gaining a communal identity tethered to territorial stability associated with home. And for

Sulca, Pueblos Unidos represents *his* community: it is a space for which he fought, braved the devastating consequences of being kicked off the land, and has had to build a productive model along with other *militantes* that could eventually lead to self-sufficiency.

Conclusion

Community might be a rather vague concept, invented and reinvented as people move to new locations, as they transition from rural to urban life, from farming to new modes of production. But with such massive displacements and relocations, community as envisioned by MST workers is about both self-sufficiency (reclaiming the means of production) and permanence (maintaining rights to land and territory). Perhaps, as they buy into or think about large-scale soy production or ecotourism as possible options for immediate cash, their wonderful imaginings of Pueblos Unidos as an Andean utopia will begin to unravel. The point, however, is not to dwell on these contradictions. Rebuilding community is not about returning to the past in a pure form, but about using selective parts of the historic record and memory and reassembling them in order to build a meaningful future. Some of the now commonplace discussions about Andean indigeneity in Bolivia have come to argue that the past and future are envisioned differently in Andean language and cosmologies than they are in Western norms of time and space (Hylton and Thomson 2007; Kohl and Farthing 2006). Although perhaps exaggerated, it is argued that Andeans, rather than view the past being "behind" and the future "ahead," see the past in front of oneself, because we have already witnessed the events that have taken place. This suggests—without arguing for a conservative traditionalism—that we may return to the past as a means of moving forward or, perhaps more accurately, that we may move forward while looking back critically at the path already traveled, a concept referred to as *nayra pacha* in Aymara. As such, looking both back and forward from this communal space, Pueblos Unidos represents the hope and possibility of a better life for future generations, a place where there will be access to healthy food, education, and healthcare, a permanent place for the reproduction of peasant culture and farming communities. And perhaps that is all we can hope for in terms of utopia in this era as a country, a region, and a farming village struggle to undo the legacy of three decades of neoliberal reform.

Notes

1. As the United States funneled money into the agro-industrial development of the regional economy, there was a need for a steady stream of laborers on sugarcane plantations. This "forced

colonization" was intended to redistribute the population more evenly throughout the country and relieve heavy population pressure in the highlands.

2. Although the movement does not affiliate with a particular political party, MST intellectuals have worked alongside members from the Morales administration to rethink agrarian laws. Leaders such as Silvestre Saisari (the national president of MST) drafted the proposal for the Community Redirection Law.

3. For more on ayllu as a social and political-economic structure in ancient Andean communities, see Godoy 1986; Murra 1975, 1978; Zuidema 1977.

4. The activist ayllu represents a departure from an earlier generation's self-definition based much more directly on questions of livelihood, such as the ability to handle ox and plow or ownership of a truck. As a cultural heritage, indigenous identity is now something that can be claimed or reclaimed in a rapidly growing percentage of indigenous-descended popular and urban social sectors (Albro 2006).

5. Although it is illegal to turn food crops into biodiesel in Bolivia, gasoline shortages have created a crisis that has led farmers to do just that. Morales has taken a firm stance against biofuel, but regional elites have been transforming large extensions of land into production zones specifically for that purpose.

6. I borrow the subheading above from Boo 2004, after Schumpeter 1975.

7. This was a result of the approval of GMO soya resistant to the herbicide glyphosate in 2005.

8. Undated quotes are from field notes, April 1, 2006.

9. "United soy republics" describes the various countries in the Southern Cone (such as Paraguay, Bolivia, Ecuador, Brazil, and Argentina) that have united in their quest for more fertile lands in which to produce soybeans for export.

10. On the ayllu as interpreted by contemporary anthropologists, see Allen (1988); Arnold (1998); Bastein (1978); Brush (1977); Isbell (1978); Orlove (1977).

8 Power Necessarily Comes from Below

Guaraní Autonomies and Their Others

Bret Gustafson

In early July of 2009, not long after a national referendum approved the new Constitution of Bolivia, several hundred people lined up along Sucre Avenue in downtown La Paz to enter the elegant grand hall of the vice-presidential building. They gathered to attend the public presentation of a book, *Indigenous Autonomies in Bolivian Reality and in Its New Constitution* (Albó and Romero 2009). For the first time in history, indigenous rights to self-determination were being inscribed in constitutional form, and the book was a detailed analysis of how the process of implementing autonomy might unfold in practice and law. Crowded into the hall, standing, seated, and lining the balconies above, the public jostled one another for viewing space as the book's authors and other invited notables took seats at a table in the front of the hall. There were three anchors of the presentation: Xavier Albó, the Jesuit Catalán-Bolivian who is one of the godfathers of Bolivian anthropology and the founder of a major peasant-indigenous rights NGO called CIPCA; his co-author, Carlos Romero, a lawyer, then Minister of Autonomies, previously an activist and intellectual of another prominent NGO, called CEJIS;[1]

and later the vice president himself, Alvaro García Linera, sociologist and former guerrilla fighter, also part of a prominent circle of scholars who in recent years were central theorists of the movements against neoliberalism. Romero, like García Linera, had paralleled this intellectual work with formal alliances with the MAS (Movement to Socialism) party. Alongside them sat Silvia Lazarte, the Quechua coca growers' leader and former president of the Constitutional Assembly, as well as other ministers of government. A local representative of the German aid agency GTZ (Gessellschaft für Technische Zusammenarbeit), which financed the volume and has long supported Bolivian decentralization (since the neoliberal period of the 1990s), was there as well. She also later took a turn commenting on the historical significance of the occasion.

Book presentations as significant ritual events tied to national policy change are unremarkable in Bolivia. In recent years, public policy processes of all sorts—from decentralization to land reform—have been imagined, defended, designed, and critiqued through such networks of knowledge production and publishing linking social movements, NGOs, and academics to state change. In this case, the contentious issue of ethnoterritorial difference and the prospects of granting autonomy to peoples who were, in fact, the majority of the country brought into evidence once again the highly intellectualized sphere of popular and indigenous politics in the country. Yet, the book and its topic—and this array of activist intellectuals —marked a shift from the past. This ritual juxtaposed the planning efforts of a "revolutionary" regime born of NGOs and social movements, rather than of the Washington Consensus technocracy, against an incredibly complex geopolitical and ethnoterritorial reality now seen through a new lens. Aid-funded books and research, a constant, were still crucial symbols of alliance and anchoring that sought to sketch out and legitimate paths for guiding contentious change.

The NGO anthropologist, Albó, and the NGO activist-lawyer-turned-minister, Romero, gave didactic presentations with vivid PowerPoint graphics and maps. They dissected conceptual terms (*autonomy*, *self-government*) and analyzed census data that showed the distributions of indigenous populations across the country. The research—basically a template for what would later become the Law of Autonomies—outlined in legal and technical terms how indigenous peoples might achieve what the recent UN Declaration on the Rights of Indigenous People and the Bolivian constitution now defend but do not describe in detail: "autonomy" or "free-determination" or "self-government" (NCPE 2009; United Nations 2007). With indigenous autonomy in Bolivia already "domesticated" (Garcés, chapter 3, this volume) into the template of existing municipalities, the text included an exhaustive study of where indigenous peoples were more or less the majority in municipal jurisdictions (about 57 percent, or 187 of 327 municipalities) or near majorities (about 16 percent) and where they were clear minorities.

Albó described two procedural paths through which indigenous territories might become Autonomous Indigenous-Originary-Peasant Territorial Entities or autonomous ETIOCs (Entidad Territorial Indígena-Originario-Campesino), now more commonly called AIOCs (Indigenous-Originary-Campesino Autonomies).[2] AIOCs, in some cases, could emerge from existing municipal structures. Indigenous peoples could call a referendum at the municipal level to acquire *autonomía*, leading to new municipal governance structures, in which nonindigenous residents would also participate. Presumably, municipalities with an indigenous majority would be the most likely to approve such a referendum, which could yield new forms of governance, justice, representation, and participatory procedures (or grant legality to de facto forms emerging in practice). The other path to autonomy, Albó explained, was by way of the TCOs (*tierras comunitarias de origen*), an existing legal category of collectively titled lands that was created by the 1994 Land Reform law during the neoliberal era. Until now, TCOs were simply demarcations of territory with few legal or administrative attributes of self-government or resource control. With the new law, TCOs, through a yet to be determined process, can become autonomous AIOCs by detaching themselves from existing municipal jurisdictions. Such a move would be difficult, especially in much of the eastern lowlands, where native peoples are minorities in municipal jurisdictions. Like the municipality option, the TCO option would have to negotiate opposition from nonindigenous municipal authorities and residents and gain approval at the national legislative level, confronting the exceedingly complex political limitations described by Garcés (chapter 3, this volume). Nonetheless, the fact that this is now possible suggests shifts in standardized models of decentralization that had emerged from years of indigenous and intellectual struggle and were facilitated by the victory of Evo Morales and the MAS party.

Vice President García Linera himself soon appeared in the hall and took the podium. We, the audience, had passed through no metal detectors or security as we entered, yet we were now in intimate proximity to cabinet ministers and the vice president in this Bolivian equivalent of a town hall. With a stern-faced *edecán*—a uniformed military officer and personal bodyguard—posed like a motionless mime directly behind him, García Linera rose and spoke to much applause. The impressive orator gave an overview of Bolivia's unfinished history of indigenous struggle. He spoke extemporaneously, based on notes he was scribbling at the table just prior to the talk, weaving them into a seamless lecture. He began with a question of terms.

To "talk of autonomy," he said, "is to talk of power, of how the power of the state is organized, how the distribution of power is organized, and how power is institutionalized." He went on to speak of indigenous autonomies and the plurinational state as a move against the "violent impositions of colonialism," a historic attempt "to transcend, to resolve, the problem of the coloniality of the state." A radical shift from the multiculturalist rhetoric of neoliberalism, his focus on coloniality placed the indigenous autonomy question within a history of several centuries. García Linera recounted how indigenous revolutions of the past had also pursued modes of coexistence (convivencia) with the whites. Yet, these historic efforts, he suggested, were always met by the violence of the Spanish colony (which crushed the rebellion of Tupak Katari and drew and quartered its leader in 1781) and later of the neocolonial state (with the uprising and later assassination of the Aymara leader Zárate Willka at the end of the nineteenth century). "[Today,]" he said, "two hundred years after Katari, we are looking for ways to [resolve this issue of convivencia...of asking] how do different cultures live within the same state space? How do different productive and technological structures coexist within the same geographic and state space? It appears," he said, turning with a pause for effect to Albó, a Jesuit priest, "that the third time is the winner, Padre. From the Katarista effort, to the Willkista effort, "and to give it a name now, to the Evista effort," referring to President Evo Morales.

As this text went to press a year later, in mid-2010, with the Law of Autonomies recently approved, Minister Romero and Vice President García Linera were at the front lines of a wider MAS government conflict with the very subjects who were to benefit from indigenous "autonomy"—the indigenous confederation of the eastern lowlands, CIDOB (Confederación Indígena de Bolivia). CIDOB was unhappy with the outcome of the autonomy law, which not only limited possibilities for the indigenous (as described by Garcés in chapter 3) but also declared outright that populations smaller than one thousand people—like the populations of many indigenous peoples of the east—could not aspire to autonomy at all. They were deemed inviable autonomies. CIDOB also wanted the right—to self-determination, as it were —to declare its territories autonomous without submitting to the referendums and votes of nonindigenous municipal elites or the assembly. In truth, this would be self-determination, though technically, as argued by Romero, outside the constitution. There were also conflicts over indigenous representation to the national assembly, a crucial space for exercising influence and "autonomy" at the national level. Somewhat shocking, given that international observers had applauded the MAS turn toward indigenous rights, the MAS regime and Evo Morales himself were accusing CIDOB of being an agent of USAID, the US Agency for International Development. By then, attacks on CIDOB also came from García Linera and Romero, suggesting that CIDOB was a "traitor" to the process of change, attempting to bring down the MAS regime. This conflict was eventually settled through negotiation. Yet, against the largely Andean-centric narrative of indigenous decolonizing revolutions, these deep rifts with the indigenous peoples of the east were a sign that indigenous rights and indigenous autonomy were far from being resolved in the third, "Evista" era. How might this ongoing struggle over convivencia and power—in García Linera's terms—unfold in the future remapping of Bolivia?

Knowledge and Power in a Social Movement State

This chapter examines Bolivia's turn to redistributive plurinationalism and indigenous autonomy through ethnographic sketches of knowledge production and reterritorializing processes in the southeastern Guaraní region. The Guaraní, like CIDOB, are involved in their own set of conflictive negotiations over autonomy and resources. They live across an area of southeastern Bolivia between the Andes and the Chaco. Much of their actual and ancestral territory is the region that is also the source of most of Bolivia's immense natural gas reserves (see figures 1 and 2). Over the past decade, this relatively poor agrarian region has seen the eruption of a complex scenario of gas development and geopolitics tied to the nationalization process, with multinational firms hungry for gas and intensifying intra-regional and inter-regional competition over the real and imagined benefits of this boom. Though an in-depth account of the gas regime and the Guaraní is beyond the scope of this chapter, the following discussion highlights the contending visions of change and transformation that ground themselves in the region. These echo, I suggest, the issues and ideas that will shape wider territorial and resource conflicts across the country as a whole.[3] The subtext considers a deeper challenge that crosscuts all the chapters of this book: How does a developmentalist state rich with resources and pursuing a centralized form of sovereignty and redistribution engage a plurality of indigenous demands for territorial self-determination in tandem with efforts to address the material expectations of a largely poor population? And do emergent moves toward indigenous autonomy transcend the managerial neoliberal multiculturalism inherited from the recent past? Or does the MAS regime's "democratic and cultural revolution" promise only a China model, a state-centric version of neoliberalism with a market-friendly strategy of managerial control and extractivist fury?

Although certain socioterritorial spaces of the state (both indigenous and not) enjoy a kind of de facto autonomy through local enactments of sovereignty (whether through extrajudicial law or violence), in legal terms there are at this writing no "autonomous" indigenous territories of "self-determination" in the country. Further, despite the exaggerated opposition to indigenous autonomy from the business-led right and the hyper-nationalist left, there is no impending cataclysm of ethnoterritorial "balkanization." The December 2009 election cycle saw only 12 out of 187 indigenous-majority municipalities participate in the first municipal-level referendum votes on autonomy. There was no rush to autonomy. In many municipalities, especially in the Andes, indigenous Bolivians already dominate local institutions. Radical changes of municipal structures or existing relationships with party-mediated representation were not, for the moment, a priority. In much of the eastern lowlands, municipal jurisdictions run against indigenous interests and territorialities. Becoming an autonomous municipality was neither feasible nor desirable. Here the TCO option is preferred, though hindered by the autonomy law itself. Of the 12 municipalities that moved to convert themselves into "indigenous autonomies"—the referendum passed in 11; 9 Andean (3 Quechua, 4 Aymara, 1 Uru); and 2 Guaraní municipalities in the southeast. Things were further complicated when conflicting indigenous authorities emerged in some of these municipalities. Some supported autonomy; others had been elected in regularly scheduled municipal voting and sought to defend the status quo. Others were tied to peasant unions (sindicatos) or ayllus, the territorialized "traditional" authority structures in the Andes. In general, this suggests a latent tension between parties, in some cases the dominant MAS itself, and other indigenous authorities. The split has many legitimate origins but is also encouraged by the right-wing opposition and, some evidence suggests, foreign (US and oil-company) intervention (Chumacero 2010; Plata 2010:250).[4] Though these 11 municipalities represent a small percentage of the indigenous population (roughly 100,000 out of more than 4 million), the process is revelatory of future conflicts to come (Colque 2009). Regimes of de jure indigenous "autonomy" are far from achieved. Any robust indigenous autonomy may threaten to erode the hegemony of the MAS in some regions. This potential is counterbalanced by the ways that resource rents might be used to maintain alliances and articulations between these regional formations and the state. These conflicts will revolve around issues that echo conflicts of the neoliberal era: control of resources, juridical rights to territory and political authority, and participation in resource projects, with the full range of indigenous rights to prior consultation, consent, and monitoring of extractive projects.

What must be emphasized is that, as sketched out in the constitution, an ethnic reterritorialization is not underway. Rather, we see the creation of procedures for potential long-term shifts that protect the authority of a centralized state and make difficult, if not impossible, the consolidation of substantive ethnoterritorial formations (even if such entities were desired by indigenous peoples, and they are not, at least in any uniform sense). The question of what indigenous "autonomy" or self-determination actually is—and with what other processes and power relations it might ultimately articulate—is in many ways still unanswerable, though the new dynamics certainly demand a transformation of research practice and orientation.

During the neoliberal 1990s, anthropologists and other observers, as well as indigenous and popular movement activists, grappled with the contradiction between neoliberal policies tied to the dispossessing effects of structural adjustment and the turn toward indigenous cultural rights and recognition under the mantra of "interculturalism" (Gustafson 2002, 2009a). From this perspective, as Hale (2002) warned, the progressive-sounding language of multiculturalism was to be assessed critically. Its managerial goals and soft forms of cultural recognition did little to address structural inequalities and hard questions of material redistribution. What was particular to the ethnographic engagement with neoliberal multiculturalism during this period was its modality as *critique*, that is to say, ethnographic research and writing aimed at revealing the effects of neoliberalism and thereby exposing its violences and exclusionary outcomes. The emphasis was on (generally rural or periurban) subjects as exemplars of those excluded by neoliberalism and on ongoing indigenous marginalization despite the formal embrace of cultural rights. Neoliberal multiculturalism did not grant robust indigenous rights but worked (as it still does, through new tactics) to distinguish an *indio permitido* (permitted or docile Indian) from an *indio prohibido* (a prohibited or radical Indian) (Hale 2002, 2006a; Sawyer 2004). The former was one whose demands fell within the purview of neoliberal managerialism: participating in a standard municipal template, embracing the rhetoric of individual opportunity, and reconciling cultural alterity with the mantras of markets, technocracy, and growth. The latter was an indio whose radical demands were seen as threatening to the neoliberal project—whether because they advocated the redistribution of land and power or because they expressed subjectivities that ran contrary to neoliberal governmentality. This critique marked a limit point of ethnography, building on a Gramscian model of resistance, and, often paradoxically, a Foucaultian skepticism of statecraft. Yet, in the euphoria of the 2000s, with the smiling and humble Evo Morales thronged by thousands of jubilant Bolivians wherever he appears, now speaking directly about redistribution, as well as indigenous recognition and strong state sovereignty, where does our critical ethnographic lens turn in its encounter with the state and the indigenous? And what, given that Evo himself was in many ways once an indio prohibido (and is now president), does this imply for research and thinking on indigenous-inspired territorial transformations? What directions should engaged research take as movements now resist both older and newer expressions of coloniality while also working to reconstitute the state itself?

In hindsight, observers were more troubled by the paradoxes than were members of the movements themselves, who appropriated neoliberal reforms to the extent possible while maintaining de facto grassroots strategies that eventually led to the rise of the MAS and the weakening of the traditional parties. Bolivia appears to be set on a new course. Yet, it is not altogether clear that it is a course imagined by those who critiqued neoliberalism and saw hope in the MAS rise to power. As illustrated in the book presentation described at the beginning of this chapter, this is a regime still deeply inflected by the intercultural policies of the prior era and their embeddedness in a nexus of NGOs, academics, movements, and development aid. But at the level of national policy, as evidenced in the constitution—and positions like that of Vice President García Linera—there is a clear shift away from the blind embrace of the market and its rhetoric of competition, liberalization, and individualism. Leaders and intellectuals now embrace a social movement-inspired (and academically-inspired) language of decolonization, articulation, economic and social plurality, redistribution, and sovereignty. If the neoliberals cited Jeffrey Sachs and Adam Smith, then the MAS cites Katari, Guattari, and Marx. On the ground, Bolivia's plural movements continue generating their own knowledge and reterritorialization projects rooted in a plethora of local histories and "social memories of struggle" (Gordon, Gurdián, and Hale 2003). These plural histories articulate and clash with the emerging hegemony of the state regime of plurinational decolonization and a new kind of socialism built on resource extraction, industrialization, and state-led development.

Now capitalizing, quite literally, on the influx of gas rents and the negotiated support of a mosaic of social movements, state tactics of governance and rule are shifting. Understanding the ongoing politics of territory requires situating analyses within this state of flux. Indigenous claims are as likely to be embraced or rejected selectively, and for tactical reasons, as they are to be addressed in some uniform way out of a principled concern with indigenous rights or decolonization rhetoric. This may change as—and if—the social-movement-backed project is consolidated over the longer term. However, at the moment, uncertainty, various wars of position, and experimentalism are the order of the day. One Guaraní colleague framed it thus, commenting on the irony that, on my return visits since 2003, I always seemed to encounter a blockade, march, conflict, or referendum vote: "We do not live in tranquility here. We do not just get up and go to work every day like you do."

At the heart of these transformations are social movements. Boaventura de Sousa Santos has argued for the primacy of social movements—as opposed to traditional party politics—in the recent transformative shift in Latin America. This process, he writes, led to the introduction of "experimentalism in the very sphere of the state, transforming the state into an absolutely new social movement" (de Sousa Santos and Avritzer 2005:xlv). According to Santos, this makes of the search for a new social grammar and relation between state and society the "order of the day," a fact illustrated in events like the book presentation described above. Yet, social movements are not only popular, labor, and indigenous movements with some affinity to the MAS project. As described throughout this volume, regional and provincial elites have also mobilized the language and practice of social movements. They are equally experimentalist and often violent in their pursuit of new relations of de facto authority. But, replicating colonial dualities, these elites eschew the label *social*—deemed too close to the rural, the dark-skinned, the poor, and the *social(ist)* MAS. They embrace instead the label *civic*, deemed closer to the citizen, "civilized" and "modern," of the urban town or city. These competing projects emerge nationally, as detailed in a number of chapters, and in multiple local and regional forms in places like Guaraní country. Experimentalism emerging from above thus collides with the intensification of potentially transformative and experimental cultural-political practices from "civics" and "socials" below.

These dynamics offer a challenge to conventional understandings of indigeneity in relationship to state sovereignty, whether understood in its colonial forms of territorializing violence or its expressions in managerial and biopolitical containment of selves in liberal multicultural states. Here indigeneity, as part of the state's emergent public identity and emergent legal form, is conceived less as the expression of a particular kind of subject to be managed through biopolitical techniques (or violence) and more as social, historical, and territorial subjects carrying out their own unfinished historical projects of decolonization. At least in ideal terms, when Romero, in the book presentation, referred to indigenous peoples as the "living communities" (*comunidades vivas*) that preceded the founding of the state, he intimated that indigenous sociohistorical formations would not be managed through universalizing templates but would, through new forms of self-government and alongside other expressions of Bolivian plurality, be articulated with the state in a shared exercise of power. This pushes us to move beyond our tendencies to view indigenous peoples as only subject to, or resistant to, the biopolitical and violent modes of sovereignty (the prohibido and the permitido). Can we think of this yet existing "thing" called the pluri-national state and imagined to be a "living" articulation of pluralities in some new form? Is this possible? Is it naïve to think that Bolivia might be on the path toward a new model of plurinational sovereignty with room for sub-stantive indigenous autonomies and the maintenance of a redistributive sov-ereign nation-state? How are indigenous organizations and their various allies and opponents positioning themselves in relation to this emergent reality? For the moment, an anthropology of state and movement processes must be content with identifying key points of conjuncture and disjuncture, outlining how emerging dynamics of the present are shaped by, or depart from, continuities of the past, and identifying how competing cultural-political projects might lay the groundwork for change. I offer some ideas in what follows.

Gas and Redistributive Dreams

According to the 2000 World Petroleum Assessment, carried out by the United States Geological Survey (USGS) in collaboration with major oil companies, Bolivian gas lies within a geologic province recently named the Santa Cruz–Tarija Basin (Ahlbrandt 2000). The name chosen for the basin is a bit suspicious, given that Santa Cruz and Tarija are the two cities whose conservative business classes are spearheading the regional autonomy agenda. Until the late 1990s the gas-rich formation was labeled as the "Altiplano" or "Sub-Andean" basin. This suggests that USGS scientists and companies affiliated with the Bolivian oil industry may have colluded in a geohistorical detachment of "Andeanness" from subsoil hydrocarbons in the east (compare Baby et al. 1995 and Lindquist 1998). Three megafields hold most of Bolivia's reserves in this basin: San Alberto and San Antonio, oper-ated by Brazil's Petrobras, and Margarita, operated by Spain's Repsol-YPF. Critics of the nationalist turn often warn of the coming depletion of Bolivian gas. Yet, the USGS estimated that between 30 and 170 more undiscovered fields exist, with an estimated 4 billion barrels of oil equivalent, much of it gas (Lindquist 1999).

In Bolivian public discourse, the gas-rich region is not known as the Santa Cruz–Tarija Basin, but the Chaco, a cultural, ecological, and histori-cal space that intersects segments of the Santa Cruz, Tarija, and Chuquisaca departments. The Chaco is intimately articulated with the national imagi-nary through the remembering of the Chaco War, fought between Bolivia and Paraguay from 1932 to 1935. It was Bolivia's first oil war, motivated in part by the machinations of Standard Oil and Royal Dutch Shell, leading to a bloody conflagration that left thousands dead. As the Bolivian intellectual René Zavaleta (1967:37) lamented, it was a war between "multitudes" of "naked soldiers," a "phenomenon after which began the consciousness [raising] and the rebellion of the national classes." Evidencing a longer Bolivian intellectual concern with the geographic shaping of state power, Zavaleta (1967:43) called the war a "cartographic" failure of liberalism's alliance with imperialism. In the case of the Chaco War, fought by Andean and lowland indigenous and poor foot soldiers who were its main protagonists, indigenous claims to citizenship after the war unsettled the caste-like colonial society of the country and ultimately propelled peasant and labor mobilizations that led to the Bolivian Revolution of 1952 (H. Klein 2003). We might also apply Zavaleta's phrasing of cartographic failure to the conditions and alliances between (neo)liberalism and global capital that led to the 2003 Gas War, itself an event that presaged a new "remapping" of the country.

The nationalist memories of the Chaco War disrupt regionalist remappings of territory and history led by Santa Cruz and Tarija. These elite regionalists seek to delineate histories (and geologies and resources) as detached and free from the "Andean" state. Yet, for nationalists, the Chaco fits into a wider narrative of Bolivia's frustrated nation-building history. This history is marked by territorial losses facilitated by the *entreguismo* (the servile "hand-it-over" attitude) of Bolivian elites. Speaking of the Chaco, the war, and gas thus yields a deep anti-imperialist discourse about an unfinished historical process, about a set of *national* political relations (between the people and popular state and against regional oligarchs), and about memories of a series of failed nationalizations (the first, of Standard Oil in 1937, and the second, of Gulf Oil in 1969, both followed by reprivatization phases). The neoliberal dismantling and privatization of Bolivia's national oil company, YPFB (Yacimientos Petrolíferos Fiscales Bolivianos), in the 1990s is, in this reading, the latest expression of a long history of "handing over" of Bolivian resources to foreign powers. When President Evo Morales renationalized gas in 2006, he did so at a grandiose ceremonial "retaking" of the Petrobras-controlled San Alberto field in the eastern Chaco. Nationalization was inscribed through a decree titled the "Heroes of the Chaco," and banners reading "Property of All Bolivians" were hung on the Petrobras tanks. Evo's re-nationalization is thus the "third" nationalization, and as García Linera said of the pursuit of indigenous autonomy, perhaps the third time is, in Bolivian terms, the victorious.

Rising expectations about gas rents and their distribution complicate tensions between nationalist, regionalist, and indigenist projects. Of approximately 41 million cubic meters of gas produced each day, about 15 percent is for domestic consumption, 12 percent is exported to Argentina, and the rest (more than 70 percent by contract obligation) goes to Brazil, where it generates electricity for domestic and industrial consumption and fuels cars from Mato Grosso to São Paulo and points farther south (Jironda Cuba 2007). Rents, in turn, flow into state coffers. Prior to nationalization, the state received between 18 and 50 percent of hydrocarbon revenues, depending on the concession block (very few received 50 percent). After 2006 the state continued to take at least 50 percent from smaller and older fields and up to 90 percent of revenues from mega-fields. Annual flows into state coffers increased from $188 million in 2001 to more than $1.5 billion in 2009 (*Jubileo* 2009). Some of this money is to go to the rebuilding of the YPFB, the national oil company. Talk of the industrialization of gas is booming, and, given the now widely celebrated lithium reserves, Bolivia's leaders speak of themselves as a continental "energetic center" surrounded by consuming markets. Like neighboring Brazil, Bolivia is now embarking on distributive policies based on direct transfers from the central government to targeted sectors of society (school children, the elderly, expectant mothers, veterans of the Chaco War) (Müller 2009). The new hydrocarbon laws also established a special Indigenous Fund in answer to indigenous mobilizations before the election of Evo Morales. Thus, a series of redistributive logics and dynamics are unfolding in a complex, multiscalar, geopolitical shift tied to state-led resource control and multiple forms of regional reorderings.

Constituting Autonomy as an Administrative Process

In the wider context of the gas boom, redistributive contests, and state change, multiple local struggles over territoriality and power unfold. Ongoing maneuvers to redesign local forms of government, adjust territorial arrangements, and dismantle local hierarchies merge questions of redistribution with new modes and claims to recognition. These unfold at a quite different pace and scale than the relatively more simple politics of direct transfers. In the sections that follow, I explore some of these expressions in Camiri, formerly known as the Oil Capital of Bolivia, now a town positioned at the crossroads of nationalist resurgence, indigenous autonomy, and regionalist defense of privilege (see figures 16–20).

A glimpse at the oral histories of the region sheds light on some of these contemporary dilemmas. In conversations with retired oil workers and their wives and families, aimed at sketching out what things were like during Camiri's oil-rich era from the 1930s to the 1980s, oil workers wax nostalgic about their contributions to the *patria* (the fatherland), their patriotism, and the toughness of their work. Amid accidents at the well sites and on the road, long days of hard work on the rig, and the travails of living in rustic conditions, images of oil were central to the ideal of conventional monocultural nation-building. These visions are distinct from the relations between resources and plurinational decolonization today. The old workers are undoubtedly proud of this past, highlighting moments such as the period of gasoline sovereignty achieved in the 1950s. Yet, oilmen also joke when they retell the underside—the petty pilfering that made its way into local construction techniques, yielded oil pipes and artifacts that are visible in most Camiri homes today; the corrupt dealings with mounds of "cash on the table," as one fellow recalled, that shaped union, military, and state relations; and the raucous, baroque, and often erotic accounts—which really animate memories—of the debauchery (and alcohol-fueled modes of generating masculine labor solidarity) that marked oil-worker exuberance when they returned to town from two- or three-week stints in the rural *campamento* (oil camp). Most of the older wives, many now widowed or divorced, are less enamored with this golden past, recounting stories of broken families, brutal domestic violence, and fist fights with angry mistresses over the chits that gave families' rights to goods in the oil workers' commissary.[5] A husband's arrival at home was often followed by his quick departure as he went off drinking with companions at La Bonanza, one of the city's (now disappeared) bordellos. It was, as in oil towns elsewhere, a particularly fragmenting social history, despite its illusions of wealth, grandeur, and nation-building (Apter 2005; Coronil 1997).

For contemporary understandings, what is significant, in addition to the familiar ways that extractive industries exacerbated gendered forms of exclusion and violence, is how this prior era of nationalization also largely excluded—while deeply affecting—Guaraní lives and spaces in the rural oil fields. In the rural camps and well sites that dot much of Guaraní country, another kind of exclusion and violence, one that fuses the gendered and raced character of oil work, is less remembered by workers themselves but often recalled by the indigenous Guaraní. When asked by one of my Guaraní colleagues about relations between criollo Bolivian oil workers and local indigenous women, one elderly Guaraní woman answered, "Did they leave kids here? Sure they did, several! So-and-so's son, the one they call 'blondie,' he is a child of Yacimientos...and the others, I don't remember, all those [women] who worked in the campamento, as laundry women, cooks, they all brought children home from there."[6] Another Guaraní woman was incorporated into the labor of the campamento through her patrón, her boss, evidencing how one type of semi-feudal colonial arrangement (between peon and patrón) blurred into labor in the highly capitalized and proletarianized regime of oil extraction. "We worked hard," she recalled, "[but] lots of women were tricked. The oil workers said they were unmarried, but [the women] were tricked [into sexual relations] in exchange for diesel, for trinkets. It was no good."

Back in town, oil memories also motivate thinking among a new generation of Camiri's post-boom, nonindigenous urban elites. On the one side, a cluster of local nonindigenous notables, most of them attached in some way to the local municipal government, represent a political mafia of sorts. Having captured the municipality, this family mobilizes connections with relatives in Santa Cruz and in the national congress, seeking to control various channels of funding that flow into the municipality now that oil is no more and the riches of gas are yet to come. This unsurprisingly merges local kin-based ties of an anti-indigenous provincial elite with shifting tides of national party politics. A conversation with a group of young men tied to these networks outlined the economic dilemmas and conflicts of the present. Dreams of recovering the age of oil merge with new schemes for development that are largely blind—again—to rising indigenous claims for autonomy and to alternative visions of regional economies. For this provincial growth-elite, development—understood as the local capture of circulating wealth and the acceleration of exploration and extraction—is the cure. They explained, echoing the memories of the older men, that "there used to be *circulación* [circulation]…*movimiento* [movement]," referring to the ways that money as oil wages circulated through social and economic exchange. "Now it's just pensioners' and teachers' checks that sustain this town." Camiri has yet to benefit from the gas boom, and Villamontes and Yacuiba, cities to the south, are more favorably positioned in relation to the megafields run by Petrobras and Repsol. Flows of rents to the municipality come only in part from the national government and rely on alliances with the department capital at Santa Cruz from which special projects and investments might derive. "We have to find a new economic base, to defend the municipality. Do you think you could bring tourists here?" they ask. They were also dreaming of projects to turn Camiri into a region of services (hospitals, schools, a local university) and perhaps even damming the local river to irrigate the dry Chaco, all projects that would bring people, and circulación, to the town.

These dreams were largely hostile to both the MAS regime and issues of indigenous rights and autonomy. The MAS represents challenges to local power, with new claimants on gas rents and prospects generated by nationalization. Guaraní claims on autonomy also upset these provincial growth visions, because autonomous regions might divert circulating flows of rents and power away from the traditional centers of provincial power. It is a recipe for seething rentier conflict. In self-defense, the local elite embraced the right-wing Santa Cruz–based autonomist elites, seen as protection from both indigenous and local subaltern threats to the status quo. They were also hard at work countering indigenous and nationalist agendas with their own attempts to take control of the "true history" of the region. They met in the little office of Camiri's House of Culture (Casa de la Cultura) to talk about the region's past, populated as it was with uncomfortably revolutionary figures like Che Guevara and Regis Debray. These figures bring "garbage tourists," backpackers with no money, I was told. They also engaged the equally problematic "indigenous" with familiar tactics that reaffirmed existing exploitative relationships with the Guaraní. In one tourist scheme, the Guaraní were represented as local "ethnics" to dance and attract tourism. "We have lots of plans," they told me, "but this [MAS] government is the problem."

On other occasions, oil stories led in a different direction, to the nationalist and left-leaning locals who spoke in the register of union struggle and resistance to imperialism while showing some sympathy for the MAS project. Eusebio Vargas, an old former union leader, was typical. In response to a colleague's question about the nationalism of the past, he answered with gusto:

> That time [post 1969] was a nationalization with honors for Bolivia. Because it was a true and legitimate nationalization, where the gringos of Gulf [Oil] had to leave with their ponchos under their arms and without taking a single screw with them. That was the nationalization carried out by the paladin of democracy, the socialist Marcelo Quiroga Santa Cruz, whose deeds still today continue to serve as the true example of the true Bolivian who recovered Bolivian oil from the claws of the transnationals. [And thirty years later, with the neoliberal privatization,] we were lacerated and wounded, not so much by the transnationals but by the sell-out-your-country [entreguista] government of Sánchez de Lozada. That was national shame, but we went on [hunger] strike anyway, for several days, but unfortunately, as you know, when money rules, the truth is silenced.[7]

Photos of Che and Fidel Castro—whom he referred to as "those who have lighted the way for future workers' leaders"—lined his living room. He finished the conversation by extending greetings of revolutionary solidarity to the indigenous Guaraní.

In Camiri, this small cluster of nationalists expresses itself through a shifting array of alliances and battles for control of the town's Civic Committee—historically held by the local elite yet now disputed by MAS and other popular sectors, including the nationalist circles. Through a series of protest events, these popular civics have staged blockades against the MAS government—and against the Santa Cruz autonomists—demanding that the state return to Camiri that which it deserves: its true legacy as the Petroleum Capital of Bolivia. One of the more vocal of this local circle is Mirko Orgaz (see Orgaz 2005), who has led the charge against the MAS by demanding the restoration of oil activities in the hills around Camiri, the establishment of national offices of YPFB in the town, and the creation of jobs, to restore Camiri's position in the circuits of hydrocarbon rent circulation, that is, the distribution of public monies to various spaces and scales of government.

Whereras the more conservative political mafia allies with Santa Cruz, the local nationalists express themselves as part of an ongoing history of the national left, only selectively—and cautiously—aligned with the decolonizing struggle of indigenous peoples. They cite a pantheon of heroes and martyrs—Marcelo Quiroga, gunned down by the military dictatorship in 1980; Carlos Montenegro, the first theorist of nationalization; and René Zavaleta, the brilliant theorist of the revolution of the masses. They mobilize a stable of villains—the long list of oil barons (Rockefeller, Standard Oil, and so forth) and their local cronies, such as neoliberals and the Santa Cruz oligarchic elite —against whom the unfinished project of recovering Bolivian property and sovereignty continues. Their critiques also point to long-standing imperialist oppressors (the United States and its interventionist development and clandestine activities), as well as emerging imperial threats, most prominently, Brazil, the behemoth next door.

But not all of the left-leaning nationalists look kindly on the Guaraní and other indigenous peoples as part of this MAS-led process of change. Many are as blind to Guaraní issues as is the provincial growth elite and as was the prior generation of oil workers. On the far left, a sustained critique against the MAS accuses the regime of carrying on neoliberal politics while threatening to break down the country with indigenous autonomies. In this view, Evo and the MAS are overseeing a "false" nationalization that has so far failed to truly recover control of oil and gas for the people of Bolivia (see figure 16). Here the emergent growth elites and the nationalist circles share a skeptical stance regarding the indigenous question. To be sure, works like that of Orgaz (2005), in line with national left intellectuals such as Andrés Soliz Rada, voice a limited solidarity with lo indígena, as part of a wider "indo-mestizo" generic subjectivity of a subaltern popular-nationalist pueblo. Yet, proposals for decolonization, indigenous autonomy, and plurinationalism are vehemently opposed. This stance views both oligarchic regionalism (as in Santa Cruz–style autonomy) and indigenous self-determination (as in plurinationalism) as reactionary projects that threaten to disintegrate the country (Orgaz 2005:19). The privileging of indigenous territorialities, they argue, is congruent with the "tribalizing" policies of imperial colonial states and oil companies in the Middle East and Africa. They blame the NGOs—and here organizations such as CIPCA (of Xavier Albó) and CEJIS (of Carlos Romero) are frequently mentioned—suggesting that they are tied to US interests, funded by George Soros (among others), threatening an "Africanization" or a "Balkanization" of the country (Orgaz 2005:45; Solíz Rada 2007).

For example, against the empires that seek to crush Latin American resistance and in support of the liberatory projects of Bolivarian inspiration, Soliz Rada writes:

> The alienators of the empire affirm that nationalism in the oppressed countries is like that of Franco, Hitler, and Mussolini. They do not admit that the defensive nationalism of the oppressed countries is antagonistic to the expansive and exploitative nationalism, the one that transforms into imperialism, of the oppressor countries. This rejection is intensified as the articulation of our defensive nationalisms advances in search of an endogenous socialism, with transparency and participatory democracy, without indefinite reelections or cults of personality, but capable of affirming national self-determination and achieving the effective re-investment of the economic surplus in benefit of our peoples [de los excedentes económicos en beneficio de nuestros pueblos]. [Soliz Rada 2007]

There are obvious articulations with the wider MAS agenda. In fact, Solíz Rada was the regime's first Minister of Hydrocarbons, later resigning after a dispute with the MAS over a contract with Brazil. Yet, in this view, redistributive nationalism conflictswith indigenous autonomy and plurinationalism. Against more robust indigenous claims to "plurinationalism" and "self-determination," the national left mobilizes the concepts of "indo-mestizo" and "interculturalism" (the latter a term also embraced by the neoliberals). Here the revindication of lo indio in a more generic, racialized, deterritorialized, and nonethnically specific sense is firmly ensconced within the national popular, part of a wider alliance of indio and mestizo, distinct from the framing of some (not all) indigenous thinkers who juxtapose indigeneity as opposed to the conjoined categories of blanco-mestizo (white-mestizo) (for example, Mamani, chapter 2, this volume). If, for Solíz Rada, the "indigenist" turn of Evo Morales threatens to mobilize the indigenous against both "whites" and "mestizos,"—then the only hope for Bolivia lies in an "indo-mestizo" alliance against imperialism and its local representatives, the regional oligarchs. (For their part, some regional oligarchs on the right have also embraced the category "mestizo," as discussed in the introduction).

This position maintains a defiant defense of a strong, unitarian model of the nation-state and a deep skepticism and distrust regarding indigenous epistemological, linguistic, and territorial projects for rethinking and decolonizing territorial orders. These positions—from both left and right—question in distinct ways the territorial and historical specificities of indigeneity, setting the stage for plurinational remappings to unfold in a tentative way.

Guaraní Imaginings

Settled across the Chaco and Andean foothills long before either Bolivians or Chaqueños existed, the indigenous peoples of the southeast face a complex set of contradictory political-territorial options. The largest population, the Guaraní (between sixty thousand and one hundred thousand) are politically significant though still political minorities in the region that was once theirs. They comprised almost a quarter of the region's population and have been at the forefront—or more accurately, have borne the brunt—of the rapid expansion of gas activities in the Bolivian southeast. Today, Guaraní territories exist in archipelago-like fragments with some established TCOs but no uniform or consolidated basis for exercising anything like autonomy or self-determination (see figures 1 and 2). The acceleration of gas development activities of the 1990s spurred a new phase of mobilization when Guaraní began confronting foreign companies and experiencing ecological and social dislocations (as well as the corruption of their leadership) as gas companies moved in to explore and extract gas on their lands (Humphreys Bebbington and Bebbington 2009; Humphreys Bebbington and Catari n.d.; Perrault 2008b). Some TCOs nonetheless wrangled concessions of money from the gas companies, though rarely was this redirected toward sustained productive initiatives. TCOs are thus important templates of struggle but are imagined both by the indigenous and by their detractors as potential competitors with municipalities and departments for gas royalties. The war of percentages—as the competition for gas rents is called—thus threatens to absorb indigenous agendas into rentier logics. With nationalism, things are not necessarily better. Companies such as Gazprom and Total have joined the rush on the region through joint ventures with YPFB, and some Guaraní say that it was easier dealing with multinationals in the neoliberal era than it is with the state. However, as evidenced in recent critiques of the eastern indigenous peoples by the MAS (including harsh statements by Morales and García Linera), any contestation is now taken as national betrayal. At this writing, indigenous organizations confront the state, the national oil company (YPFB), and a putatively indigenous president who appears to have backed off from the radical defense of indigenous rights to consultation. One

Guaraní friend said, "At least with the multinationals, we knew we had the enemy in front of us. Now the state is all around us." Lest these observations be taken as criticism of the MAS and a nostalgia for neoliberalism, I should add that the Guaraní nonetheless represent a key bastion of MAS support in the southeast.

Throughout mobilizations following 2003, indigenous organizations first demanded constitutional change and now, in the wake of its approval, are working to put into practice and writing their local visions of autonomy. With the new figure of the autonomous AIOCs inscribed in the constitution, their efforts focus on specific strategies and forms. In a handful of munici-palities (four out of fifteen with Guaraní presence), there is the possibility of moving forward through the municipal path. In most cases, however, Guaraní are not demographic majorities in municipal spaces—such as the Guaraní of the Itika Guasu region in O'Connor Province to the south, whose letter to regional elites is reproduced in the Visions section following this chapter. Their hopes lie in consolidating control over their TCO and ensur-ing the rights to consultation, compensation, monitoring, and some share in the benefits. Though challenging, the prospects of achieving some kind of self-determination in articulation with the state project are still central and real to a wider Guaraní dream of "reconstituting the Guaraní nation." What appears to be emerging, then, is a partial and modified decentralization in which the indigenization of some municipalities might advance and other territorial spaces will as yet see dramatic shifts. All of this unfolds against local opposition by both nationalist and civic elite regionalist groups, sug-gesting that while the spatialization of political logic intensifies, a "tribal-ized" ethnoterritorial reordering like that seen in oil-rich Nigeria is unlikely.

Provincial elites like those in Camiri are resisting these turns tooth and nail. When the Guaraní of the municipality to the north, Lagunillas, sought to convene the municipal council to call a referendum on indigenous autonomy, the non-Guaraní council members simply left town and headed to the site of their patrons—Santa Cruz. This echoes the ongoing strategy of the regionalist right: to resist the MAS by obstructing and undermining the im-plementation of legal procedures, through violence if necessary. In another case, that of the TCO of Alto Parapeti, provincial cattlemen, again backed by the elites of Santa Cruz, mobilized a region-wide blockade, arguing that the TCO was a plot by the MAS to bring in kollas and "amputate" spaces of the territories of the municipality (Gustafson 2010). Against this opposition, the Guaraní have tried to engage the more popular, MAS-aligned activists of the region—including, at times, the more militant nationalists—to negoti-ate articulations despite deeply divergent interests and imaginaries about the future of the region.

Productivist States and Pluralist Territorialities

I have tried to illustrate through juxtaposition the expressions of local and ultimately conflictive, reterritorializing agendas: the municipal elites who cling to their posts with the backing of wealthy Cruceño patrons; the nationalists who dream of rebuilding the glory days through state largesse and jobs in the new gas industry; and the Guaraní, who maneuver within and between to exploit the spaces opened to them by the state. Each articulates in a distinct way with other scales of power, "scale-making projects" (Tsing 2004) emanating from elsewhere, while each locally clashes and colludes through legal and extralegal measures and mobilizations. For the moment, because of the Guaranís' crucial geopolitical location, they have maintained the selective support of the state for portions of their agenda. Yet, beyond the talk of "indigenous autonomies" and the sympathies of influential intellectuals like Albó and Romero and the wider networks of advocacy they represent, there is another side of the state, the "productivist" one, which also confronts attempts to embrace pluralism.

The vice president, Alvaro García Linera, is equally versed and fluent in that expression of the "national popular will." Though there is not space here for a full engagement with the more complex formations of ideas and debates over economic pluralism in Bolivia (but see Wanderley 2008), García Linera's recent discourses on the Bolivian economy are revealing in this sense. In a recent address to the Bolivian Central Bank, García Linera (2009:12) selectively dismantled neoliberalism with a withering critique of its legacies and of the illusory idea that the free market would bring national development and salvation to Bolivia. "It was a racket [*estafa*]," he said, "the swindle of the century." In an economically centered register sprinkled with references to Marx and Hegel—distinct from his temporalization of indigenous resistances around Katari, Willka, and Evo—he elaborated on how the state would assume a role in facilitating the modernization of the country's plural economies, setting out an unwavering stance on the centrality of the state as the primary actor in development:

> We lost twenty years under the illusion that foreign capital was going to create a prosperous national economy, with equality and equity, when it has never done that in any part of the world and never will…. That is not its function, nor its task. They do not come for that. [Nor] can the small local bourgeoisie, rentier, and intermediary [achieve this]…what remains is the general popular and national will, that is to say, what we call the State. [García Linera 2009:12]

This would not be by replicating mistakes of state capitalism, nor by becoming a producer of goods, but by facilitating and articulating the array of premodern, mercantile, peasant, and artisanal modes of production that provide subsistence to more than 70 percent of the country.

> Our objective is a State that intervenes selectively and specifically [puntual] in the modern nuclei of the strategic production of surplus of the country and, at the same time, transfers technology, resources, infrastructure, and financing to other pockets [bolsones], axes [ejes], and spaces [espacios] of traditional noncapitalist, semi-capitalist, semi-mercantile, [artisanal], and communitarian economy. In the end, it will clearly be the State that takes leadership in all of this process, without obstructing economic activity but rather awakening internal potentialities, pushing forward internal development. [García Linera 2009:18]

Here is a crucial intellectual-political articulation, a space of heterogeneity and polyvocality within the state project that simultaneously pursues the National Productive Model for achieving modernity, through the embrace of economic pluralities, and the indigenous resurgence, which argues for its own kind of decolonizing plurality, pluralities whose possibilities may come into conflict with the hydrocarbon regime that sustains the entire transformative project. Here the developmentalist state clashes with more decolonizing visions of the plurinational. Is there the possibility that the state will open space for emergent economies linked to variegated modes of territorial use, occupation, and self-government? In a positive sense, the possibilities are twofold: first, that Bolivia might move away from the imposition of homogeneity or a singular model of economic extraction and accumulation as the goal and defining logic of sovereignty, toward a redistributive and democratizing political-economic project; second, that such a possibility will leave space for indigenous and other territorializing projects to remake society from the base of locally rooted symbolic and social particularities (Escobar 2008). This is neither radical nor utopian but is within the realm of possibility because it activates and legitimates—albeit with a reordering of power relations—already underlying and existing realities, the "living communities" on the ground. However, it does suggest that indigeneity, rather than decolonize and re-create the entirety of society in some non-Western way, will thrive as part of a wider composite of pluralities. As Carlos Romero described it at the event that opens this chapter, autonomy is something other than absolute "self-determination" as suggested by its English term (*auto-determinación* in Spanish). It is aimed more at "self-government" (autogobierno), with the latter implying articulation with the state and a circumscribed set of "attributes" (*competencias*). In a negative sense, the possibility also exists that the capitalization of the state by way of the surplus of gas yields a more sacrificial approach to indigenous rights, as suggested in the ongoing weakness of rights to prior consultation in Bolivia (Bebbington 2009).

Along with the other chapters in this volume, which examine this tension between territorializing projects and wider national articulations, I have explored interactions of state policy and local strategizing. While local movements like the Guaraní mobilize from below in pursuit of new modes of governance, they also, like all citizens, seek access to resources and social rights coming from above. This entails engaging and rethinking traditional frames of autonomy and self-determination in ways that transcend crude imaginaries of "ethnoterritorial" rights (Gustafson 2009a). Guaraní views of autonomy contrast somewhat with those of García Linera, although they are not mutually incompatible. In the series of workshops that fed into the writing of an initial autonomy statute, built on the concept that "power necessarily comes from below," Guaraní intellectual Felipe Román made an intense and evocative statement about what this might mean, situating it, as did García Linera, in the context of an unfinished history of decolonization:

> Since the Spanish arrived, they have displaced our way of life...taken our territory, our resources, appropriated what was always ours, and on top of it they subjugate us, they oppress us. When we go to milk their cows at four in the morning, when we cut the cane in the fields, when the women work in their homes, that is the wringing out of our labor. So what does Indigenous Autonomy mean? That we are going to free ourselves from oppression and live without conditions...that is the dream, to have our own lives, to live from our resources, from our own labor, to return again to drink kägui.[8] That is autonomy—to live in freedom, be free, sovereign, and independent.

Whether this convergence of the strong developmentalist state and robust forms of pluralist indigenous (and nonindigenous) "autonomy" is possible in the face of the resource boom sets out a challenge for researchers and activists in the coming years. With the ideal of a redistributive state that is able to utilize resources to pursue economic diversification while maintaining a principled stance on decolonization, indigenous and environmental rights, and social justice come the risks that might lead Bolivia into a Nigerian-style resource curse tied to the communalization of citizenship, a

Peruvian-style authoritarian extractivism, or a Chinese model of state-led developmentalism. But it is also, as imagined by Guaraní leaders such as Felipe Román, possible that there will emerge some day a new reality that transcends other ways of being to generate the utopia of "living well." For the Guaraní, this will be based both on territorial groundings and on the ability to move among the karai (whites) in cities and towns without replicating the colonial relations of extraction and nationalist models of exclusion that generated the reality of today. This is, in short, the conviv-encia that is yet to come. As state-led development and state-led regional planning become the new "consensus" in Latin America, engaged critical research must move beyond critiquing (only) state power to articulate the cultural-political and the economic across distinct scales, merging concerns that attempt the rethinking of regionalized models of sociality and economic production articulated with wider state visions of transformation (sovereignty, redistribution, equality, decolonization, and a new view of nature). Here lies a challenge to think of recognition and redistribution—both of material goods and epistemic rights to rethink and reorder territory—as inseparable components of indigenous self-determination in alliance with broader popular and national frameworks of state change. To work within and to maintain spaces for pluralist possibility, without seeking to reassert control over "prohibited" and "permitted" indigenous subjectivities, are tasks for scholars and activists alike.

Notes

1. CIPCA, Centro de Investigación y Promoción del Campesinado (Center for Research and Promotion of the Peasantry), is an NGO supported by the Catholic Church. CEJIS, Centro de Estudios Jurídicos Institucionales y Sociales (Center for Juridical, Institutional, and Social Studies), was a significant backer of and legal advisor to indigenous and rural farmers' movements and initially of the MAS project.

2. See Garcés, chapter 3, this volume, for a discussion of this terminology.

3. For background on the Guaraní movement, see Gustafson 2009a; Postero 2006.

4. There is some evidence of foreign (US) and right-wing infiltration or influence in indigenous organizations (a long-time strategy), yet recent attacks on eastern indigenous movements by the MAS regime have used the accusation in a hyperbolic way, sparking criticism of both Evo Morales and García Linera from within the MAS itself.

5. The comparison between the more conservative oil workers of the east and the revolutionary Andean miners of the period of the 1960s is yet to be written, but see Nash 1979, on the paradoxes of gender, militance, indigeneity, and dependency in the mines during this era.

6. This interview was carried out by Felipe Román, June 2009.

7. Eusebio Vargas, 82 years old, in an interview with Ubaldo Padilla September 2009.

8. Kãgui is a fermented corn-based beverage (*chicha*), whose moments of consumption for the Guaraní are marked by celebratory sociality, redistribution, and economic abundance.

Visions from the Ground
"Those Who Begrudge What They Have Deserve the Respect of No One"

In December 2007, Bolivia was in the midst of violent assaults on state institutions led by the right-wing proponents of departmental autonomy. These movements aimed at destabilizing and delegitimizing the national Constitutional Assembly in its final phases leading to the vote for its approval that month. The right wing was mobilized through civic committees, unelected bodies similar to chambers of commerce that present themselves as the organic representatives of the people in large cities such as Tarija and Santa Cruz. These urban-centered civic committees opposed the MAS and the constitution and were generally aligned against the movements of indigenous and nonindigenous poor in rural provinces, most of whom supported constitutional change. Nonetheless, the civic committees and autonomists often represented themselves as encouraging indigenous participation.

The letter reproduced below, written by a Guaraní organization to the Civic Committee of Tarija, questions how nonindigenous elites spoke for, rather than with, indigenous organizations.[1]

In addition to rejecting the legitimacy of the Civic Committee, this letter reveals in a profound way a distinctly Guaraní style of discourse surrounding an ideology of generosity and dialogue, a critique of self-centric autonomy. It is a clear illustration of how indigenous peoples—under whose ancestral lands lie most of the country's gas reserves—have chosen to pursue articulation and solidarity within a plurinational state rather than make demands for radical self-determination and absolute control over natural resources, a position generally attributed to indigenous peoples but one, in fact, closer to that held by the more exclusionary urban elites.

From the Assembly of Guaraní People to the Civic Committee of Tarija
Entre Ríos (Guaeye)
December 14, 2007

Mssrs.
Reynaldo Bayard
Patricia Galarza
Provincial Civic Committees
Members of the Civic Committee for the Interests of Tarija

Mssrs:

We received your letter of 11 December 2007, in which you summon us for the "grand Assembly of the People of the Department of Tarija" to be held in the Plaza de Armas, in Tarija. With respect to this, we, the 800 Guaraní families who have survived the colonial State and who continue to occupy the ancestral territory that our grandparents left to us in the jurisdiction of O'Connor Province, organized in 36 Captaincies and making up the Assembly of Guaraní People of Itika Guasu [APG-IG], we take the word [*tomamos la palabra*], and in the most respectful way, we direct ourselves to you, but also to all of those who for different reasons do not feel represented by the Civic Committee for the Interests of Tarija.

...In your invitation, you mention a resolution from your "Assembly of Tarija" in which the "originary peoples" participated. We have absolutely no knowledge of such a resolution, and we deny, as Guaraní people, having been present at such a meeting. We have never approved resolutions like those indicated in your invitation in support of departmental autonomy.

We want to remind you publicly that the Assembly of Guaraní People of Bolivia and we of the Itika Guasu have NEVER been in agreement with Departmental Autonomies, because the departments have divided us as Guaraní people, because the departments represent the colonial State that massacred our grandparents at Kuruyuki in 1892 and that subjected us to servitude, a system under which many of our Guaraní families continue living because their patrones control them with the whip and the stomach, in plain sight of corregidores, sub-prefects, prefects, deputies, senators…. This abuse has been documented by the United Nations, in the person of Mr. Rodolfo Stavenhagen, the special representative for indigenous rights, who visited the captive communities and saw with his own eyes the semi-slavery and was also a witness to the racism manifest in Sucre and other cities against indios and indígenas.

…In addition to defending our position of our indigenous autonomy [nuestra autonomía indígena], we have serious doubts about the promises of the civic leaders and authorities…and about departmental autonomy, because on the one hand, you "summon" us, as if giving us orders to go to a Grand Assembly, and on the other, violent groups threaten our leaders if we do not obey, just as the landlords did with our grandparents.

As Guaraní, [we] did not invent autonomy a year or two ago. Historically, we were autonomous, and for that in our political and cultural principles we speak of being *IYAMBAE* [Guaraní, "without masters"], and although it is taking us more than a century, our struggle is to liberate ourselves from all masters. We cannot think about departmental autonomy when our own way of being is signaling to us that we should struggle for our self-determination [auto-determinación] as indigenous people.

…We Guaraní, having been marginalized by the Bolivian state, have proposed the RE-FOUNDATION of Bolivia. Nonetheless, throughout the process of the Constitutional Assembly…we ceded in our demands. For example, [we acquiesced to] maintaining the nine departments that create boundaries among Guaraní, to accepting the idea of departmental autonomies that concentrates power in the capital cities and marginalizes provinces and communities, and to accepting that natural resources should remain in the hands of the State when we believe that the true owners are indigenous peoples.

We recount this situation so that you know that the Guaraní respect the rights and the way of life of other peoples and that we only ask the same respect that is given to a human being, that our culture be respected, our community life, our collective production, that we not be obligated to dress or speak like *karai* [Guaraní, "nonindigenous, whites"] to be heard, that our authorities be given credence, and that our customs be given value. We only want, like most people, to live well, to benefit from the natural resources that come from our territory, such as wood, fish, salt, and hydrocarbons, such that the territory not be exploited like wind that at its passing leaves us only destruction.

We have listened until our ears hurt about how the Civic Committee defends the territorial integrity of its department, even declaring itself independent and producing many words about [gas] royalties and taxes, and we still do not understand. For the past [twenty] years, we have been demanding our territory, the return of lands that were taken from us by force or by law of the colonial State, appropriated by single powerful families or handed over to cattlemen by the [1952] land reform, making them owners of our land and our new bosses. We have been fighting since 1996 for our TCO [communal lands of origin] and until now have not achieved our rights. This is because you [the Civic Committee] have been fighting against it.

We know that the department will receive 11 [percent] of gas royalties…but we Guaraní of Itika Guasu are the direct victims of the damages and effects that the exploitation of gas in the Margarita field is causing. We have been demanding of REPSOL-YPF for ten years that it respect us, and in all those years, we NEVER heard a word from the Civic Committee in defense of our rights. The authorities and civics have fought among themselves, but not to improve the lives of those of us who live in the rural area, only to control the money of the royalties of the Margarita field. We have asked to participate, but they have never given us the word;[2] they have even denied our existence.

Because we, the Guaraní, are the most affected, we should most benefit from royalties or taxes. But as a sign that we are not self-centric [egoistas], we have never complained of the fact that from the gas that is taken out of Itika Guasu, many brothers and sisters are eating in La Paz, Pando, Santa Cruz, or the city of Tarija. If there are resources, our culture teaches us that one has to show solidarity, that we should share. We think that the elderly should benefit from the gas payments of the special tax,[3] and if we were to deny that the money that comes out of the hydrocarbons of our territory should be used to pay them this pension, we would not be able to look them in the face—we would have to live in shame and run around hiding ourselves until our death. That is how our culture is: those who begrudge what they have deserve the respect of no one, because what our Tüpa [god] has given us, nobody can appropriate. It belongs to all.

Finally, we want to thank you for the invitation that you sent us to attend the Grand Assembly of Tarija, because we have thus been able to know your heart and understand better your ideas. Because we refuse to participate in such a meeting, we ask that you not feel offended by this reply, because just as we have read with patience your words, we hope that you will also do so with ours. Thanks to this *tupapire* [paper], we are repeating many things that we have said to other people, but perhaps for the first time to some, and do so only with the desire to know ourselves better and with true respect.

Just as we have ceded demands…we ask that you open your hearts and minds, because this moment in which everyone is heated up is going to pass and we and you will continue here and our children and grandchildren will continue here, so it is not good that we show them destruction and violence…. That we understand and respect ourselves depends on our no longer living in poverty, that we eliminate discrimination and racism that we have suffered for centuries and still feel. On you, on us, and on all depends the construction of a new State: unitary, which takes all into account, indigenous and nonindigenous; strong, with departmental and indigenous autonomies; diverse and unified, unlike any others because it is ours; a State made to our measure, without imitations or recipes.

That is what we feel and think. *Yasurupay* [Thank you].

Signed [leaders of the APG-IG]

P.S. Because we believe that our word should not be confined within the four walls of the Civic Committee, we submit this letter for the consideration of national and international public opinion.

Notes

1. Letter received by email, December 2007. Capitalization from the original.

2. To give us the word, the right to speak.

3. The Guaraní refer here to the Dignity Payment (Renta Dignidad), a universal pension for elderly financed with monies from a special tax on natural gas and oil. The payment was opposed by department elites, from whose share of royalties some of these monies were taken.

9 *Epilogue*

Charles R. Hale

The arc of the moral universe is long, but it bends toward justice.
—*Dr. Martin Luther King Jr.*

"…So that my daughter will not end up being your servant."
—*Response of the Aymara leader Felipe "el Mallku" Quispe when Bolivian journalist Amalia Pando asked him why he joined an armed guerrilla movement in the 1980s*

There is much in the past three decades of Bolivia's history that provides eloquent backing for Dr. King's prophetic image, and this book echoes that conclusion while also nudging us to rethink the metaphor. The transformations achieved through the cumulative effects of three decades of social movements, culminating with the Morales presidency, are remarkable: powerful indigenous collective voice and citizenship; radical political alternatives debated in high-stakes public arenas such as the Constitutional Assembly; adamant commitments emanating from the state to eliminate historic inequities. The "voices from the ground" in this volume—interludes among the academic chapters in which frontline actors speak—dramatize the contrast: from the president himself, to indigenous intellectuals in the Chaco, these voices convey a collective power and an historic self-confidence unimaginable, for example, in Domitila Chungara's inspiring testimony of the 1970s, "*Si me permiten hablar*." But there is also a whole lot in this book that complicates any linear account of progressive change: contradictions between state- and community-driven paths of social transformation; virulent (often racist) backlash, which requires negotiated concessions; outright failures in political practice, especially painful for those who, in 2006, had such soaring aspirations. Dr. King's majestic arc, with a gentle, reassuring bend toward justice, starts to look much more like a crooked line: still confirming the conclusion, if you squint from a distance, but constantly threatening to turn back on itself.

The year 1980 is a somewhat arbitrary point of historical reference chosen mainly because that was the last year I spent any significant time in the country. But it could also represent a political "ground zero" of sorts, when the bloody military coup led by Garcia Meza decimated the democratic left, suppressed all civil society–based political mobilization, and set the stage for a particularly draconian program of neoliberal economic reform. Working as a neophyte activist anthropologist, under the tutelage of an Aymara intellectual and community organizer named Max Paredes, I researched a senior thesis on a fledgling association of llama and alpaca herders based in a remote zone of provincia Pacajes. The association's principal goals revolved around economic empowerment: fair market conditions for wool, opportunities to make and sell artisan goods, an end to racist prohibitions on the sale of llama meat in the cities. The truly visionary element in Don Max's leadership was to pursue economic empowerment while rejecting sindicatos and cooperatives as Western impositions and to insist on a recuperated and revitalized ayllu as the association's organizational foundation (Healy 2001). In accompanying this effort, I fancy having caught a glimpse of the formative phase of one principal current of political mobilization that would bring Morales to power twenty-five years later.

I experienced the contrast very directly during a brief visit to La Paz in July 2010, exactly thirty years after the Garcia Meza coup. With Evo Morales entering the second term of his presidency, the military remained in the barracks, and army leaders appeared to have made their peace with the "Movimiento al Socialismo," whatever that actually means. The government operated under a new constitution, the achievements and implications of which are deeply contested (including in these pages) but which represents a momentous step away from the "constitutive exclusions" of its predecessors toward the endorsement of cultural pluralism and equality, with at least rhetorical openings for radical alternatives. Although aspirations outstrip political practice at every turn, I was deeply impressed to find spaces of the state that had been transformed in ways that are bound to have material and symbolic reverberations for years to come: indigenous universities devoted to expanding educational opportunities to the marginalized majority; a Vice Ministry of Decolonization, charged with transforming the "colonial" political culture of state and society; a Defensor del Pueblo (literally, Defender of the People, a human rights ombudsman) who has taken substantive steps to place anti-Indian racism at the top of the agenda; a school for future diplomats, housed in the Foreign Ministry and run by an Aymara intellectual with deep roots in the indigenous movement, whose boss, the Foreign Minister, is also a leading Aymara intellectual. Whatever the particular outcomes, a good deal of "remapping" of state and society is no doubt going on.

This book's broad purpose is to describe these processes and to help us gauge their repercussions, with a particular emphasis on the spatial. Although the principal contributions are—very appropriately—close to the ground, fully engaged with the urgent and momentous unfolding political drama, this parallel theoretical project should not go unnoticed. In a cumulative and highly interdisciplinary fashion, the chapters yield an approach for using spatial differentiation—in its material and symbolic dimensions—as a window on political contention. The macroregional division between the media luna departments and the highlands is the most evident spatial backdrop for this contention, and some of the chapters trace how the historic regional divide has been reframed as a contest between incommensurable identities, which at times even overshadow economic interests. Debates on autonomy encapsulate this divide and go much further, raising the possibility of a true remapping of Bolivian democracy: not just decentralization, but spatially differentiated forms of governance. More broadly still, some contributions show how space—quite apart from the political-administrative project of autonomy—becomes the focus of politics: urban vendors' struggles for rights to occupy locales favorable to market their wares (Kirshner, chapter 5); islands of land rights for dispossessed workers amid a sea of soy agribusiness (Fabricant, chapter 7); equal public services for El Alto, whose residents feel they were deprived a fair shake on racial grounds (Revilla, chapter 6). Finally, as Revilla's study makes explicit, to address the politics of space in Bolivia inevitably involves coming to terms with how spatial differentiation is imbued with racial meanings. If, as critical geographers have taught us in recent years, maps embody and express power relations, then this book may be thought to offer a corollary: to remap these power relations, in a society like Bolivia, inevitably brings racial inequalities and political dialogue about race pointedly to the fore.

Here is where the line turns especially crooked. These processes, which the book's rich contents trace, are anything but linear: their outcomes often are surprising, highly variable, and in many ways profoundly uncertain. Using these contributions as empirical base and analytical sounding board, I will reflect briefly on four topics that I found especially resonant, situated in rough chronological order along the crooked line.

The first concerns the previous regime, epitomized by the first (relatively successful) and the second (disastrous) terms of Sánchez de Lozada. In what ways did this classic example of neoliberal multiculturalism set the stage for the transformations that would follow? As a target of repudiation only? Or also, paradoxically, as an incubator of dissent? Second, after Morales took office in 2006, political contention soon took on a dramatically *racialized* form of polarization. How can this be explained without recourse to an action-reaction reasoning, which makes this fundamentally contingent outcome appear natural or inevitable? Third is the question of autonomies—adamantly in the plural because so many different meanings of the term swirl around the debate that the multiplicity at times threatens incoherency. Did the right, and its particular version of autonomy, hijack the debate? Finally, returning to the theoretical insights about race and space, there is a question about political horizons: if indigenous empowerment remains central to the broader vision of social transformation unleashed by the Morales presidency, can this be achieved without racial polarization? Can the protagonists "de-racialize" politics without falling back on well-known liberal solutions that depoliticize race?

What Did Neoliberal Multiculturalism Do?

The first question calls out for attention, even if it is not the book's central focus. A number of authors, including me, have made forceful arguments over the past decade about the "menace" of Latin America's multicultural turn (see Hale 2002). Although hardly deterministic in their message or uniform in their normative implications, these arguments have generally emphasized the governance effects of conjoined regimes of multicultural recognition and neoliberal economic reforms. The phrase "governance effects," as I use it at least, is focused primarily on subject formation: how these regimes open spaces that shape and channel the subjectivities of those who come to occupy them. They become "pragmatic," compliant, and accustomed to the pleasant benefits of working in such spaces, distanced from the communities and community-based processes that produced them as leaders, disinclined toward the radical tactics and demands that helped to produce the spaces in the first place. Did these governance effects take hold under Sánchez de Lozada? And if so, how did they unravel so quickly in 2003?

In the introduction, Gustafson and Fabricant provide a general answer, which in part plays out empirically in the book's chapters, but also calls out for additional scrutiny. They suggest that the problem is merely theoretical: a preoccupation of outsider academics, who have dwelled on the contradictions between neoliberalism and multiculturalism and worried excessively about governance effects, in marked contrast to the protagonists who simply appropriated the openings while maintaining de facto movement autonomy. These protagonists, one infers, played the multicultural moment for whatever they could get and at the same time were integral to the protests and mobilization that brought the MAS to power. Revilla's chapter 6 account of political organizing in El Alto does give some credence to this narrative. Neoliberal policies of decentralized participation resulted in political fragmentation for many years, he reports, but at a crucial moment activists were able to weave together a collective project that offered a "space for cohesion among ideologically diverse leaders." Fabricant's chapter 7 also shows how peasant migrants from the highlands reconstituted themselves as a land rights movement in lowland Santa Cruz, inspired by collective memories of the ayllu, and they advanced militant collective agendas undeterred by neoliberal subject formation. Gustafson's work on the Guaraní, in this volume (chapter 8) and other publications, makes the point most extensively; he follows Guaraní language and bilingual education activists who relocate to La Paz to take World Bank–funded jobs in the Ministry of Education, all the while keeping their eyes on the prize, using the openings for ends very different from what the architects of these reforms intended.

My sense is that Gustafson and Fabricant's corrective is welcome but the careful work of theoretical revision has yet to be accomplished and the unraveling of the Sánchez de Lozada regime in the first years of the new century is a crucial empirical setting for such an effort. It will be especially important that this revisionist analysis focus on the subjects of neoliberal multicultural policies *and* the primary protagonists of the protests and mobilizations, making sure that they were, in fact, one and the same. What first comes to mind with some of these protagonists—*cocaleros* (coca farming peasants organized in defense of their rights), indigenous migrants and unemployed miners in El Alto, displaced highlanders of the MST—is an incorrigible subject, more inclined to militant mestizaje than the neatly bounded identity categories of indigeneity that neoliberal multiculturalism promotes. Put differently, if "Indianist" consciousness was less central in Morales's rise to power than militant mestizaje, then the puzzle becomes a lot less salient. To seal the counter-argument advanced in the introduction, Gustafson and Fabricant needed an account of a quintessentially highland indigenous organization such as CONAMAQ or the Bartolinas, the national women's peasant and indigenous union.[1] As composed, the book does not provide quite enough empirical substance to dislodge the paradox, which leaves the reader wondering whether the editors' counter-argument might be driven, in part, by wishful thinking.

Where Did the Racial Eruptions Come From?

Whatever the role of Indianist consciousness in the undoing of Goni, there is no doubt about its growing importance once Evo came to power and about the virulently racist reaction against the preposterous idea that Bolivia would have an Indian president. The documentary *Humillados y ofendidos* (Brie 2008), which covers one such racial eruption, leaves two indelible images in the mind: the brutal, ritualized public torment of indigenous peasants, carried out by urban youth who in phenotypic terms could barely be distinguished from their victims, and the criollo-mestizo "expert" clearly pained by what happened but assiduously avoiding reference to racism, explaining the acts as part of a long history of urban–rural tensions in Chuquisaca. The chapters in this book—especially Soruco Sologuren's moving analysis of the Pando massacre (chapter 4)—offer a welcome corrective to this dissimulation, examining carefully how spatial differentiation is historically constituted, infused with power relations, and (at least in the cases we have before us) thoroughly racialized. Soruco Sologuren walks us through the logic of this racialization: how the regional "Camba" identity slips easily into a bald assertion of whiteness; how this whiteness carries a naturalized premise of supremacy in relation to darker-skinned and culturally different Bolivians; how even moderate indigenous ascendancy provokes indignation, then fear, which "rapidly turns into hatred...that at times appears to exude from every pore of eastern society." Although the book does not include as systematic an account of elite or middle-class responses to the Morales government in other parts of the country, there are inklings in Mamani Ramirez's chapter 2, and a general sense that race is never far from the surface in how political contention is signified.

The question that follows is whether this basic observation—that Bolivia is a society historically structured in racial dominance (to paraphrase Stuart Hall [1980])—is enough. Is this enough to explain the horrifically excessive racial eruptions, such as the Pando massacre that Soruco Sologuren narrates, or the spectacle of racial hatred in Sucre? Soruco Sologuren apparently thinks not. After laying the groundwork of what I would call a racial formation argument, her reasoning takes a (Fanonian?) psychological turn. When the constitutive master–slave (that is, white–Indian) relationship is called into question, she argues, in an arresting turn to the first person: "My subjectivity crumbles, and I do not attempt to articulate anything more than naked violence, panic, decadence, and defeat." I am not sure what to do with this line of explanation. On the one hand, these eruptions do cry out for something more than a structural analysis of racial hierarchy, challenged and defended in a predictable action-reaction pattern. On the other hand, I worry about a psychological analysis that could lead us to pass too quickly over these structural dimensions. As Kirshner's chapter 5 on contention over urban space shows nicely, basic material issues (such as who gets to sell their goods in prime locations) lurk just beneath the surface of extravagant accusations of "Colla invasion" and "avasallamiento." Revilla makes a similar point in chapter 6, tracing the racially charged differentiation between the two sectors of El Alto to perceived inequities in the distribution of public goods. Rather than venture an argument on this question, the editors, perhaps wisely, leave it to the readers themselves to sort out the different positions that the authors put forth.

I am highly receptive in intellectual terms to Soruco Sologuren's inclination to delve deeper, but practical political considerations would lead me to prioritize basic ethnographic description (what people do and the stories they tell about what they have done) and racial formation analysis. This surely leaves out many layers of complexity associated with deeper psychological processes, but it lays out an ample agenda of high-priority work to be done. The response to Amalia Pando's question, reproduced in the epigraph, makes the argument nicely. Felipe Quispe's quip is both a vast simplification of a complex social field and a brilliant encapsulation of the central problem that seems to haunt Bolivian politics. It would not help much if we had to explain how his urbanized grandchildren could become the tormentors of their rural cousins or even to explain why elites would react with such venom to such a moderate and universalist call for equality. But it does reiterate a basic fact of Indianness (to paraphrase Fanon [1967]), which must hold a key to the pervasive racialization of Bolivian politics. Even without understanding the problem completely, the first remedial steps to follow are pretty clear.

Has the Racial Right Hijacked the Autonomy Debate?

If race has become both a focus of contention and something of a "floating signifier" in its political deployment, then autonomy goes even further, pushing the axiom past its breaking point. At least four distinct meanings of the term animate the various narratives in these pages, at times in direct engagement with one another but often in separate arenas and radically different political conversations. Garcés (chapter 3) explicates the first two in his fascinating account of the Constitutional Assembly: a "liberal decentralization" defined and controlled by the state—which eventually won out in the Constitution's text—versus a radical pluralist autonomy, predicated on a deterritorialization of the state, driven by a distinctly indigenous notion of temporal-spatial organization and governance. Other chapters, especially

Fabricant's chapter 7, introduce a third, quite different notion, grounded in community, constituted in struggle, outside the bounds of readily recognized indigenous traditions, and probably too fluid to be codified by the state as a "right." Fourth and finally, various authors allude to and provide sketches of the Camba claims for autonomy: regional in reach; a historically recent response to having lost disproportionate influence in the state; having thinly disguised racial underpinnings, in relation both to indigenous people within and to the specter of Colla-instigated avasallamiento. (I can add a fifth variant —espoused by my former mentor Max Paredes, now an octogenarian, still going strong as the intellectual force behind the Aymara Parliament—which claims sovereignty in relation to all four "neocolonial" nation-states home to the Aymara [Peru, Chile, Bolivia, and Argentina].) The first observation to make about this bewildering array of significations is that it complicates the political dialogue immensely to have all four (or five?) simultaneously at play. This analytical question follows: has the right managed to frame the narrative (to use a notion current in US politics) so that the different meanings of autonomy have all been subordinated to its own? If so, how and with what consequences?

The conclusion that surely is the most comfortable for anyone with political inclinations like those of the authors (or for that matter my own) is yes, the racial right has, in effect, poisoned the well. The Media Luna elite represents immensely powerful economic interests, with an already well-developed discourse of regional identity, which neatly stands as the Morales government's antithesis. Following a well-trodden path of Latin American nation building, they even discovered mestizaje as the essential idiom of regional/national identity formation, finding it much more effective than the crude, polarizing eruptions of white supremacy. Regional autonomy also provides an ingenious means to confound long standing Oriente indigenous demands for autonomy, dramatized by the plaintive letter from the Guaraní leaders, who report having listened to the Cruceños's statements in support of "territorial integrity" of the department "until [their] ears hurt" and they still "did not understand." Given the Morales state's principled support for "autonomy" and its virtual obligation to negotiate with rather than suppress the Cruceño uprising, the racial right gets its solution on a silver platter. Once this regional (departmental) version of autonomy wins official endorsement, it becomes nearly impossible for any of the others to prosper in the Media Luna departments and difficult even in the highlands. Autonomy is resignified as sedition; to support indigenous empowerment, one must, first and foremost, defend the state.

Another, much less comfortable story also comes through in these pages. It places greater emphasis on the Morales state's ambivalence about indigenous autonomy from the start. Garcés's account (chapter 3) of the demise of the "plural-territorial" version of autonomy in the Constitutional Assembly is especially eloquent in probing this contradiction. Residual national-popular ideological commitments and state-centered development strategies do not sit well with expansive notions of autonomy, which tend to have, in Garcés's words, other "civilizatory horizons." Ambivalence turns to outright refusal in areas where autonomy might interfere with rents from resource extraction, a point that Gustafson makes clear in his discussion (chapter 8) of Guaraní territorial politics in the petroleum-rich Chaco. Although media luna sedition could not have been too far from anyone's minds in the Constitutional Assembly, Garcés leaves the distinct impression that the defeat of the peasant-indigenous Unity Pact had more to do with the state-centered political logic, in general, than the poisoned well effect of regional autonomy. His recommended antidote follows: return to the grass-roots mobilization that brought Morales to the presidency, focus on the "recovery of power for the popular and indio civil society," *not* for the salvation of the state.

This second line of explanation is another quintessential example of the crooked line. Garcés's critical analysis, like those of Arturo Escobar (2010) and Raquel Gutiérrez (2008) , is compelling and in some respects definitive. If the collective voices favoring the "radical pluralist" version of autonomy, embodying the alternative times, knowledges, and spaces of popular and indigenous struggle that Gutiérrez calls the "ritmos del Pachakuti," (the rhythms of Upheaval), are squeezed out by a state-centered concentration of power and resources and by a top-down economic strategy that clings to worn-out notions of "development" and "progress," then the Morales–Garcia Linera project will sooner or later be drained of its inspiring potential. Yet, at present (September 2010), especially because the media luna departments have succeeded in framing the narrative around autonomy, to assert that the state now has become the enemy would be to miss the mark. Beyond the obvious collective interest in fending off a "reconquista" from the Oriente, there is the key question of how much the Morales state allows, and perhaps even enables, the spaces of "radical pluralist" autonomy, despite its ambivalence in the realm of constitutionally endorsed rights. A parallel question applies for the admittedly discouraging image of a Morales state firmly committed to policies of economic redistribution and equality, which are sustainable only with revenues from state-controlled extractive business-as-usual. If the state follows this compromised but pragmatically coherent path, will historians thirty years from now note the contradiction but still portray its arc as having been bent toward justice?

Gustafson's answer to this last question, like that of Garcés, is an emphatic "maybe." The best-case scenario that he sees is an unwieldy articulation: that utopian visions, necessarily coming from below, stay mobilized and true to their principles and find ways to take advantage of the limited spaces that remain open, amid the general turn to a state-driven extractivist economy. Ironically enough, at least for the Guaraní, this scenario sounds a lot like the strategy they fashioned in response to the previous era's contradictory terrain of neoliberal multiculturalism. This irony is not lost on the Guaraní themselves, who report to Gustafson that "it was easier dealing with multinational companies in the neoliberal era," when the enemy was clear, as opposed to now, when the state labels "any contestation as national betrayal." But this irony needs to be paired with another, focused on the indigenous majority of the highlands. Given the character of the Morales state and the formidable political threat from the Oriente, it may well be that *autonomy* has lost its traction as a keyword in their struggles for social transformation. Silvia Rivera Cusicanqui (2008) has identified the most expansive political aspiration of the movement that brought Morales to power, after all, as the elaboration and implementation of a "logic of the majority," which would subordinate all questions of local or regional autonomy to a thoroughgoing "Indianization" of the polity. Granted, a call for "Indianization" leaves many questions unanswered and raises concerns as well, especially if the state were to retain a role as agent of change. But it does open at least the theoretical possibility of a political project for indigenous empowerment that makes no necessary recourse to autonomy.

Can Bolivia "Indianize" and at the Same Time "De-racialize" Politics?

Amid much debate about the extent to which "indigenous" collective actors have taken center stage in Bolivian politics and about the implications this Indianization might have, the hope has come to the fore that political relations could be "de-racialized." In some discourses, such as the interview excerpt with Evo Morales near the beginning of this volume, the idea remains implicit. He and Garcia Linera advocate an Andean capitalism with a socialist ethos, with the strong hand of the state to assure the overall direction of change, but not to meddle excessively with market forces, with state authority as counter-weight to the powerful political-economic interests of the Oriente but otherwise as a guardian of pluralism. This political vision grows a little more charged, however, when it becomes clear that pluralism comes with empowerment of the Indian majority, with proportionate indigenous representation in the state and the economy, including all political variants of Indianismo, from the Aymara *ponchos rojos* (red ponchos) of Achacachi and the Indian-accented MST communities in the midst of Santa Cruz "soyscapes," to the much less threatening identity politics of, say, Victor Hugo Cárdenas. When this expression of pluralism gets the nod, the racial right cries foul, and the "racialization" of politics summarizes all that has gone wrong. While one response to this hyperbole is simply to reiterate the thoroughly liberal principles of electoral democracy (after all, Morales won the second round with a remarkable 64.2 percent of the popular vote), but the ethnic demography and historic racial formation of Bolivia inevitably give these principles a sharp edge. Mamani Ramirez drives the point home in a succinct summary of the principal message of his chapter 2: "We are establishing an ethnic democracy to break with the white-mestizo ethnic dictatorship." When Indians have a solid majority, the basic principles of liberal democracy could be all that is needed for "Indianization" to win the day.

This analytical question follows: is it reasonable, theoretically and politically, to speak of "Indianization" and "de-racialization" as parts of the same utopian horizon? In some respects, this question, like the first one I posed on neoliberal multiculturalism, stands outside the authors' primary gaze. But, implicitly at least, it emerges powerfully from these pages. Most of the authors refer to the ugly racialization of politics from the right, which they understand in some measure as a response to indigenous political ascendancy. Gustafson quotes Vice President Garcia Linera as invoking the rebellion of Tupak Katari, saying essentially that Bolivian politics has been in search of *modos de convivencia* (means of coexistence) ever since. Then, following on direct references to long-standing racial polarization, deepened in current times by the collective assertion of the subordinated group, culture swoops in to the rescue. Indigenous political assertion is not about race, but culture; cultural convivencia (often referred to as *inter-culturalidad*) is perfectly conceivable, but interracial coexistence apparently is not; racialization comes solely from the history of racial hierarchy and from the defensive over-reaction of the right, but not from indigenous collective assertion (unless, perhaps, the protagonists stray from the script).

We can heartily endorse the aspirations expressed in this chain of assertions (dialogue and coexistence, without sacrificing principled antiracism and indigenous empowerment) while at the same time raising some doubts about the underlying premises. In the first place, it is hard to imagine how indigenous ascendancy could be achieved without, at least initially, sharpening the boundaries between Indians and those who historically have occupied positions of privilege in the racial hierarchy. To be sure, neither the boundaries nor the identities they enclose need to be conceived in essentialist terms. They could well embody the kind of mestizo Indianization of which Silvia Rivera Cusicanqui writes and could challenge each and every premise that traps Indians in the static space of tradition or the romanticized discourse of new age *cosmovisión* (or pachamamismo, as discussed in the introductory chapter).[2] Still, or perhaps especially, this collective militancy would challenge the inherited racial privilege of white-mestizos, a challenge almost inevitably perceived by the white-mestizos themselves as racial. Perhaps it would help to emphasize that this is about the political ascendancy of a cultural project, not the empowerment of all those who have a certain skin tone. But this distinction—valid and crucial as it may be—does grow a little tenuous, given that the great preponderance of those who adhere to the cultural project do, in fact, have that skin tone and the great preponderance of their adversaries do not.

My point is not to deny the potential of "cultural politics" to transcend the double-bind of racialization, but rather to highlight how the call for "de-racialization" implicitly becomes a proposal for unilateral disarmament. This is certainly a common pattern in other places where I have lived and worked: everyone agrees to privilege culture; continued collective assertions of rights and empowerment by the historically subordinated group are denounced as a violation of that agreement; if these persist, the subordinated group is guilty of "reverse racism." Moreover, historically and contemporarily, in most places, among most peoples, there is massive slippage between race and culture, such that cultural reasoning often rests upon racial premises and racial discourse often erupts only to retreat onto the safer and more acceptable terrain of cultural difference. Although it would be more politically comfortable to maintain that only the right racializes, in the face of adamant indigenous-popular attempts to keep politics cultural, it is almost certainly more accurate to say that both sets of premises infuse the language of contention, with unpredictable ebbs and flows, eruptions, and retreats on both sides.

The broader message of this argument is not to take recourse to some kind of relativism in which everyone is playing the race card on everyone else. To the contrary, it is to ask about the risks involved if "de-racialization" became an unquestioned descriptive feature of the Morales political project. On at least two occasions during a week of public events in July 2010, Enriqueta Huanca, an activist-intellectual from the Bartolina Sisas, insisted that we cannot/should not "depoliticize race," because to do so would be to ignore history. Whether or not it follows that we cannot/should not "de-racialize politics" depends centrally on our understanding of race. If race inevitably calls forth biologically fixed human characteristics, then by all means, let's give culture a whirl. However, if race is deployed and understood as a social construction, with ample possibilities for fusion and change, then keeping politics "racialized"—in the sense of explicitly naming the sensibilities, fears, identities, and hierarchies at play—could become a means to affirm Huanca's insistent statement of principle. The key here is the phrase "understood as," a reference not to theory but to popular consciousness. Ultimately, the question is how to keep forward motion toward a society in which the grandchildren of Amalia Pando and Felipe Quispe have roughly equivalent life chances. If anyone can think of a plausible means to achieve this social change, while banning race and its many euphemisms from the political lexicon of all those involved, now would be a good time to speak.

Notes

1. CONAMAQ is the (Andean) National Council of Aymara and Quechua Ayllus and Mallkus. The Bartolinas, named after the anticolonial heroine Bartolina Sisa, are the Bartolina Sisa National Confederation of Indigenous, Peasant and Originary Women (Confederación Nacional de Mujeres Campesinas Indígenas Originarias de Bolivia "Bartolina Sisa"). It is the women's counterpart to the largely Andean, although national in scope, CSUTCB (Confederation of Peasant Workers of Bolivia).

2. See, among others, Rivera Cusicanqui 2008.

About the Contributors

Nicole Fabricant is an assistant professor of anthropology at Towson University in Maryland. She received her PhD from Northwestern University in 2009 in socio-cultural anthropology. Her scholarship focuses on the cultural politics of resource wars in Bolivia. She is completing a manuscript on the rise of the Landless Peasant Movement (MST-Santa Cruz) and the political use of invented traditions from the Andes to shape alternative ideology and new agro-ecological models of development in lowland Bolivia. Her current research centers on resource battles over scarce water resources in El Alto, Bolivia, and the struggles of organizing around issues of climate change.

Fernando Garcés is a linguist and pedagogue with an MA in social sciences from FLACSO (La Facultad Latinoamericana de Ciencias Sociales) in Quito, Ecuador, and a PhD in Latin American cultural studies from the Universidad Andina Simón Bolivar in Quito. He has worked for many years with issues of indigenous territorial governance and bilingual intercultural education in Bolivia and Ecuador and was part of the technical team of the Indigenous Unity Pact during the Bolivian constitutional reform. He is currently a fellow at CLACSO (El Consejo Latinoamericano de Ciencias Sociales) in Buenos Aires, Argentina, and an affiliated researcher at the Institute of Anthropological Research at the Universidad Mayor de San Simón in Cochabamba, Bolivia.

Bret Gustafson is an associate professor of anthropology at Washington University in St. Louis. He has studied state transformation and worked with and for indigenous organizations in Bolivia since 1992. His book *New Languages of the State: Indigenous Resurgence and the Politics of Knowledge in Bolivia* (Duke, 2009) examined the politics of bilingual and intercultural education, neoliberal reform, and indigenous rights. His current research focuses on the cultural geopolitics of energy resources, indigenous territorial rights, and state-led developmentalism in Bolivia and Brazil.

Charles R. Hale is professor of anthropology, director of the Teresa Lozano Long Institute of Latin American Studies at the University of Texas, Austin, and former president of the Latin American Studies Association. He is the author of *Resistance* *and Contradiction: Miskitu Indians and the Nicaraguan State, 1894–1987* (Stanford, 1994) and *Más Que un Indio: Racial Ambivalence and Neoliberal Multiculturalism in Guatemala* (SAR Press, 2006), and editor of *Engaging Contradictions: Theory, Politics and Methods of Activist Scholarship* (UC Press, 2008). His research examines themes of identity politics, racism, neoliberalism, and resistance of indigenous peoples of Latin America.

Joshua Kirshner is a lecturer in the Geography Department at Rhodes University in Grahamstown, South Africa. Kirshner received a PhD in city and regional planning from Cornell University in 2009 and wrote a dissertation on urban development and migration in Santa Cruz, Bolivia. Kirshner lived and worked in Bolivia for three years and conducted research in Bolivia, Mexico, Brazil, the United States, and South Africa. His current research focuses on migration, regional development, and extractive economies in South Africa and Mozambique.

Pablo Mamani Ramirez is a Bolivian sociologist. He has an MA from FLACSO (Ecuador) and is completing a PhD in Latin American studies at the Universidad Nacional Autónoma de México (UNAM). Mamani Ramirez is the author of several influential works, including *El rugir de las multitudes* (Aruwiyiri-Yachaywasi, 2004), and *Microgobiernos barriales* (CADES-IDIS-UMSA, 2005). He teaches at the Public University of El Alto (UPEA) and is the founder and current editor of the journal *Willka*.

Carlos Revilla is a Bolivian anthropologist. He graduated from the Universidad de San Andrés in La Paz with a licenciatura in anthropology in 2007 and is currently completing an MA in development and globalization. He works as a researcher and popular educator at the Bolivian Institute of Research and Action for Integral Development (IIADI), a grassroots organization focused on urban socio-economic development in El Alto, Bolivia. His scholarship focuses on power relations, neighborhood organizing, and urban development in the Bolivian Andes.

Ximena Soruco Sologuren received her PhD from the University of Michigan in 2006. She is the author of *The City of the Cholos: Bolivia in the Nineteenth and Twentieth Centuries* on national racist projects and the circulation of images of the *cholo* (IFEA, 2011). Her book *Los Barones del Oriente* (Fundacíon Tierra, 2008) examines uneven landholding patterns in eastern Bolivia with a focus on soy, elite power, and the history of the rubber boom. She has taught at the Universidad de San Andres and the Universidad Andina Simón Bolívar in Bolivia, and various universities in Ecuador, including Cuenca, Azuay, and Guaranda.

References

Ahlbrandt, Thomas
2000   U.S. Geological Survey World Petroleum Assessment 2000. Compiled PowerPoint
        Slides. U.S. Geological Survey Open File Report 99-50-Z. Vol. 2006. Denver: USGS.

Albó, Xavier
2002   Los pueblos indios en la política. La Paz: Plural Editores / CIPCA.
2006   El Alto, La vorágine de una ciudad única. Journal of Latin American Anthropology
        11(2):329–350.
2007   El Alto: Mobilizing Block by Block. NACLA Report on the Americas. July/August
        2007:34–38.
2008   The "Long Memory" of Ethnicity in Bolivia and Some Temporary Oscillations. In
        Unresolved Tensions: Bolivia, Past and Present. John Crabtree and Laurence
        Whitehead, eds. Pp. 13–34. Pittsburgh: Pittsburgh University Press.

Albó, Xavier, y Franz Barrios
2006   Por una Bolivia plurinacional e intercultural con autonomías. La Paz: PNUD Bolivia.

Albó, Xavier, and Carlos Romero
2009   Autonomías indígenas en la realidad boliviana y su nueva constitución. La Paz:
        Vicepresidencia del Estado Plurinacional de Bolivia.

Albro, Robert
2005   The Water Is Ours, Carajo! Deep Citizenship in Bolivia's Water Wars. In Social
        Movements: An Anthropological Reader. June Nash, ed. Pp. 249–271. Oxford:
        Blackwell Publishing.
2006   The Culture of Democracy and Bolivia's Indigenous Movements. Critique of
        Anthropology 26(4):387–410.

Allen, Catherine J.

1988   The Hold Life Has: Coca and Cultural Identity in an Andean Community. Washington, DC: Smithsonian Institute Press.

Almaráz, Alejandro

2010   En defensa de la propiedad comunitaria de la tierra. La Paz: CEJIS / CENDA / CEDIB. Electronic document, http://www.constituyentesoberana.org/3/noticias/tierra/042010/300410_1.pdf, accessed July 14, 2010.

Andia Fernandez, Jose Luis

2002   Politica de mercados y gremiales de la Ramada. In Gobernabilidad en Santa Cruz de la Sierra. Jose Luis Andia Fernandez, Hedim Cespedes Cossio, Jean Paul Feldis Bannwart, and Francisco Mendez Eguez, eds. Pp. 23–40. Santa Cruz: SINPA / UAGRM.

Antelo, Sergio

N.d.   Vade retro, Satanás. Electronic document, http://www.nacioncamba.net/articulos/satanas.htm, accessed October 11, 2009.

APG (Asamblea del Pueblo Guaraní)

2007   Ñamometei ñande ñemongeta: Construcción del estatuto de autonomía de la Nación Guaraní. Territorio Guaraní Kaami: Grupo Ñeeñope.

Apter, Andrew

2005   The Pan-African Nation: Oil and the Spectacle of Culture in Nigeria. Chicago: University of Chicago Press.

Arbona, Juan

2002   Managing Social Policy Failures: Social Mobilization in Bolivia. Unpublished ms.

2006   Neoliberal Ruptures: Local Political Entities and Neighborhood Networks in El Alto, Bolivia. Geoforum 3:127–137.

2008   Sangre de Minero, Semilla de Guerrillero: Histories and Memories in the Organization and Struggles of Santiago II Neighborhood of El Alto, Bolivia. Bulletin of Latin American Research 27(1):24–42.

Arbona, Juan, and Benjamin Kohl

2004   La Paz–El Alto. Cities 21:255–265.

Archondo, Rafael

2000   Identidad Cruceña: Entre Collas tropicalizados e himnos al imperio. T'inkazos 7:111–116.

2001   Ser "chango" en El Alto: Entre el rock y los sikuris. T'inkazos 5:87–97.

Aretxaga, Begoña

2005   States of Terror. Joseba Zulaika, ed. Reno: Center for Basque Studies.

Arguedas, Alcides

1982[1910]   Pueblo enfermo. Barcelona: Tasso.

Arias Castro, Juan Manuel

2009   Ciudad limpia. El Dia, March 6.

Arnold, Denise
1998   Matrilineal Practice in a Patrilineal Setting: Ritual and Metaphors of Kinship in an Andean Ayllu. PhD dissertation, Department of Anthropology, University of London.

Arnold, Denise, and Juan de Dios Yapita
2006   The Metamorphosis of Heads: Textual Struggles, Education, and Land in the Andes. Pittsburgh: University of Pittsburgh Press.

Assies, Willem
2002   From Rubber Estate to Simple Commodity Production: Agrarian Struggles in the Northern Bolivian Amazon. Journal of Peasant Studies 29(3):83–130.

2003   David versus Goliath in Cochabamba: Water Rights, Neoliberalism, and the Revival of Social Protest in Bolivia. Latin American Perspectives 30(3):14–36.

Auyero, Javier, and Deborah Swinston
2008   The Social Production of Toxic Uncertainty. American Sociological Review 73(3):357–379.

Ayra
2006   Rebelión Kolla impone un Presidente Aymara, 9(97). Ayra: La Paz.

Baby, P., I. Moretti, B. Guillier, R. Limachi, E. Mendez, J. Oller, and M. Specht
1995   Petroleum System of the Northern and Central Bolivian Sub-Andean zone. *In* Petroleum Basins of South America. A. J. Tankard, R. Suárez S., and H. J. Welsink, eds. Pp. 445–458. AAPG Memoir 62.

Balboa, A.
1993   La juventud Alteña: Entre la integración e identificación socio-cultural aymara occidental y sus formas de relación social. *In* Memorias de la Reunión Anual de Etnología, vol. 1. Pp. 75–84. La Paz: MUSEF.

Barth, Frederik
1969   Ethnic Groups and Boundaries: The Social Organization of Cultural Difference. Boston: Little and Brown.

Bastein, Joseph W.
1978   Mountain of the Condor: Metaphor and Ritual in an Andean Ayllu. St. Paul, MN: West Publishing Co.

Bebbington, Anthony
2009   The New Extraction: Rewriting Political Ecology in the Andes. NACLA 42(5):12–20.

Becker, Marc
2008   Indians and Leftists in the Making of Ecuador's Modern Indigenous Movements. Durham: Duke University Press.

Bedoya, Eduardo, and Alvaro Bedoya
2005   Enganche y servidumbre por deudas en Bolivia. Ginebra: OIT.

Bello, Álvaro, y Marta Rancel
2000   Etnicidad, "raza" y equidad en América Latina y el Caribe. Santiago: CEPAL.

Benería, Lourdes
2001   Shifting the Risk: New Employment Patterns, Informalization, and Women's Work. International Journal of Politics, Culture, and Society 15(1):27–53.

2003   Gender, Development, and Globalization: Economics as if All People Mattered. New York: Routledge.

Benería, Lourdes, and Martha Roldán
1987   The Crossroads of Class and Gender: Industrial Homework, Subcontracting, and Household Dynamics in Mexico City. Chicago: University of Chicago Press.

Bengoa, José
2000   La emergencia indígena en América Latina. Mexico, DF: Fondo de Cultura Económica.

Bigenho, Michelle
2002   Sounding Indigenous, Feeling Bolivian: Authenticity in Music Performance. Houndmills: Palgrave Press.

Blanchard, Sophie
2006   Migración y construcción de la identidad: Los Collas en Santa Cruz. Sociológicas 5:1–12.

Boo, Katherine
2004   The Churn: Creative Destruction in a Border Town. The New Yorker, March 29. Pp. 139–151.

Brie, Cesar
2008   Humillados y ofendidos. Documentary film, http://www.youtube.com/watch?v= 27i9SsZOFT0, accessed April 20, 2011.

Bromley, Ray
1997   Working in the Streets of Cali, Colombia: Survival Strategy, Necessity, or Unavoidable Evil? In Cities in the Developing World: Issues, Theory and Policy. J. Gugler, ed. Pp. 124–139. Oxford: Oxford University Press.

Brown, Alison, ed.
2006   Contested Space: Street Trading, Public Space, and Livelihoods in Developing Countries. Warwickshire: ITDG.

Brush, Stephen B.
1977   Mountain, Field, and Family: The Economy and Human Ecology of an Andean Village. Philadelphia: University of Pennsylvania Press.

Cabezas, Marta
2006   ¡A Chonchocoro! Testimonis de dones bolivianes afectades per la guerra del gas. Barcelona: Instituto Català de les Dones. Electronic document, http://www.acsur.org/ IMG/pdf/A_chochoncoro__cat.pdf, accessed October 11, 2009.

Cabrales Barajas, Luis Felipe
2006   Gated Communities Are Not the Solution to Urban Insecurity. In State of the World's Cities 2006/7. UN Habitat, ed. Pp. 146–147. London: Earthscan.

CAINCO
2004 Santa Cruz consolida su liderazgo productivo y competitivo en Bolivia. Santa Cruz de la Sierra: Camera de Industria, Comercio, Servicios, y Turismo (CAINCO).

Caldeira, Teresa
2000 City of Walls: Crime, Segregation, and Citizenship in Sao Paulo. Berkeley: University of California Press.

Calderón, Fernando, and Alicia Szmukler
1999 La política en las calles. La Paz: CERES / PLURAL / UASB.

Catacora, Georgina
2007 Soya in Bolivia: Production of Oilseeds and Dependency. In United Soy Republics: The Truth about Soy Production in South America. Javiera Rulli, ed. Pp. 233–253. Grupo de Reflexión Rural (Argentina). Electronic document, www.lasojamata.org.ar, accessed September 1, 2010.

Casaus Arzú, Marta Elena
1992 Guatemala: Linaje y Racismo. San José (Costa Rica): FLACSO.

Castells, Manuel, and Alejandro Portes
1989 World Underneath: The Origins, Dynamics and Effects of the Informal Economy. In The Informal Economy: Studies in Advanced and Less Developed Countries. A. Portes, M. Castells, and L. A. Benton, eds. Pp. 11–40. Baltimore: Johns Hopkins University Press.

CEDLA
2008 El empleo en tiempos de cambio. La Paz: CEDLA.

CENDA
2009 Periódico Conosur Ñawpaqman, N° 133, marzo.

Chatterjee, Partha
1993 La nación y sus campesinos. In Debates Post-Coloniales: Una introducción a los Estudios de la Subalternidad. Silvia Rivera and Rosana Barragán, eds. Pp. 195–210. La Paz: Historias.

Chumacero, Juan Pablo, ed.
2010 Reconfigurando territorios: Reforma agraria, control territorial y gobiernos indígenas en Bolivia. La Paz: Fundación Tierra.

Cingolani, Pablo
2008 A propósito del masacre de El Porvenir: Un homenaje al pueblo Tacana. Electronic document, http://www.ecoportal.net/content/view/full/81389, accessed June 15, 2009.

Collier, Paul
2010 The Plundered Planet: Why We Must—and How We Can—Manage Nature for Global Prosperity. New York: Oxford University Press.

Colloredo-Mansfeld, Rudi
1999 The Native Leisure Class: Consumption and Cultural Creativity in the Andes. Chicago: University of Chicago Press.

2009   Fighting like a Community: Andean Civil Society in an Era of Indian Uprising. Chicago: University of Chicago Press.

Colque, Gonzalo
2009   Autonomías indígenas en tierras altas: Breve mapeo para la implementación de la Autonomía Indígena Originaria Campesina. La Paz: Fundación Tierra.

Conaghan, Catherine, J. Malloy, and Luis Abugattas
1990   Business and the Boys: The Origins of Neoliberalism in the Central Andes. Latin American Research Review 25(2):3–30.

Coronil, Fernando
1997   The Magical State: Nature, Money, and Modernity in Venezuela. Chicago: University of Chicago Press.

Cosgrove, Denis E.
1998   Social Formation and Symbolic Landscape. Madison: University of Wisconsin Press.

Cottle, Patricia, and Carmen Beatriz Ruiz
1993   La violenta vida cotidiana. *In* Violencias encubiertas en Bolivia. Xavier Albó and Raúl Barrios, eds. Pp. 81–192. La Paz: CIPCA.

Council on Foreign Relations
2004   Andes 2020: A New Strategy for the Challenges of Colombia and the Region. New York: Council on Foreign Relations.

Crabtree, John, and Laurence Whitehead, eds.
2008   Unresolved Tensions: Bolivia Past and Present. Pittsburgh: University of Pittsburgh Press.

Cross, John
1998   Informal Politics: Street Vendors and the State in Mexico City. Palo Alto: Stanford University Press.

CSUTCB, CONAMAQ, CIDOB, CSCB, FNMCB-BS, CPESC, CPEMB, MST, APG
2006   Propuesta para la nueva Constitución Política del Estado. Sucre, 5 de agosto.

CSUTCB, CONAMAQ, CIDOB, CSCB, FNMCIOB "BS", CPESC, MST, ANARESCAPYS, Movimiento Cultural Afrodescendiente
2007   Propuesta consensuada del Pacto de Unidad. Constitución Política del Estado Boliviano. "Por un Estado Unitario Plurinacional Comunitario, Libre, Independiente, Soberano, Democrático y Social." Sucre, 23 de mayo.

Dangl, Benjamin
2007   The Price of Fire: Resource Wars and Social Movements in Bolivia. Edinburgh: AK Press.

Davis, Mike
2006   Planet of Slums. New York: Verso.

Dean, Bartholomew, and Jerome Levi
2003   Introduction. *In* At the Risk of Being Heard: Identity, Indigenous Rights, and Postcolonial States. Bartholomew Dean and Jerome Levi, eds. Pp. 1–44. Ann Arbor: University of Michigan Press.

de Certeau, Michel
2002   The Practice of Everyday Life. Berkeley: University of California Press.

De Soto, Hernando
2010   The Peruvian Amazon Is Not Avatar. Washington, DC: Center for International Private Enterprise. Electronic document, http://www.cipe.org/regional/lac/pdf/The%20Peruvian%20Amazon%20is%20not%20Avatar.pdf, accessed September 1, 2010.

de Sousa Santos, Boaventura
2007   La reinvención del Estado y el Estado plurinacional. Cochabamba: Alianza Interinstitucional CENDA, CEJIS, CEDIB.

de Sousa Santos, Boaventura, and Leonardo Avritzer
2005   Introduction: Opening Up the Canon of Democracy. *In* Democratizing Democracy: Beyond the Liberal Democratic Canon. Boaventura de Sousa Santos, ed. Pp. xxiv–lxivv. London: Verso.

del Valle Escalante, Emilio
2009   Maya Nationalisms and Postcolonial Challenges in Guatemala: Coloniality, Modernity, and Identity Politics. Santa Fe: SAR Press.

di Leonardo, Micaela
2008   Introduction: New Global and American Landscapes of Inequality. *In* New Landscapes of Inequality: Neoliberalism and the Erosion of Democracy in America. Jane Collins, Micaela di Leonardo, and Brett Williams, eds. Pp. 3–19. Santa Fe: SAR Press.

Domic, Jorge
1999   Niños trabajadores. La Paz: PIEB.

Douglas, Mary
1966   Purity and Danger: An Analysis of Concepts of Pollution and Taboo. New York: Praeger.

Dunkerley, James
1984   Rebellion in the Veins: Political Struggles in Bolivia, 1952–1982. London: Verso.
2006   Bolivia: Revolution and the Power of History in the Present. London: Institute for the Study of the Americas.

El Deber (Santa Cruz, Bolivia)
2010a   Pelea campal entre gendarmes y gremialistas causa más de diez heridos. June 8.
2010b   Gremialistas seguirán vendiendo en las calles. June 21.
2010c   La Ramada, ¿'turística'? June 21.

Escobar, Arturo
2001   Culture Sits in Places: Reflections on Globalism and Subaltern Strategies of Localization. Political Geography 20(2001):139–174.

2008   Territories of Difference: Place, Movements, Life, Redes. Durham: Duke University Press.

2010   Latin America at a Crossroads: Alternative Modernizations, Postliberalism, or Postdevelopment? Unpublished ms.

Escobar, Arturo, and Sonia Alvarez
1992   The Making of Social Movements in Latin America: Identity, Strategy, and Democracy. Boulder: Westview Press.

Escobari, Silvia
2001   Caciques, yanaconas y extravagantes. La Paz: Plural Editores.

Espósito, Carla, and Walter Arteaga
2007   Movimientos sociales urbano-populares: Una lucha contra la exclusión económica, social y política. La Paz: UNITAS.

Fabricant, Nicole
2009   Performative Politics: The Camba Countermovement in Eastern Bolivia. American Ethnologist 36(4):768–783.

Fanon, Frantz
1967   Black Skin, White Masks. Translated by Charles Lam Markmann. New York: Grove Press.

Farthing, Linda
2009   Bolivia's Dilemma: Development Confronts the Legacy of Extraction. NACLA 42(5):25–30.

Farthing, Linda, and Benjamin Kohl
2001   The Price of Success: The Destruction of Coca and the Bolivian Economy. NACLA 34(7):35–41.

Fernandes, Leela
2004   The Politics of Forgetting: Class Politics, State Power and the Restructuring of Urban Space in India. Urban Studies 41(12):2415–2430.

Fernandes, Sujatha
2010   Who Can Stop the Drums? Urban Social Movements in Chavez's Venezuela. Durham: Duke University Press.

Fernandez, Bernardo Mancano
2001   The Occupation as a Form of Access to Land. Paper presented at LASA International Congress, Washington, DC, September 6–8.

Fernández, Hermán
1984   Nosotros y otros: Ensayos sobre la identidad Cruceña. Santa Cruz: Plural.

Fifer, Valerie
1970   The Empire Builders: A History of the Bolivian Rubber Boom and the Rise of the House of Suarez. Journal of Latin American Studies 2(2):113–146.
1982   The Search for a Series of Small Successes: Frontiers of Settlement in Eastern Bolivia. Journal of Latin American Studies 14(2):407–432.

Finnegan, William
2002   Leasing the Rain: The world is running out of fresh water, and the fight to control it has begun. The New Yorker, April 8.

Flores, Freddy Gonzales, Fernando Justiniano Arteaga, Alex Linares Cabrera, and Juan Justiniano Viruez
2002   Comite Civico Pro–Santa Cruz: Grupos de Poder y Liderazgo Regional. La Paz: Programa de Investigacion Estrategica de Bolivia.

Foucault, Michel
2000   Power: The Essential Works of Foucault, 1954–1984. Paul Rabinow, ed. New York: New Press.

Gamarra, Eduardo A.
2007   Bolivia on the Brink. Council Special Report 24. New York: Center for Preventive Action / Council on Foreign Relations.

Garcés, Fernando
2008a   Ordenamiento territorial, recursos naturales y Asamblea Constituyente en Bolivia: ¿Hacia un Estado Plurinacional? In Estados y autonomías en democracias contemporáneas: Bolivia, Ecuador, España y México. Natividad Gutiérrez Chong, ed. Pp. 141–154. México: UNAM / IIS / Plaza y Valdés.
2008b   Asamblea Constituyente, Estado Plurinacional y democracia intercultural: La experiencia boliviana. In Seminario Regional Andino: Democracia, interculturalidad, plurinacionalidad y desafíos para la integración andina. Raúl Peñaranda, ed. Pp. 51–63. La Paz: CEBEM.
2009a   Los esfuerzos de construcción descolonizada de un Estado Plurinacional en Bolivia y los riesgos de vestir al mismo caballero con otro terno. Unpublished ms.
2009b   ¿Colonialidad o interculturalidad? Las representaciones de la lengua y el conocimiento quechuas. La Paz: PIEB / UASB-Q.

García, María Elena
2005   Making Indigenous Citizens: Identities, Education, and Multicultural Development in Peru. Stanford: Stanford University Press.

García Linera, Álvaro
2005   Estado Plurinacional: Una propuesta democrática y pluralista para la extinción de la exclusión de las naciones indígenas. In La transformación pluralista del Estado. Álvaro García Linera, Luis Tapia, y Raúl Prada, eds. Pp. 190–198. La Paz: Muela del Diablo.
2009   El papel del Estado en el Model Nacional Productivo. Discursos & Ponencias 3(6). La Paz: Vicepresidencia del Estado Plurinacional.

García Linera, Álvaro, Marxa Chávez León, and Patricia Costas Manje, eds.
2004   Sociología de los movimientos sociales en Bolivia: Estructuras de movilización, repertorios culturales y acción política. La Paz: Plural.

García Paz, Ricardo
N.d.   Santa Cruz es hermoso, pero.... Electronic document, http://www.nacioncamba.net/articulos/jovenes/ jovenes%20-%20santa%20cruz%20hermosa.htm, accessed September 15, 2007.

Gill, Lesley

1987   Peasants, Entrepreneurs and Social Change: Frontier Development in Lowland Bolivia. Boulder: Westview Press.

2000   Teetering on the Rim: Global Restructuring, Daily Life, and the Armed Retreat of the Bolivian State. New York: Columbia University Press.

GMEA (Gobierno Municipal del El Alto)

2005   Informe Cumbre Distrital. Unpublished ms.

GMSC

1990   Ordenanza Municipal sobre Politicas Generales de Mercados Municipales. Santa Cruz de la Sierra: Direccion de Abastecimiento, Construccion de Mercados. Gobierno Municipal de Santa Cruz de la Sierra.

2004a   Plan de Ordenamiento Territorial (PLOT). Santa Cruz: Gobierno Municipal de Santa Cruz de la Sierra.

2004b   Ordenanza Municipal para el Uso del Espacio Publico. Santa Cruz de la Sierra: Oficialia Mayor de Planificacion. Gobierno Municipal Santa Cruz de la Sierra.

Godoy, Ricardo

1986   Fiscal Role of the Andean Ayllu. Man 21(4):723–741.

Goldstein, Daniel

2004   The Spectacular City: Violence and Performance in Urban Bolivia. Durham: Duke University Press.

Gomes, Luis

2004   El Alto de pie: Una insurrección aymara en Bolivia. La Paz: Textos Rebeldes.

Goodale, Mark

2008   Dilemmas of Modernity: Bolivian Encounters with Law and Liberalism. Stanford: Stanford University Press.

2009   Reclaiming Modernity: Indigenous Cosmopolitanism and the Coming of the Second Revolution in Bolivia. American Ethnologist 33(4):634–649.

Gordon, Edmund, Galio Gurdián, and Charles Hale

2003   Rights, Resources, and the Social Memory of Struggle: Reflections on a Study of Indigenous and Black Community Land Rights on Nicaragua's Atlantic Coast. Human Organization 62(4):369–381.

Gordon, Gretchen, and Aaron Luoma

2008   Petróleo y gas: La riqueza ilusoria debajo de sus pies. *In* Desafiando la globalización. Historias de la experiencia boliviana. Jim Schultz and Melissa Crane Draper, eds. Pp. 87–129. La Paz: El Centro para la Democracia / Plural.

Gray Molina, George

2005   Crecimiento de base ancha: Entre la espada y la pared. T'inkazos 15:95–101.

Grindle, Merilee, and Pilar Domingo, eds.

2003   Proclaiming Revolution: Bolivia in Comparative Perspective. Cambridge: David Rockefeller Center for Latin American Studies.

Guerrero, Andrés

2000   El proceso de identificación: Sentido común ciudadano, ventriloquia y tranescritura. *In* Etnicidades. Andrés Guerrero, ed. Quito: FLACSO-ILDIS.

Guha, Ranahit

1997   Sobre algunos aspectos de la historiografía colonial de la India. *In* Debates Post Coloniales. Una introducción a los Estudios de la Subalternidad. Silvia Rivera and Rossana Barragán, eds. Pp. 25–32. La Paz: Historias, SEPHIS, Ayuwiyiri.

Gustafson, Bret

2002   Paradoxes of Liberal Indigenism: Indigenous Movements, State Processes, and Intercultural Reform in Bolivia. *In* The Politics of Ethnicity: Indigenous Peoples in Latin American States. David Maybury-Lewis, ed. Pp. 266–306. Cambridge: Harvard University Press.

2006   Spectacles of Autonomy and Crisis: Or, What Bulls and Beauty Queens Have to Do with Regionalism in Eastern Bolivia. Journal of Latin American and Caribbean Anthropology 11(2):351–379.

2008   By Means Legal and Otherwise: The Bolivian Right Regroups. NACLA 20(7):20–25.

2009a   New Languages of the State: Indigenous Resurgence and the Politics of Knowledge in Bolivia. Durham: Duke University Press.

2009b   Manipulating Cartographies: Plurinationalism, Autonomy, and Indigenous Resurgence in Bolivia. Anthropological Quarterly 82(4):985–1016.

2009c   Bolivia 9/11: Bodies and Power on a Feudal Frontier. Caterwaul Quarterly 2 (Spring–Summer). Electronic document, http://www.caterwaulquarterly.com/node/85, accessed October 9, 2009.

2010   When States Act Like Movements: Dismantling Local Power and "Seating" Sovereignty in Post-Neoliberal Bolivia. Latin American Perspectives 37(4):48–66.

Gutiérrez Aguilar, Raquel

2008   Los ritmos del Pachakuti: Movilización y levantamiento indígena-popular en Bolivia. Buenos Aires: Tinta Limón.

Hale, Charles

2002   Does Multiculturalism Menace? Governance, Cultural Rights and the Politics of Identity in Guatemala. Journal of Latin American Studies 34(3):485–524.

2006a   Más que un indio: Racial Ambivalence and the Paradox of Neoliberal Multiculturalism in Guatemala. Santa Fe: SAR Press.

2006b   Activist Research v. Cultural Critique: Indigenous Land Rights and the Contradictions of Politically Engaged Anthropology. Cultural Anthropology 21(1):96–120.

Hall, Stuart

1980   Race, Articulation, and Societies Structured in Racial Dominance. *In* Sociological Theories: Race and Colonialism. UNESCO, ed. Pp. 305–345. Paris: UNESCO.

Harvey, David

2000   Spaces of Hope. Berkeley: University of California Press.

2003   The New Imperialism. Oxford: Oxford University Press.

2006   Spaces of Global Capitalism: Towards a Theory of Uneven Geographical Development. New York: Verso.

Healy, Kevin
2001   Grassroots Development Trekking with Alpacas, Llamas, and Ayllus. *In* Llamas, Weavings, and Organic Chocolate: Grassroots Development in the Andes and Amazon of Bolivia. Kevin Healy, ed. Pp. 189–224. Notre Dame: University of Notre Dame Press.

Heath, Douglas, Charles Erasmus, and Hans Buechler
1969   Land Reform and Social Revolution in Bolivia. New York: Praeger Publishers.

Henkel, Ray
1982   The Move to the Oriente: Colonization and Environmental Impact. *In* Modern Day Bolivia: Legacy of the Revolution and Prospects for the Future. Jerry R. Ladman, ed. Pp. 277–299. Tempe: Center for Latin American Studies, Arizona State University.

Hertzler, Douglas
2002   Agrarian Cultures of Solidarity: Campesino Unions and the Struggle for Land and Community Development in Santa Cruz, Bolivia. PhD dissertation, Department of Anthropology, University of Iowa.

Holston, James
2008   Insurgent Citizenship: Disjunctions of Democracy and Modernity in Brazil. Princeton: Princeton University Press.

Humphreys Bebbington, Denise, and Anthony J. Bebbington
2009   Governing Inequities: Extraction and Territorial Dynamics in Bolivia. Unpublished ms.

Humphreys Bebbington, Denise, and Umber Catari
N.d.   Expansión de la actividad hidrocarburífera en el PNANMI Aguarague. Unpublished ms.

Hunt, Stacey
2009   Citizenship's Place: The State's Creation of Public Space and Street Vendors' Culture of Informality in Bogota, Colombia. Environment and Planning D: Society and Space 27(2):331–351.

Hurtado, Javier
1986   El Katarismo. La Paz: Hisbol.

Hvalkof, Soren
2008   Privatization of Land and Indigenous Communities in Latin America: Tenure Security or Social Security? Danish Institute for International Studies Working Paper 2008/21. Copenhagen: DIIS.

Hylton, Forrest, and Sinclair Thomson
2007   Revolutionary Horizons: Past and Present in Bolivian Politics. New York: Verso.

INE (Instituto Nacional de Estadística)
2001a   Censo Nacional de Poblacion y Vivienda. La Paz: Instituto Nacional de Estadística.
2001b   Santa Cruz: Proyecciones de Población, Por Sexo, Según Municipio, 2000–2010. Electronic document, http://www.ine.gov.bo/indice/visualizador.aspx?ah=PC20407 .htm, accessed February 9, 2010.

2002a   Bolivia: Censo de Población y Vivienda, Autoidentificación con Pueblos Originarios o
         Indígenas de la Población de 15 años o más de edad. Electronic document,
         http://www.ine.gov.bo:8082/censo/make_table.jsp, accessed October 6, 2009.

2002b   Autoidentificación con Pueblos Originarios o Indígenas de la Población de 15 años o
         más de edad. Electronic document, http://www.ine.gob.bo:8082/censo/entrance.jsp,
         accessed October 6, 2009.

2003   Bolivia. Características sociodemográficas de la Población Indígena. La Paz: INE-
         UNFPA-VAI.

2005   Estadísticas del Municipio de El Alto—2005. La Paz: INE. Electronic document,
         http://www.ine.gov.bo/pdf/Est_Dptales/Depto_2005_10.pdf, accessed December 10, 2009.

2007   Anuario Estadístico. La Paz: Instituto Nacional de Estadística.

Isbell, Billie Jean
1978   To Defend Ourselves: Ecology and Ritual in an Andean Village. Austin: University of
         Texas Press.

Jironda Cuba, Rafael
2007   ¡No tenemos gas! Energy Press, July 2. Electronic document, http://www.energypress
         .com.bo/OpinionesAnteriores/351.htm, accessed July 2, 2007.

Jubileo
2009   Revista Jubileo 14 (March–April). La Paz: Jubileo Foundation. http://www.jubileo
         bolivia.org.bo/recursos/files/pdfs/REVISTA_JUBILEO_N_14.pdf, accessed July 2, 2009.

Karriem, Abdurazack
2009   The Rise and Transformation of the Brazilian Landless Movement into a Counter-
         Hegemonic Political Actor: A Gramscian Analysis. Geoforum 40(2009):316–325.

Klein, Herbert
1982   Bolivia: The Evolution of a Multi-ethnic Society. New York: Oxford University Press.

2003   A Concise History of Bolivia. Cambridge: Cambridge University Press.

Klein, Naomi
2010   A New Climate Movement in Bolivia. The Nation, May 10.

Kohl, Benjamin, and Linda Farthing
2006   Impasse in Bolivia: Neoliberal Hegemony and Popular Resistance. London: Zed Books.

Kudva, Neema
2006   Informality in Urban Space: Spatial Implications and Political Challenges. In
         Rethinking Informalization: Poverty, Precarious Jobs and Social Protection. Neema
         Kudva and Lourdes Beneria, eds. Pp. 163–181. Ithaca: Cornell University Open Access
         Repository.

Kymlicka, Will
1995   Multicultural Citizenship: A Liberal Theory of Minority Rights. Oxford: Oxford
         University Press.

La Razón
2003   Los vecinos de El Alto cercaron a La Paz por dos formularios. September 16, A9.

2009   La ONU dice que en Pando "se habría" ejecutado a campesinos. March 26, A17.

Lacombes, Zéline

N.d.   Nación camba, del regionalismo al nacionalismo. Electronic document, http://www.nacioncamba.net/articulos/zeline_lacombe.htm, accessed September 20, 2009.

Lagos, María, y Pamela Calla, eds.

2007   Antropología del Estado. Dominación y prácticas contestatarias en América Latina. La Paz: PNUD.

Lazar, Sian

2004   Personalistic Politics, Clientelism and Citizenship: Local Elections in El Alto, Bolivia. Bulletin of Latin American Research 23(2):228–243.

2006   El Alto, Ciudad Rebelde: Organisational Bases for Revolt. Bulletin of Latin American Research 25(2):183–199.

2008   El Alto, Rebel City: Self and Citizenship in Andean Bolivia. Durham: Duke University Press.

Limpias, Victor Hugo

2003   Arquitectura y Urbanismo en Santa Cruz. Santa Cruz: Universidad Privada de Santa Cruz.

Lindquist, Sandra

1998   The Santa Cruz–Tarija Province of Central South America: Los Monos-Machareti (!) Petroleum System. Open File Report 99-50-C, vol. 2007. US Geological Survey and US Department of the Interior.

1999   Sub-Andean Fold and Thrust Belt Assessment Unit 60450101. In U.S. Geological Survey World Petroleum Assessment 2000—Description and Results. Washington, DC: US Geological Survey.

López, José Luis

2007   El derecho a la libre determinación de los pueblos indígenas en Bolivia. Oruro: CEPA.

Lowrey, Kathleen

2006   Bolivia Multiétnico y Pluricultural, Ten Years Later: White Separatism in the Bolivian Lowlands. Latin American and Caribbean Ethnic Studies 1(1):63–84.

Lucero, José Antonio

2008   Struggles of Voice: The Politics of Indigenous Representation in the Andes. Pittsburgh: University of Pittsburgh Press.

Madison, Soyini

2007   Co-performative Witnessing. Cultural Studies 21(6):826–831.

Máiz, Ramón

2002   Nacionalismo, federalismo y acomodación en estados multinacionales. In Identidad y autogobierno en sociedades multiculturales. William Safran and Ramón Máiz, eds. Pp. 67–96. Barcelona: Ariel.

2008   XI tesis para una teoría política de la autonomía. In Estados y autonomías en democracias contemporáneas: Bolivia, Ecuador, España y México. Natividad Gutiérrez Chong, ed. Pp. 17–41. México: UNAM, IIS, Plaza y Valdés.

Mallon, Florencia
1995 Peasant and Nation: The Making of Postcolonial Mexico and Peru. Berkeley: University of California Press.

Malloy, James M.
1970 Bolivia: The Uncompleted Revolution. Pittsburgh: University of Pittsburgh Press.

Mamani, Julio
2006 Octubre. Memorias de Dignidad y Masacre. El Alto: CEDLA / APA.

Mamani Ramirez, Pablo
2003 El rugir de la multitud: Levantamiento de la ciudad Aymara de El Alto y la caida del gobierno de Sánchez de Lozada. OSAL 4(12):15–26.
2004 El rugir de las multitudes: La fuerza de los levantamientos indígenas en Bolivia/Qullasuyu. La Paz: Aruwiyiri-Yachaywasi.
2005 Microgobiernos barriales: Levantamiento de la ciudad de El Alto (October 2003). La Paz: CADES-IDIS-UMSA.
N.d. Cuartel de Qalachaka. El poder aymara y violencia estatal en Jach'a Omasuyu, Bolivia (2001–2009). Unpublished ms.

Mamani Ramirez, Pablo, Máximo Quisbert, and Carlos Callizaya
N.d. Universidad y Multiversidad. Entre la realidad social y la educación superior. Unpublished ms.

Mansilla, H. C. F.
2004 El carácter conservador de la nación boliviana. Santa Cruz: Editorial El País.

Martinez-Alier, Joan
2002 El ecologismo de los pobres: Conflictos ambientales y lenguajes de valoración. Barcelona: Icaria.

Massey, Doreen
1994 Space, Place, and Gender. Cambridge: Polity Press.

Mayer, Enrique
2002 Articulated Peasant: Household Economies in the Andes. Boulder: Westview Press.

Mayorga, Fernando
1997 ¿Ejemonías? Democracia representativa y liderazgos locales. La Paz: PIEB.
2007 Acerca del Estado Plurinacional. Electronic document, www.plazapublica.org/documentos/EstadoPlurinacional%5B1%5D.doc, accessed December 23, 2007.

Mendoza, Omar, Zedin Manzur, David Cortez, and Aldo Salazar
2003 La lucha por la tierra en el Gran Chaco tarijeño. La Paz PIEB.

Mignolo, Walter
2005 The Idea of Latin America. Malden: Blackwell.

Mosqueira, Gustavo Pinto
N.d. La nación Camba y el Estado. Electronic document, http://www.nacioncamba.net/articulos/nacion%20camba%20y%20el%20estado.htm, accessed April 15, 2009.

Müller, K.
2009   Contested Universalism: From Bonosol to Renta Dignidad in Bolivia. International Journal of Social Welfare 18:163–172.

Murra, John V.
1975   Formaciones económicas y políticas del mundo andino. Lima: Instituto de Estudios Peruanos.
1978   La organización económica y política del estado Inca. México: Siglo XXI.

Nash, June
1979   We Eat the Mines and the Mines Eat Us. New York: Columbia University Press.
1992   Interpreting Social Movements: Bolivian Resistance to the Economic Conditions Imposed by the International Monetary Fund. American Ethnologist 19(2):275–293.

NCPE (Nueva Constitución Política del Estado)
2009   Nueva Constitución Política del Estado: Texto final y compatibilizado. Electronic document, http://www.comunicabolivia.com/nueva-constitucion-bolivia, accessed October 6, 2009.

Negri, Antonio
1999   Insurgencies: Constituent Power and the Modern State. Minneapolis: University of Minnesota Press.

Negri, Toni, and Michael Hardt
2001   Empire. Cambridge: Harvard University Press.

Nordenskiöld, Erland
2001   Exploraciones y aventuras en Sudamérica. La Paz: APCOB / Plural.

Offen, Karl H.
2003   The Territorial Turn: Making Black Territories in Pacific Colombia. Journal of Latin American Geography 2(1):43–73.

Olivera, Oscar, and Tom Lewis
2004   Cochabamba: Water War in Bolivia. Cambridge: South End Press.

Orduña, Victor
2001   La Hora de Las Ocupaciones: El Desembarco de Los Sin Tierras. *In* La lucha por la tierra y el territorio. Carlos Romero Bonifaz, Ana Cecila Bentacur, Jose Percy Paredes Coimbra, Marco Antonio Aimaretti, and Leonardo Tamburini, eds. Pp. 89–93. Santa Cruz: CEJIS Artículo Primero.

Orgaz García, Mirko
2005   La nacionalización del gas. La Paz: CEDLA / C&C Editores.

Orlove, Benjamin
1977   Alpacas, Sheep, and Men: The Wool Export Economy and Regional Society in Southern Peru. New York: Academic Press.

Orta, Andrew
2004   Catechizing Culture: Missionaries, Aymara, and the New Evangelization. New York: Columbia University Press.

Pacheco, Diego
2007   An Institutional Analysis of Decentralization and Indigenous Timber Management in Common-Property Forests of Bolivia's Lowlands. PhD dissertation, Department of Geography, Indiana University.

Pacto de Unidad
2004   Hacia una Asamblea Constituyente soberana y participativa. Unpublished ms.
N.d.   El Pacto de Unidad y el proceso constituyente en Bolivia. Unpublished ms.

Painter, Michael
1985   Ethnicity and Social Class Formation in the Bolivian Lowlands. Binghamton: Institute for Development Anthropology.

Paley, Julia
2001   Marketing Democracy: Power and Social Movements in Post-dictatorship Chile. Berkeley: University of California Press.

Palmer, Robert
1979   Politics and Modernization: A Case Study of Santa Cruz, Bolivia. Unpublished PhD dissertation, UCLA.

PAR
2005   El Alto: 9 aspectos que configuran la ciudad. El Alto: UE / GMEA / PAR.

Patzi Paco, Felix
2004   Sistema Comunal. Una propuesta alternativa al sistema liberal. La Paz: CEA.

Paz, Sarela
2008   Autonomías territoriales y democracia plural en Bolivia. In Estados y autonomías en democracias contemporáneas: Bolivia, Ecuador, España y México. Natividad Gutiérrez Chong, ed. Pp. 125–140. México: UNAM, IIS, Plaza y Valdés.

Peluso, Nancy, and Michael Watts
2001   Violent Environments. Ithaca: Cornell University Press.

Peña, Paula, Rodrigo Barahona, Luis Enrique Rivero, and Daniela Gaya
2003   La Permanente Construcción de lo Cruceño: Un Estudio Sobre la Identidad en Santa Cruz de la Sierra. La Paz: PIEB.

Pérez Carrillo, Carmen
2009   Sucia, asi se ve la ciudad en los mercados y vias. El Deber, January 26.

Pérez Sáinz, Juan Pablo
2003   Exclusión laboral en America Latina: Viejas y nuevas tendencias. Sociologia del Trabajo 47.

Perrault, Thomas
2006   From the Guerra de Agua to the Guerra de Gas: Resource Governance, Neoliberalism and Popular Protest in Bolivia. Antipode 38:150–172.
2008a   Custom and Contradiction: Rural Water Governance and the Politics of *Usos y*

Costumbres in Bolivia's Irrigators' Movement. Annals of the Association of American Geographers 98(4):834–854.

2008b   Natural Gas, Indigenous Mobilization, and the Bolivian State. UNRISD. Electronic document, http://www.unrisd.org, accessed June 12, 2009.

Plata, Wilfredo
2008   El discurso autonomista de los élites de Santa Cruz. *In* Los barones del Oriente: El poder en Santa Cruz ayer y hoy. Ximena Soruco, Wilfredo Plata, and Gustavo Medeiros, eds. Pp. 107–132. La Paz: Fundación Tierra.
2010   De Municipio a Autonomía Indígena: Los once municipios que transitan a la Autonomía Indígena Originaria Campesina. *In* Reconfigurando territorios: Reforma agraria, control territorial y gobiernos indígenas en Bolivia. Juan Pablo Chumacero, ed. Pp. 247–272. La Paz: Fundación Tierra.

PNUD (Programa de las Naciones Unidas para el Desarrollo)
2004   Informe de Desarrollo Humano Regional Santa Cruz. La Paz: PNUD / Plural.

Polanyi, Karl
1944   The Great Transformation: The Political and Economic Origins of Our Time. Boston: Beacon Press.

Popke, Jeffrey, and Richard Ballard
2004   Dislocating Modernity: Identity, Space and Representations of Street Trade in Durban, South Africa. Geoforum 35(1):99–110.

Poupeau, Frank
2009   El Alto: Una ficción política. Unpublished ms.

Postero, Nancy
2006   Now We Are Citizens: Indigenous Politics in Post-multicultural Bolivia. Stanford: Stanford University Press.
2007   Andean Utopias in Evo Morales's Bolivia. Latin American and Caribbean Ethnic Studies 2(1):1–28.

Prada, Fernando
2007   Articulaciones de la complejidad: Estado plurinacional. Electronic document, http://www.bolpress.com/art.php?Cod=2007022803, accessed March 2, 2007.

Prado, Fernando, Susana Seleme, Isabella Prado, and Carmen Ledo
2005   Santa Cruz y su Gente: Una vision critica de su evolucion y sus principales tendencias. Santa Cruz: Centro de Estudios para el Desarrollo Urbano y Regional.

Pribilsky, Jason
2007   La Chulla Vida: Gender, Migration, and the Family in Andean Ecuador and New York City. Syracuse: Syracuse University Press.

Pruden, Hernán
2003   Santa Cruz entre la post-guerra del Chaco y las postrimerías de la Revolución Nacional: cruceños y cambas. Historias: Revista de la Coordinadora de Historias 6:41–61.

Qayum, Seemin, María Luisa Soux, and Rosana Barragán
1997   De terratenientes a amas de casa: Mujeres de la élite de la primera mitad del Siglo XX. La Paz: Ministerio de Desarrollo Humano.

Quisbert, Máximo
2003   FEJUVE El Alto 1990–1998: Dilemas del Clientelismo Colectivo en un Mercado Político en Expansión. Aruwiyiri, La Paz: THOA.

Quispe, Marco Alberto
2004   De Ch'usa Marka a Jach'a Marka. El Alto: Wayna Tambo.

Radcliffe, Sarah, and Sallie Westwood
1996   Remaking the Nation: Place, Identity and Politics in Latin America. London: Routledge.

Rakowski, Cathy A., ed.
1994   Contrapunto: The Informal Sector Debate in Latin America. Albany: State University of New York Press.

Rappaport, Joanne
2005   Intercultural Utopias: Public Intellectuals, Cultural Experimentation, and Ethnic Pluralism in Columbia. Durham: Duke University Press.
2008   Beyond Participant Observation: Collaborative Ethnography as Theoretical Innovation. Collaborative Anthropologies 1(1):1–31.

Regalsky, Pablo
2003   Etnicidad y clase: El estado boliviano y las estrategias andinas de manejo de su espacio. La Paz: CENDA / CEIDIS / Plural.
2009   Las paradojas del proceso constituyente boliviano. Cochabamba: CENDA.

René Moreno, Gabriel
1989[1885]   Nicómedes Antelo. In Bolivia y Argentina. Notas biográficas y bibliográficas. La Paz: Banco Central.

Revilla, Carlos
2007   Visibilidad y obrismo: La estrategia del Plan Progreso en la Ciudad de El Alto. In Avances de Investigación, No. 1, Programa Desarrollo del Poder Local. UNITAS, ed. La Paz: UNITAS.

Rivera Cusicanqui, Silvia
1984   Oprimidos pero no vencidos, luchas del campesinado aymara y Quechua: 1900–1980. La Paz: HISBOL-CSUTCB.
1993   La raíz: Colonizadores y colonizados. In Violencias encubiertas en Bolivia. X. Albó and R. Barrios, eds. Pp. 27–131. La Paz: CIPCA.
1996   Trabajo de mujeres: Explotación capitalista y opresión colonial entre las migrantes aymaras de La Paz y El Alto, Bolivia. In Ser mujer indígena, chola y birlocha en la Bolivia postcolonial de los años 90. Silvia Rivera, ed. Pp. 163–279. La Paz: Ministerio de Desarrollo Humano.
2004   La noción de 'derecho' o las paradojas de la modernidad postcolonial: Indígenas y mujeres en Bolivia. Aportes Andinos 11:1–15.

2008   Violencia e interculturalidad: Paradojas de la etnicidad en Bolivia de hoy. Willka 2(2):201–226.

Roca, José Luis
2001   Economía y Sociedad en El Oriente Boliviano. Siglos XVI–XX. Santa Cruz: COTAS.

Rodríguez, Mario
2003   Cómo lo ven los jóvenes de barrios populares. Cuarto Intermedio 67–68:106–122.

Rojas Rosales, Antonio
1988   Mercado laboral y trabajadores por cuenta propia. In Santa Cruz: Cuestion Urbana y Problematica Municipal. Manuel de la Fuente, ed. Pp. 95–111. Santa Cruz: SURPO / Cabildo.

Romero, Carlos
2005   El proceso constituyente boliviano: El hito de la cuarta marcha de tierras bajas. Santa Cruz: CEJIS.

Rossel, Pablo, and Bruno Rojas
2002   Destino incierto: Esperanzas y realidades laborales de la juventud Alteña. La Paz: CEDLA.

Ruddick, Susan
1996   Constructing Difference in Public Spaces: Race, Class, and Gender as Interlocking Systems. Urban Geography 17:132–151.

Rudovsky, Noah Friedman
2009   Muestra de Fotografía "Tierra Abajo." La Paz: Ministerio de Cultural de La Paz.

Ruíz, Igor
2009   Las Aceras y calles siguen tomadas por los comerciantes. El Deber, January 27.

Rulli, Javiera
2007   The Refugees of the Agro-Export Model: Impacts of Soy Monocultures on Paraguayan Peasant Communities. In United Soy Republics: The Truth about Soy Production in South America. Javiera Rulli, ed. Pp. 220–234. Grupo de Reflexión Rural (Argentina).

Safran, William
2002   Dimensiones espaciales y funcionales de la autonomía. In Identidad y autogobierno en sociedades multiculturales. William Safran and Ramón Máiz, eds. Pp. 19–45. Barcelona: Ariel.

Salek, Nadine
2007   Plan Municipal Nueva Red de Abastecimiento, Mercados y Ambulantes. Santa Cruz de la Sierra: Oficialía Mayor de Planificación.

Samanamud, Jiovanny
2008   El ejercicio de la razón autonomista. Unpublished ms.

Sanabria, Harry
1999   Consolidating Status, Restructuring Economies, and Confronting Workers and Peasants: The Antinomies of Bolivian Neoliberalism. Comparative Study of Society and History 41:535–562.

Sandóval, Godofredo
1999   Rasgos del proceso de urbanización de las ciudades en Bolivia. *In* Sociólogos en el umbral del siglo XXI. Colegio de Sociólogos, ed. La Paz: Plural.

Sandoval, Godofredo, and Fernanda Sostres
1989   La Ciudad prometida. La Paz: ILDIS.

Sanjinés, Javier
2004   Mestizaje Upside-Down: Aesthetic Politics in Modern Bolivia. Pittsburgh: University of Pittsburgh Press.

Sanyal, Bishwapriya
1991   Organizing the Self-employed: The Politics of the Urban Informal Sector. International Labour Review 130(1):39–56.

Sawyer, Suzana
2004   Crude Chronicles: Indigenous Politics, Multinational Oil, and Neoliberalism in Ecuador. Durham: Duke University Press.

Schumpeter, Joseph
1975   Capitalism, Socialism and Democracy. New York: Harper.

Sieder, Rachel, ed.
2002   Multiculturalism in Latin America: Indigenous Rights, Diversity, and Democracy. London: Palgrave Macmillan / ILAS.

Smith, Anthony
2003   ¿Gastronomía o geología? El papel del nacionalismo en la reconstrucción de las naciones. *In* Nacionalismos y movilización política. Anthony Smith and Ramón Máiz, eds. Pp. 7–41. Buenos Aires: Prometeo.

Smith, Neil
1990   Uneven Development: Nature, Capital, and the Production of Space. Athens: University of Georgia Press.

Solíz Rada, Andrés
2004   Montenegro y el problema nacional y colonial. Bolpress. Electronic document, http://www.bollpress.com/art/php?Cod=2002076132, accessed October 14, 2009.
2007   Entre petroleras y ONG. Bolpress, December 18. Electronic document, http://www.bol-press.com/art.php?Cod=2007121801, accessed January 12, 2008.

Soruco Sologuren, Ximena
2008   De la goma a la soya: El proyecto historico de la élite cruceña. *In* Los barones del Oriente: El poder en Santa Cruz ayer y hoy. Ximena Soruco, Wilfredo Plata, and Gustavo Medeiros, eds. Pp. 1–100. La Paz: Fundación Tierra.

Soruco Sologuren, Ximena, Wifredo Plata, and Gustavo Medeiros
2008   Los barones del Oriente: El poder en Santa Cruz ayer y hoy. La Paz: Fundación Tierra.

Springer, Simon
2009   Violence, Democracy, and the Neoliberal "Order": The Contestation of Public Space in Posttransitional Cambodia. Annals of the Association of American Geographers 99(1):138–162.

Spronk, Susan
2007   Roots of Resistance to Urban Water Privatization in Bolivia: The "New Working Class," The Crisis of Neoliberalism and Public Services. International Labor and Working-Class History 71:8–28.

Spronk, Susan, and Jeff Webber
2007   Struggles against Accumulation by Dispossession in Bolivia: The Political Economy of Resource Contention. Latin American Perspectives 34(2):31–47.

Staeheli, Lynn A., and Albert Thompson
1997   Citizenship, Community, and Struggles for Public Space. The Professional Geographer 49:28–38.

Stapff, Andres
2009   Prosecutor Says Bolivian Opposition Backed Plot. Electronic document, http://www .democraticunderground.com/discuss/duboard.php?az=view_all&address=102x386 1649, accessed October 1, 2009.

Starn, Orin
1992   Rethinking the Politics of Anthropology: The Case of the Andes. Current Anthropology 35(1):13–28.
1999   Nightwatch: The Politics of Protest in the Andes. Durham: Duke University Press.

Stearman, Allyn
1985   Camba and Kolla: Migration and Development in Santa Cruz, Bolivia. Gainesville: University Press of Florida.

Stefanoni, Pablo
2008   Masacre de campesinos en Bolivia: "Los mataban como a chanchos." Clarín, September 21.
2010   Indianismo y pachamamismo. La Paz, May 4. Electronic document, http://www.rebe-lion.org/noticia.php?id=105233, accessed September 3, 2010.

Swanson, Kate
2007   Revanchist Urbanism Heads South: The Regulation of Indigenous Beggars and Street Vendors in Ecuador. Antipode 39(4):708–728.

Tamburini, Leonardo, and Ana Cecilia Betancur
2001   El Proceso para la titulación de la TCO Monte Verde. In La lucha por la tierra y el territorio. Carlos Romero Bonifaz, Ana Cecila Bentacur, Jose Percy Paredes Coimbra, Marco Antonio Aimaretti, and Leonardo Tamburini, eds. Pp. 5–26. Santa Cruz: CEJIS Artículo Primero.

Tapia, Luis
2000   Condiciones, problemas y capacidad de proyecto en la representación política. In Retos y dilemas de la representación política. Cuadernos de Futuro, no. 8. La Paz: PNUD.

Thomson, Sinclair
2003   We Alone Will Rule: Native Andean Politics in the Age of Insurgency. Madison: University of Wisconsin Press.

Toranzo Roca, Carlos
2008   Let the Mestizos Stand Up and Be Counted. *In* Unresolved Tensions: Bolivia Past and Present. John Crabtree and Laurence Whitehead, eds. Pp. 35–50. Pittsburgh: University of Pittsburgh Press.

Tsing, Ana
2004   Friction: An Ethnography of Global Connections. Princeton: Princeton University Press.

UNASUR
2008   Informe de la Comisión de UNASUR sobre los sucesos de Pando: Hacia un alba de justicia para Bolivia. Santiago: UNASUR. Electronic document, http://alainet.org/images/INFORME%20UNASUR%20FINAL.pdf, accessed October 9, 2009.

UN Habitat
2006   State of the World's Cities 2006/7: The Millennium Development Goals and Urban Sustainability. London: Earthscan.

United Nations
2007   United Nations Declaration on the Rights of Indigenous Peoples. A/61/L.67. New York: United Nations.
2009   Informe Público de la Oficina del Alto Comisionado para los Derechos Humanos en Bolivia sobre los hechos de violencia ocurridos en el departamento de Pando en Septiembre de 2008. La Paz: OACNUDH. Electronic document, http://bolivia.ohchr.org/informe_pando.htm, accessed October 9, 2009.

Urban, Greg, and Joel Sherzer, eds.
1991   Nation-States and Indians in Latin America. Austin: University of Texas Press.

Urioste, Miguel, and Cristobal Kay
2005   Latifundios, avasallamientos y autonomias. La reforma agraria inconclusa en el Oriente. La Paz: Fundación Tierra.

Urzagasti, César
1986   Organización y lucha vecinal en la coyuntura democrática, el caso de El Alto de La Paz. *In* Historia y evolución del movimiento popular. L. Antezana, ed. Cochabamba: CERES.

Van Cott, Donna Lee
2000   The Friendly Liquidation of the Past: The Politics of Diversity in Latin America. Pittsburgh: University of Pittsburgh Press.

Varese, Stefano, ed.
1996   Pueblos indios, soberanía y globalismo. Quito: Ediciones Abya Yala.

Vilas, Carlos
1998   Actores, sujetos, movimientos: ¿Dónde quedaron las clases? *In* Antropología Social y Política. María Rosa Neufeld, ed. Pp. 315–328. Buenos Aires: Eudeba.

Wall, Allan
2004   Is Miss Bolivia Racist? Electronic document, www.vdare.com/awall/miss_bolivia.htm, accessed August 12, 2008.

Walsh, Catherine
2009   Interculturalidad, estado, sociedad. Luchas (de)coloniales de nuestra época. Quito: UASB, Abya Yala.

Wanderley, Fernanda
2008   Beyond Gas: Between the Narrow-Based and Broad-Based Economy. *In* Unresolved Tensions: Bolivia, Past and Present. John Crabtree and Laurence Whitehead, eds. Pp. 194–212. Pittsburgh: University of Pittsburgh Press.

Warren, Kay
1998   Indigenous Movements and Their Critics: Pan-Maya Activism in Guatemala. Princeton: Princeton University Press.

Warren, Kay, and Jean Jackson, eds.
2002   Indigenous Movements, Self-Representation, and the State in Latin America. Austin: University of Texas Press.

Watts, Michael
2004   Antimonies of Community: Some Thoughts on Geography, Resources, and Empire. Transactions 29(2):195–216.

Watts, Michael, and Richard Peet
1996   Liberation Ecologies. London: Routledge.

Weismantel, Mary
2006   Ayllu: Real and Imagined Communities in the Andes. *In* Seductions of Community: Emancipations, Oppressions, and Quandaries. James F. Brooks, ed. Pp. 77–99. Santa Fe: School of American Research Press.

Whittman, Hannah K.
2005   Social Ecology of Agrarian Reform: The Landless Rural Workers' Movement and Agrarian Citizenship in Mato Grosso, Brazil. PhD dissertation, Department of Sociology, Cornell University.

Wilson, Fiona
2004   Indian Citizenship and the Discourse of Hygiene/Disease in Nineteenth-Century Peru. Bulletin of Latin American Research 23:165–180.

Wright, Lawrence
2010   Lithium Dreams. The New Yorker, March 22.

Yampara, Simón
2001   El Ayllu y la territorialidad en los Andes. Una aproximación a Chambi Grande. El Alto: UPEA-CADA.

Yashar, Deborah
2005   Contesting Citizenship in Latin America: The Rise of Indigenous Movements and the Post-liberal Challenge. Cambridge: Cambridge University Press.

Zavaleta, René
1967   Bolivia: El desarrollo de la conciencia nacional. Montevideo: Editorial Diálogo.
1986   Lo nacional-popular en Bolivia. La Paz: Plural.
1989   El Estado en América Latina. Cochabamba: Los Amigos del Libro.

Zibechi, Raul
2003   Los movimientos sociales latinoamericanos: Tendencias y desafíos. OSAL (January):185–188.
2006   Dispersar el poder: Los movimientos como poderes antiestatales. La Paz: Textos Rebeldes.

Zuidema, R. Tom
1977   The Inca Kinship System: A New Theoretical View. *In* Andean Kinship and Marriage. Ralph Bolton and Enrique Mayer, eds. Pp. 248–292. Washington, DC: American Anthropological Association.

Zulawski, Ann
2007   Unequal Cures: Public Health and Political Change in Bolivia, 1900–1950. Durham: Duke University Press.

Index

of, 188; racialized, 19; of vendors, 98, 115; of
women, 125, 127
exocentric networks, 122–123
exploitation, 132; economic, 41; of indigenous
peoples, 31–32, 70; of labor, 43, 75–76, 129;
of land, 157, 193; of natural resources, 40,
43, 58, 95, 193; systems of, 19
export, 81, 97, 101, 148–151, 156, 163, 165n9.
See also gas; natural resources; soy
extractivism, 7, 188

Fabricant, Nicole, 5, 23, 27
farmers, 163, 165n5, 188n1; attacks against,
89n1, Fig. 7; of coca, 18; displaced, 151, 153;
as disposable labor, 154; and land ownership,
84; and land reform, 142–143; and Landless
Movement (MST), 146–147; protect land/
resources, 151; small-scale, 23, 26, 52, 68,
84, 152–153, 156, 161; unions for, 12, 68
farming: and ancient methods, 160–161; and collective work, 159; communities/collectives,
17, 19, 23, 147, 149, 164; expansion of, 143;
industrialization of, 154; large-scale, 156;
mechanization of, 26; small-scale, 161; subsistence, 146, 160; without exploitation, 157.
See also agrarian; farmers
Farthing, Linda, 16
Federación de Gremialistas, 111
federalism, 57, 66n4, 92, Fig. 2
federalist system, 62
Federation of Neighborhood Councils (FEJUVE),
17–18, 119, 124, 128, 133–139
Federation of Pando Peasants, 70
Federation of Small-Scale Traders, 136–137
FEJUVE. *See* Federation of Neighborhood
Councils
FELCN (Bolivian Special Anti-narcotics Force), 144
Fernandez, Bernardo Mancano, 147
Fernández, Johnny, 108
Fernández, Leopoldo, 69–71, 87–88, 89n1
Fernández, Max, 105
Fernández, Percy, 105, 109, 111
fertilizers, 153–155, 160
FETUCRA, 136
Filadelfia, 68
fish, 193
Flores, Luis, 136
folkloric festivals, 39
food: commerce in, 98; distribution network,
109; markets, 99, 107, 109, 113; services,
124; for work programs, 121
Foreign Ministry, 197
forests, 62, 152, 154, 160
Forum for Alteño Dignity, 136
fossil fuels, 4, 150
Foucault, Michel, 42

France, 4
free market, 1–3, 7, 26, 119, 185
freedom, 78, 81, 85, 88
Friedman, Milton, 119

Galarza, Patricia, 191
Garcés, Fernando, 22–23
García Linera, Alvaro, 167–170, 173, 176, 183,
185–187, 188n4, 203–205
gas, 8, Figs. 17–18; battles over, 25n9; boom,
177, 179; companies, 183; control over, 15,
181; development, 170, 183, Fig. 20;
exploitation of, 95, 193; export of, 4, 15–16,
101, 137–138, 176–177; in Guaraní country,
183; immense natural reserves of, 4, 170,
175, 191; industrialization of, 94, 177; and
jobs, 185; location of, 175–176, 191, Figs.
1–2; nationalization of, 16, 18, 91, 135, 138,
170, 176–177, 179, 181, Fig. 16; possible
depletion of, 175; rents/royalties, 173, 176–177,
179, 183, 193, 194n3; shortages, 165n5; surplus, 18, 187; in Tarija, 150; taxes on, 193,
194n4. *See also* Gas War
Gas War (2003), 16–17, 30, 35–36, 45n7, 48,
77, 91, 94–95, 116–118, 123–124, 132,
134–140, 176, Fig. 11
gasoline, 178
Gazprom, 183
gender, 33, 73, 79, 91, 178–179, Fig. 20
geography, 8, 42, 122
geopolitics, 3, 30–31, 33, 38, 42, 44, 137, 167,
170, 177, 185, Fig. 2
global: ambition, 156; capital, 97, 176; capitalism, 3, 7, 57; center for energy/natural
resources, 16; economy, 97, 149, 151, 155;
prices of crude oil, 4; prosperity, 24n2;
soyscape, 150; struggles over natural
resources, 2, 4
gods, 40, 193
governance, 2, 5, 10, 31, 45n9, 47, 56, 64, 66n4,
69, 103, 117, 119, 168, 173, 187, 197–199,
201
government, 60, 62, 69, 71; central, 81, 94–95,
121, 177; cooperative, 53–54; departmental,
81, 84; and El Porvenir massacre, 87; indigenous, 109; and indigenous autonomies, 56;
intermediate-district level, 139; and land
issues, 142, 144, 146; lies of, 95; local-level,
134–135, 139, 177; of MNR, 96; national,
134–135, 139, 148, 179; representative, 105;
represses people, 94; of Santa Cruz, 109. *See
also* municipal; municipalities; self-government
Gran Chaco, 156, Fig. 13
grassroots, 21, 128; Alteños, 117; commission,
137; democracy, 91–92; and FEJUVE, 139;
knowledge production, 6; leadership, 117,

persecution of, 87; pride of, 37, 41; recognition of, 3, 30, 172; representation of, 16, 53, 60–61, 169, 204; struggles of, 4, 6, 40, 42, 55, 143, 168; subordination of, 2, 31, 64; symbols/motifs of, 88. *See also* originary; specific types

Indigenous People's March for Sovereignty, Territory, and Natural Resources, 47–48

indigenous projects, 16, 58, 80, 171, 176, 183, 186

indigenous resurgence, 11, 30–33, 36–37, 82, 186

indigenous rights, 173, 183, 187; claims for, 2, 12; domestication of, 50, 167; and El Alto, 23; and land ownership, 193; in Latin America, 20; and MAS, 169; opposition to, 66n4, 179–180; primary, 54; projects, 171; recognition of, 5; representatives of, 192; and self-determination, 55, 166; support for, 46–47; the turn to, 3, 172; UN declaration of, 20; unresolved, 170

indio permitido, 172, 175

indio prohibido, 172–173, 175

indios, 31–33, 40, 42, 66, 74, 77, 182, 192, 203

individualism, 29, 34, 80, 85–86, 113, 125, 130, 142, 173

"indo-*mestizo*," 181–182

industrialization, 2, 97, 154, 173, 177

Industrias Oleaginosas Limitada (IOL-SA), 150–152

inequalities, 6, 8, 21, 88; class, 5, 98; and distribution of resources/goods, 119, 201; in El Alto, 91–92; elimination of, 9, 53, 195; environmental, 23; existing, 13; and free-market policies, 2; and income, 106; between indigenous people and elites, 30; and land, 61, 147; racial/racialized, 9, 197; in Santa Cruz, 92, 97; social, 103; spatial, 103, Fig. 11; structural, 23, 124, 132; struggle against, 52

infrastructure, 100, 109–110, 121, 125, 127–128, 130, 155, 186

intellectuals, 9–11, 16, 21–22, 44n2, 56; and activism, 2, 167, 206; autonomist, 73; Aymara, 196–197, 202; and decolonization, 173; of Guaraní, 187; indigenous, 9, 195; influential, 185; of MST, 148, 165n2; of Nación Camba, 79, 105; nationalist, 24n1, 181; and natural resources, 149, 176

interculturalism, 2, 5, 57, 172, 182, 205

International Republican Institute, 29n4

invasión, 98

investment, 78, 96, 110, 113, 144, 156, 179

invisibilization, 35–36

iron ore, 4, Fig. 1

Itika Guasu region, 184, 191–194

Japan/Japanese, 4, 79, 109

Japanese International Cooperation Agency (JICA), 109

Jarro, Antonio, 129–130

juridical: organizations/institutions, 59; pluralism, 52–53, 55, 60; rights to territory/political authority, 171; security, 144; systems, 51–52

justice, 27–29

kãgui, 187, 189n8

Katari, 173, 185

Kataristas, 53, 169

Kimsa form, 137

King, Martin Luther, 24, 195–196

kinship, 19, 149, 179

Kirshner, Joshua, 23

knowledge production, 6, 21–22, 37, 167, 170

kollas. See Collas

Kudva, Neema, 104

Kurahuara de Karangas, 40–41

Kuruyuki, battle of, 72, 192

Kymlicka, Will, 54–56

La Guardia, 103

La Guerra de Gas. *See* Gas War

La Paz, 9, 35, 43, 44n5, 79, 103, 193, Fig. 12; annual march to, 27; and El Alto blockade, 138, Fig. 11; elites of, 45n11, 71, 79; as financial capital, 96; history/founding of, 118; indigenous peoples of, 38; and Landless Movement, 143; neighborhood associations of, 119; in relation to El Alto, 95, 118–120; roads to, 100, 123, Fig. 11; wealth of, 91, 118–119

La Plata, 80

La Ramada market (Santa Cruz), 105, 107, 112, 114

La Razón, 71

labor: Aymara, 91; disposable, 154; dispossessed, 197; exploitation of, 43, 75–76, 90n5, 129; family, 129, 147; indigenous, 75; informal, 18, 146; informalization, 103–104; laws, 124; and low wages, 91, 124; manual, 36; market, 104, 113, 120; and migration, 97, 101, 105, 163; mobile, 163; movements, 174; and oil extraction, 178; organized, 85, 121; relations, 62, 76; rotating supply of, 162; solidarity, 178; subjugation of, 73; and sugarcane plantations, 164n1; surplus, 97; wage, 146

labor organizations, 1, 10, 28, 48–49. *See also* unions

Lagunillas, 184

Laja, 124

land, 16, 99; access to, 146; claims to, 155–156, 193; collectively-titled, 168; commodification/

privatization of, 151; commoditization of, 15, 147; communal, 54, 61, 89n3, 159; conquered, 71, 77, 88, 156; control over, 51, 61–62, 81; distribution, 155; and elites, 83; expropriation of, 147; grants, 148; indigenous, 47, 54–55; individual holdings of, 62; invasion of, 92–93, 144, 147; for markets, 107; mercantilizing of, 156; originary, 54; ownership, 18–19, 70, 84, 88, 142, 147, 156, 163; productive, 146–147, 150; public, 84, 108, 141, 143; right to, 52, 164, 197; for small-scale production, 18, 26–27; and soy industry, 165n9; struggles over, 25n9, 77, 87, 142, 147, 159, Fig. 15; unproductive, 147–148, 150, 155–157; usage shifts, 102. *See also* cattle ranching; Landless Movement (MST); *latifundios*; *minifundios*; Movimiento Sin Tierra (MST); private property; *surcofundios*; TCOs

land occupation, 31, 70–71, 73–74, 80, 142, 147–148, 156–158, 160–162, 186

land redistribution, 18, 26–27, 55, 61–62, 84, 141–144, 147, 156, 159, 172, Fig. 13

land reform, 12, 14, 26–28, 29n2, 50, 55, 84, 142, 148, 151, 155–157, 167–168, 193

Landless Movement (MST), 17–18, 23, Figs. 13–15; and *acampamentos*, 156–157; and "community," 163–164; and displaced peoples, 199; and education, 162; and environmental consciousness, 160–161; and Evo Morales, 27–29, 165n2; and land acquisition/occupation, 38, 141–144, 147–148, 157–163; leaders of, 157–159, 165n2; members of, 149, 153, 158–159, 163; and *mit'a*, 161–162; organized attacks against, 142, 145n3, 148; as peasant movement, 49, 155–156; policies/ideas of, 157–159, 163; and soy industry, 149, 153, 161, 205. *See also* Movimiento Sin Tierra (MST)

landlords, 27–28, 38–39, 55, 143–144, 192

landowners, 28, 39–41, 61–62, 141–142, 147, 156

language, 11, 32, 37, 44n3, 122, 126–127, 164, 199

Larsen, Ronald, 86–87

latifundios, 23, 27–28, 29n3, 52, 61–63, 147, 156

Latin America, 15, 20, 31–33, 36, 63, 72, 99, 101, 119, 174, 182, 188, 198, 202

Law 2557, 77

Law for the Communitarian Redirection of Agrarian Reform, 26–27

Law of Autonomies, 167, 169, 171

Law of Decentralization (1994), 45n9

Law of Expropriation of 1874, 54

Law of Popular Participation (1994), 121–122, 128–129, 139

laws. *See* specific names

Lazar, Sian, 18, 117

Lazarte, Silvia, 167

leadership, 123, 135; alternative notions of, 133–134; changing notions of, 124–129; "civic" vs. "political," 129–131; and clientelism, 129–133, 139–140; and collective interest, 129, 132; corrupt, 183; different forms of, 134, 139, 157; economic, 57; and Gas War, 116–118; and grassroots pressure, 131–134; groups, intermediate, 138; Indianist (*indianista*), 132–134, 136, 139; Marxist (leftist), 130, 132–134, 136, 139; new discourse on, 138–139

left wing, 1, 3, 13, 66n4, 151, 171, 180–182, 196

Lewis, Tom, 15

Ley de Convocatoria a la Asamblea Constitutyente, 48–49. *See also* Constitutional Assembly

Ley de Desvinculación (1874), 25n6

Ley Marco de Autonomías y Descentralización (2010), 59

Limpias, Victor Hugo, 102

lithium, 4, 16, 177, Fig. 1

"live well" (*vivir bien*), 5, 52, 188, 193

llama meat industry, 196

Máiz, Ramón, 65

Mamani Ramirez, Pablo, 20, 22, 117, 205

Mamani, Serapio, 126

Manso, Andrés, 80

manufacturing, 92, 103, 120, 124, 152

maps, Figs. 1–3, 10

maquila model, 91, 97

March for Land and Dignity (1990), 77

March to the East program, 96

Margarita gas field, 175, 193

marginalization, 17, 104, 106, 172, 192, 196

Marinkovic, Branko, 150–151

Marinkovic, Silvo, 150–151

market: embrace of, 173; exchange, 99, 158; forces, 156, 204; networks, 97; oriented-growth, 113

market vendors, 95n1, 95n2, Fig.9; ambulatory, 99, 106, 109–110; demonstrations by, 114; fines levied on, 108; fixed, 106; and health/hygiene, 99–100; informal, 97–100, 104–106, 111; livelihoods of, 109, 111, 113; migrant, 17; organizations for, 104–105; relocation of, 99, 109–112, 114–115; rights of, 110, 113, 197; and usufruct ownership, 107, 110. *See also gremialistas*; *gremios*

markets: for food/produce, 99, 107, 109, 113; foreign, 26; informal, 106–107, Fig.9; liberalize, 149; municipal, 106–108; municipal

extraction, 178; and gender/race, 178–179; high prices of, 4, 150; nationalization of, 180–181; privatization of, 176, 180; stories about, 177–181; taxes on, 194n3; war, 175–176; workers, 177–181, 188n5, Figs. 19–20

oligarchs/oligarchy, 35, 176, 181–182

Olivera, Oscar, 15

Ordenanza Muncipal 050/2004, 112

organizaciones territoriales de base (OTBs), 128–129

Orgaz, Mirko, 181

Oriente, 23, 29n3, 70–75, 77–78, 87–88, 202–204

originarias, 48–49, 51

originary: organizations, 57–58; peoples, 43, 48–55, 63–64, 191

Oruro, 38, 58, 60, 66n7, 105

Otavalo, Ecuador, 37

Oviedo, Gabriela, 9, 11

Pacajes, 196

Pachamama (Mother Earth), 11, 25n7, 39

pachamamismo, 11, 13, 25n7, 206

Pacific Ocean harbors, 118

Pact of Programmatic Unity, 48–49. *See also* Unity Pact

Paley, Julia, 126

Pando, 23, 49, 57, 68–70, 72–73, 75–79, 84, 87, 89n2, 193

Pando, Amalia, 195, 201, 207

Paraguay, 151, 165n9, 175

Paredes, Max, 196, 202

party politics, 129, 132, 136, 140, 174, 179

patrimonio paisajístico (landscape patrimony), 113

Patzi Paco, Felix, 117

Peasant Local Union, 70

peasant movements/organizations, 23, 48–49, 51, 84, 155–156, 166. *See also* specific names

peasants, 19, 86; attacks against, 200; culture of, 164; displaced, 146–148; and economy, 118; in El Alto, 118; and El Porvenir massacre, 68–70; expulsion of, 15, 147; and farming, 147; and identity, 49; and land, 26, 47, 55, 59, 84, 141–142, 162; and land ownership, 155–156, 163; and landless movement, 17, 27–28, 146–148, 199; leaders of, 70, 84–85, 133; and making of the nation, 63; migration of, 120, 199; persecution of, 87, 151; politics of, 157; representation of, 53; reterritorialization of, 17; and small-scale production, 157–158; and solidarity, 159; and struggle for services, 162; and unions, 29n2, 49, 171, 199; use of term/category, 33, 39, 51–52

Peet, Richard, 160

Peru, 3, 8, 80, 188, 202

pesticides, natural, 160

Petrobras, 101, 103, 175–176, 179

petroleum, 100–101, 103, 203

Plan Regulador (1995), 102

plantations. *See haciendas*

Plata, Wilfredo, 155

pluralism, 66n4, 92, 185–186, 188, 196, 201, 203–205

plurality, 173–175, 186

Plurinational Assembly, 61

plurinationalism, 1–2, 8, 19, 50–56, 60–61, 63–66, 66n4, 169–170, 173, 175, 181–183, 186, 191

PODEMOS (Democratic and Social Power) party, 27, 60, 66n8

police force, 93, 95n2, 126, 132, 137–138

political, 13, 58; action, 138, 157; alliances, 57, 123, 142; alternatives, 195; capital, 127; change, 3, 8, 13, 15, 109; coalition, 52–53; contention, 39, 87–88, 197–198, 200; control, 77, 83–84; cutlure, 196–197; domination, 31; ecology, 160; economy, 92, 186; equality, 53, 65; exclusion, 105; expansion, 71; forms/models, 63, 92, 139; fragmentation, 199; identities, 13, 18–19, 51; influence, 104, 108; institutionalism, 65; issues, rights to, 53; knowledge, 139; militance, 91–92, 97; minoritization, 36; mobilizations, 106, 196; opposition, 71; orders, 3, 47; organization, 52, 97; organizing, 121, 151; patronage, 147; pluralism, 52–53; power, 32, 41, 57, 80–81, 99, 143, 150; practices, 120, 196; projects, 9, 14, 16–17, 66, 78–79, 82, 204; reforms, 121; relations, 23, 43, 176, 204; representation, 50, 65; revolution, 36; socialization, 156; spaces, 8, 33, 95, 150; status and territories, 46; strategies, 82, 149; structure, 156; struggles, 2–3, 40, 42, 82; studies, 8; subjectivities, 91–92; systems, 1, 51, 54, 56, 78, 133–134; transformation, 1, 5–6, 14

political parties, 47, 60, 64, 66n8, 81, 105, 108, 119, 129–130, 133–134, 171, 173

politics: Alteño, 117; "de-racializing" of, 198, 204–207; and environmental issues, 160; ethnic, 5; indigenous, 167; and leadership practices, 139; local, 19, 105, 134; and mobilizations, 7, 134; municipal, 119, 140; popular, 167; and race, 198, 200–201, 205–207; regional, 150; "remapping of," 91; of space, 197; state-centered, 203; territorial, 173, 203

polyvocality, 6, 186

"Popular Participation," 17–18, 37, 45n9, 121–122, 128–129, 139

84, 91; as cultural/strategic factor, 39; definition of, 40–41, 46; devolution of, 65; indigenous, 46–47, 52–53, 55–56, 58, 168; indigenous originary, 57; indigenous originary peasant, 59, 168; micropolitics of, Fig. 9; and "modern" Bolivia, 78; remapping/reordering of, 176, 188

Total, 183

tourism, 97, 103, 113–115, 164, 179–180

trade, 3, 101, 104, 149

traditions, 13, 88, 98, 202

trans-writing (*transescritura*), 36

transnational corporations, 15, 150, 180, Fig. 16

transnationalism, 8, 17

transportation, 107–108, 120–121, 124

tribute, 161

Tupak Katari, 169, 205

"two eyes" concept, 53–54

UN (National Unity) party, 66n8

unemployment, 17, 124, 144, 146–147, 151

Unión Juvenil Cruceñista (UJC), 84, 141, 151

Union of South American Nations (UNASUR), 84, 89n1

unions, 16, 18, 124, 132; 2008 gathering of, 68–70; and Camiri, 178; dissolution of, 156; for farmers, 12, 68; for meatpackers, 136; for miners, 17; organized attacks against, 69–70; and peasants, 29n2, 49, 70, 155–156, 171; Regional Workers, 137; struggles of, 10, 180; trade, 104; weakening of, 121

Unitary Plurinational State, 51

United Nations, 70–71, 84, 87, 103, 192

United Nations Commission on Human Rights, 89n1

United Nations Declaration on the Rights of Indigenous Peoples, 20, 167

United Nations Development Program (UNDP), 11

United Nations Habitat criteria, 102

United States, 25n4, 73, 86, 182; and agro-industrial development, 164n1; and "coca" wars, 15; Drug Enforcement Agency of, 144; and food aid, 121; foreign policy of, 3; Geological Survey of, 175; interventions of, 171, 181, 188n4; and labor organizations, 28; and March to the East program, 96; and natural resources, 4, 137–138; and NGOs, 66n4

United States Agency for International Development (USAID), 28, 29n4, 29n5, 170

Unity Pact (Pacto de Unidad), 47–59, 63–65, 66n1, 203. *See also* Pact of Programmatic Unity

urban, 132; belonging, 39; centered health care, Fig. 14; collective needs, 112–113; democ-racy, 117; designs/plans, 102, 108–109; economy, 108; elites, 97, 179, 191; environment, 118, 122; governance, 103; growth, 23, 97, 99–100, 104, 107–109; heterogeneity, 122–123; labor, 18, 104, 146, 149; landscape, 104, 112, 115, Fig.9; leaders, 47; life, 164, Figs. 11–12; livelihoods, 108, Fig. 9; markets, 104–106, 109–110, Fig. 9; militance, 116; mobilizing forms, 135; organizations, 48, 190; peasant autonomies, 57; politics, 105, 121–122, 136; poor, 119–120, 135; populism, 106; public health/hygiene, 97; rationality, 111; realities/spaces, 91–95; regionalist demonstrations, Figs. 5–6; and rural tensions, 200; social relations, 37; social sectors, 165n4; society, 98, 113; space, 96–100, 110, 113, 115, 117, 121, 125, 201. *See also* Santa Cruz

Uru people, 37, 171

usos y costumbres (uses and customs), 15

usufruct ownership, 107, 110

utopia, 7, 13, 78, 163–164, 188, 204–205

Valencia, Francisco, 126–127

Vanderbilt University, 11

Vargas, Ademar Valda, 152

Vargas, Eusebio, 180, 189n7

vecinos (neighbors), 119, 124, 129–130. *See also* neighborhood organizations

vendors. *See* market vendors

Venezuela, 4, 7, 144

Vice Ministry of Lands (Santa Cruz), 142–143

Viceroy Toledo as Leyes de Indias, 86

Villa Calama neighborhood, 137

Villa Tunari neighborhood, 126–127

Villamontes, 179

violence, 14, 42, 93, Fig. 7; by autonomists, 88; to demonstrators, 82; ecological, 3; and elites, 83–84, 88, 174; of exclusion, 23; extralegal, 151; and gas/oil wars, 124, 176; against Guaranís, 192; justification of, 88–89; and labor exploitation, 75; against landless movement/people, 141–142, 145n3, 148; "legitimate" physical, 32; and neoliberalism, 172; and occupiers, 156; over taxes, 135, 137; political, 43; and racism, 10; reactionary, 7; right-wing instigated, 69; social, 3; and sovereignty, 171, 175; and the state, 79, 117, 190; and street battles, 114; territorializing of, 174; against women, 148, 178. *See also* Massacre of Pananti; Massacre of Porvenir

Warisata, 138

Warnes, 102

Washington Consensus technocracy, 167